GRANDMOTHER, GRANDFATHER,
AND OLD WOLF

90

GRANDMOTHER, GRANDFATHER, ➤ AND ↝ OLD WOLF

Tamánwit Ku Súkat and Traditional Native American Narratives
from the Columbia Plateau

Edited by
Clifford E. Trafzer

Michigan State University Press
East Lansing

∞ The paper used in this publication meets the minimum requirements of
ANSI/NISO Z39.48-1992 (R 1997) (Permanence of Paper).

Michigan State University Press
East Lansing 48823-5202

03 02 01 00 99 98 1 2 3 4 5 6 7 8 9

All royalties from this volume will be donated to the Yakama Nation Library in
Toppenish, Washington, for the purchase of books for children by and about Native
Americans. Many storytellers presented in this volume were from the Yakama
Reservation or had an association with the fourteen tribes and bands of the
Confederated Tribes of the Yakama Nation. The stories are theirs.

Research for this book was made possible in part from the Faculty Research Incentive
Grant of the University of California, Office of the President.

Designed by Nicolette Rose

Library of Congress Cataloging-in-Publication Data

Grandmother, Grandfather, and Old Wolf: tamánwit ku súkat and traditional Native
American narratives from the Columbia Plateau/edited by Clifford E. Trafzer.
     p.   cm.
   Includes bibliographical references and index.
   ISBN 0-87013-445-0 (alk. paper)
   1. Indians of North America—Columbia Plateau—Folklore. 2. Oral tradition—
Columbia Plateau. 3. Tales—Columbia Plateau. 4. McWhorter, Lucullus Virgil,
1860-1944. I. Trafzer, Clifford E.
E99.C63G73 1998
398.2'089'9707961—dc21   98-22731
     CIP

To my mother who taught me to delight in stories
For my grandfather who gave me a college story
To my daughters who heard stories
For Lee Ann the storyteller

Contents

Preface

THE PRESENT WORK is an outgrowth of my interest in presenting the traditional native view that oral narratives, the ancient texts of Native Americans, are history. They are not "fish tails that grow with the telling," as a reviewer once suggested, but a body of sacred stories kept by every native group in the Americas. Native American narratives are available to all scholars and are an excellent way of learning about particular native cultures. I have chosen to offer several original stories from a fine collection as a means of illustrating the power of the stories in reference to the issues of spirit and law. The stories have provided Native Americans with the spirit and law for untold generations, and the stories remain a body of knowledge that continues to serve this purpose.

According to one of the narratives found in this collection, there was once a time on the Northwest Plateau when the Cold North Wind Brothers invaded the region and froze it, bringing only snow, ice, sleet, dark clouds, and cold winds. In the spring of the year, the ice did not melt but the Salmon Chief and his people tried to make their way up the Columbia River in accordance with the law to spawn and die. After traveling up the river a short distance, ice in the river blocked their path.

Five Wolf Brothers joined the Five Cold North Wind Brothers, challenging and killing all people that stood against them. When Salmon Chief and his people arrived at that place where the ice met the river, Salmon Chief challenged the Wolf Brothers to a wrestling match. If

Salmon Chief beat all five of the Wolf Brothers, the Cold North Wind Brothers and their allies would retreat up north. If he lost, Coyote promised to slit Salmon Chief's throat. During the course of the wrestling match, one of the Wolf Brothers threw Salmon Chief to the ground. Coyote cut his throat and a great bloodletting began. The Wolf Brothers and their allies became lost in a killing frenzy that resulted in the death of every member of the Salmon tribe. The Wolf Brothers slit open the body of every female Salmon, including Salmon Chief's wife, destroying their eggs. One of the eggs of Salmon Chief's wife became lodged between two rocks. The Wolf Brothers tried in vain to reach the egg, but they finally gave up, believing that it would dry up and die. The Creator saw what had happened and sent a rain to wash the egg from the crevice into the river.

The small Salmon egg became lodged in the sand, and semen floating in the river fertilized the egg. A small smolt emerged and swam backward to the Pacific Ocean where Young Chinook's Grandmother met and nurtured him. Grandmother Salmon trained Young Chinook to be strong and wise, instructed him so that he could meet the challenge ahead. When he was old enough, Young Chinook traveled up the Columbia and wrestled the Five Wolf Brothers, defeating each one in turn. Young Chinook reestablished the old law and broke the Cold North Wind so there would always be a time for each season.

Traditional storytellers do not interpret stories for their listeners, but elders encourage people to think about the ancient narratives and assess their meanings. The story of Young Chinook and the Wolf Brothers offers several themes important in this work. The narrative deals with death and rebirth, and like the egg becoming Young Chinook, the stories offered in this collection have never died but continue to influence history, culture, literature, and language among native people of the Northwest Plateau. There is a direct link between such stories and Native American history, since the stories establish the relationship of all the peoples—plants, animals, mountains, rivers, lakes, etc.—with each other and creation. The stories provide a basis for understanding a particular native culture.

Equally important, the ancient texts describe what Sahaptin-speaking people of the Columbia Plateau call the *tamánwit ku súkat* or the law and spirit. At the beginning of time, the Creator set the law and spirit into motion, in this case establishing the law that each year the Salmon People should swim up the Columbia River and its tributaries to spawn and die. According to the law, tiny smolts would travel backward into the ocean and return to recreate themselves in the years to come. The Cold North Wind Brothers broke the law by bringing perpetual winter to the area and allowing the Wolf Brothers to enforce this new law which was a violation of creation. This kind of law is not secular or sterile but alive with spirit and understanding of the natural balance needed within the environment to keep the things of nature in motion. Like the Cold North Wind Brothers, whites in the twentieth century broke the law by establishing dams on Northwestern rivers, and the consequences of the violation of the law have been very grave indeed. Not only have the dams violated ancient law, but they have harmed the spirit of the region and the relationship of man to plants, animals, places of nature, and other human beings.

There are several versions of the stories offered in this volume. Those presented here were preserved by an unusual white rancher and scholar named Lucullus Virgil McWhorter, known to Yakama, Nez Perce, and other tribal people as Big Foot or Old Wolf. A short biographical sketch of McWhorter is offered in the introduction, but those interested in McWhorter's life should read Steven Evans' fine volume, *Voice of the Old Wolf: Lucullus V. McWhorter and the Nez Perce Indians*. McWhorter spent many years of his life ranching near the Yakama Reservation and making friends with numerous Northwestern Indians. He was an historian who kept notes, manuscripts, maps, documents, photographs, and material culture. Over the years he collected many versions of native stories which he intended one day to publish as a book. He never had time to complete his volume of stories, and upon his death, his family placed his many documents and artifacts in the McWhorter Collection, Manuscripts, Archives, and Special Collections of the Holland Library, Washington State University, Pullman. The stories presented here are from that collection and published with the kind permission of the McWhorter family: (Mrs. Judith McWhorter Goodwin, McWhorter's granddaughter, and the descendants of L. V. McWhorter).

Mrs. Goodwin graciously wrote me that "The McWhorter Family is happy to grant you permission to use our Grandfather, L. V. McWhorter's materials in this manuscript. In it, you are doing exactly what he wanted, getting all the material he collected before the public and into the history books, so the information will not be lost." Acting on behalf of Manuscripts, Archives, and Special Collections of the

Holland Library, Washington State University, John Guido also gave me permission to use the stories found within the McWhorter Collection. The stories are those of several different native people, all deceased, from many different reservations in the Northwest, but primarily from the Yakama Reservation. For that reason, all royalties derived from the sale of this book will be donated to the Yakama Nation Library in Toppenish, Washington, to be used to purchase books for children. The presentation of this work has been a labor of love but one that might have meaning for native people, general readers, and scholars interested in Native American history.

Some of the stories presented in this volume are still told by elders on the reservations of the inland Northwest, the home of several diverse tribes and bands, but, some of the stories and the details contained within these versions of the stories are not common knowledge today among the Nez Perce, Yakama, Wasco, Wishom (also spelled Wishram), Klickitat, and Cascade. Like the small egg, the stories have survived, and this is significant since they represent seeds of knowledge from past generations. These stories are an illuminating collection of original oral traditions from the Great Columbia Plateau, collected and preserved by a meticulous man in the first decades of the twentieth century.

My work on this book began in 1977 while I was researching a tribal history of the Palouse Indians. The McWhorter Collection contained some documents useful to the Palouse project, but it also contained a wealth of other information, including several traditional stories that provided an understanding of traditional Indian "law," as Plateau Indians understood the term, and many of these stories are offered in this volume. Because of my interest in oral history and traditional stories, I was drawn to the ancient tales of Plateau Indians as a means of understanding their culture, traditions, history, and laws. I read the stories with interest and determined one day to edit them and produce a volume that would inform others about the rich oral literature of the people of the Columbia Plateau. I believe strongly that there can be little understanding of any native tribe or band without some understanding of their ancient stories—tales that Native Americans considered historical, literary, and religious. The stories contained in this volume inform us about the "law" as established by Coyote, Raccoon, Beaver, Eagle, the Huckleberry Sisters, and many more characters who lived during the time of the first creation before the arrival of humans. The stories are sacred texts, documents that delight and enlighten but contain spiritual instructions about life and death.

Versions of some stories have appeared in other works written by Mourning Dove, Donald Hines, Nashone, Richard Erdoes, Alfonso Ortiz, Ella Clark, and Margot Edmonds. In some of these accounts, editors have altered the stories. I present the stories collected by L.V. McWhorter with few changes to the texts—except punctuation—and have added interpretive annotations and explanatory notes that will help the reader understand more fully the meanings of the stories, their similarities, differences, and significances. The focus of this presentation is on native law, and the connection between law and spirit. I changed some of McWhorter's punctuation, particularly his excessive use of semicolons, but did not alter the texts. I changed his use of footnotes, providing his statements at the end of some stories, designating them, "Notes by McWhorter." I added my own notes to illuminate the texts in relation to spirit and law; this information is provided in notes so that the narratives are not interrupted by excessive annotations that might break the flow of the stories. If readers wish to see the stories in their original form, they may do so by reviewing them at Washington State University in Manuscripts, Archives, and Special Collections.

The work is also intended to offer a voice for various Indian storytellers who were sufficiently concerned about the preservation of their stories to share them with McWhorter. Other stories McWhorter heard at powwows and rodeos and then subsequently wrote them down. McWhorter's methods are discussed in the introduction and his influence on individual narratives is presented in the notes. Several drafts of the same story occasionally appear in the collection, and the most original copy was used for this book. I chose early drafts of the stories, not versions that McWhorter edited in his own hand, intending to insert his changes. If the added material seemed important, I included the information in brackets or placed it at the end of the story in "Notes by McWhorter." Most of this information, however, added little to the story and was not used. Moreover, if more than one version of a story was found (the same story provided by different storytellers), each version is presented. I have kept McWhorter's use of the term Yakima (spelled with an i) in reference to the tribe, storytellers, and reservation. In my own notes and writing, however, I have used the tribe's preferred spelling of Yakama, a spelling the Yakama Nation recently designated as its official spelling in accordance with the Yakama Treaty of 1855.

The stories are varied and rich. They are literary and historical masks that offer more than what can be seen, inviting readers to look deeper and wonder at the meaning of the words. People are asked to read the words aloud and listen to Listening Coyote, Owl Child, Blazing Bush, Black Bear, Mrs. Skouken John, and other storytellers spin their tales, listen to the elders recreate the world by retelling the first literature and history of the Americas. Much of the work presented in this volume was conducted with support from the Faculty Research Incentive Grant of the University of California, Office of the President. Some work was also presented through the assistance of the Costo Historical and Linguistics Native American Research Center at the University of California, Riverside. In addition, librarians at the Rivera Library at the University of California, Riverside, helped me locate source materials regarding Plateau Indians, and several people were instrumental in helping prepare, conceptualize, and present the work. Most of all, I thank the Native American storytellers—the Grandmothers and Grandfathers—who have shared their oral traditions with me over the years, including my mother. I also thank those Native American storytellers who shared their narratives with L.V. McWhorter, *Hemene Kawan* or Old Wolf.

Lee Ann Smith-Trafzer and Louise Smith read all the stories and helped me imagine the book. Virginia Ohr and Pamela Norman typed portions of the manuscript and offered criticisms. I express my gratitude to Carlos Vélez-Ibáñez, Max Neiman, and Carl Cranor as well as Chancellor Raymond Orbach and Vice Chancellor David Warren of the University of California, Riverside, who provided support so that I could finish this book. I thank the faculty of the Departments of History and Ethnic Studies who were supportive of my research. My colleagues Tom Avramis, Rebecca Kugel, Rob Patch, Lee Francis, Donna Akers, David Stratton, Troy Johnson, Duane Champagne, Cheryl Duran, Rick Danay, Scott Andrews, Raymond Starr, Armando Navarro, Sterling Stuckey, Richard Hanks, Steffi San Buenaventura, and Gerald Vizenor provided new insights that helped further my scholarship. I thank Mary Jim, Andrew George, Darryl Wilson, Steve Evans, Richard Scheuerman, and Eugene Hunn for their knowledge about native people of the Columbia Plateau and their help. I offer a special thanks to Fred Bohm, director of the Michigan State University Press, for his interest in Native Americans and presenting documents such as these that help us access the nature of native history. I offer my heartfelt gratitude to the editors and reviewers of Michigan State University Press for their good work and constructive criticism.

I thank my mother, Mary Lou, and grandfather, Earl Henry, for instilling in me a love of native history and our family's stories. Most important, I owe a debt of deep gratitude to my wife, Lee Ann, and our three children, Tess Nashone, Hayley Kachine, and Tara Tsaile who have woven their own stories into the fabric of my life. Thank you for giving of yourselves and your time so that I could research and write. They gave me time and support, always encouraging me to go forward with the work, and I deeply appreciate their understanding.

Clifford E. Trafzer
Yucaipa, California
August 2, 1997

Introduction

WHEN THE EARTH was young, all of the suns, stars, and moons in the universe interacted with each other like a great family. Light linking the Milky Way was alive with spirit, and everything was in motion. It was the same way on earth where rivers, mountains, plants, and animals lived with each other in a great historical drama. They spoke to each other, intermarried with one another, had their own language, told their own stories, and sang their own songs. It was a time of imagination when creative characters had a vision of a world embodying positive and negative forces as well as a host of other dualities. But like any family, all was not tranquil, all was not settled or pleasant or beautiful. To be sure there was harmony, but there was also chaos.

According to traditional beliefs of most Native Americans of the Columbia Plateau, there were two creations and both were sacred—filled with spirit. The Creator, known by many names, set the world into motion, giving life and spirit to everything. In return, everything was connected to creation through positive and negative actions that offered a lesson or teaching of the law. During the first creation, the mountains, rivers, plants, and animals interacted, creating the first laws by which the earth would function. This was the time of the *Wah-tee-tash* or Animal People, before the arrival of humans. They began the process of establishing *tamánwit ku súkat* or the law and spirit, the highest law of creation that would determine the relationships among animals, plants, mountains, and

1

rivers[1] Rules of nature and society, cultural mores, and appropriate behavior were established, and these are the *tamánwit ku súkat*—the spirit and the law—that are addressed in the ancient stories. Coyote was the major actor in the creation of the laws, but there were other heroes creating law, including Beaver, Raccoon, Wild Cat, and Grizzly Bear. Coyote established the law that the river should never be dammed and Salmon should always have free access to travel up the Columbia River and its tributaries in accordance with the laws detailed in stories. Coyote created the law by breaking the fish dam of the Five Sisters or *Tah-tah Kleah* Monsters. He created laws through his positive action for the good of the people, continually making the world ready for a new people that Coyote knew would one day come to the earth. He also created law through his negative action, marrying his own daughter who had a baby that was born ill and malformed. In this way, Coyote created the law against incest, and taught that people suffered greatly by violating incest laws.[2]

The second creation refers to the time when humans inhabited the Columbia Plateau, a creative time that is at once past and present. This time began when humans arrived—the first Native Americans. According to Mourning Dove, the famous Salish-speaking author of Swhyyaylpuh, Nicola, and Okanogan Indian blood, this was a time when "the animals ruled the world a long period of time before the event of creation of man."[3] The famous native author from the Colville Indian Reservation of Washington argued that this was a time when humans interacted closely with those elements of their world that were animate and inanimate. The relationships between humans and their relatives— the animals, plants, mountains, and rivers—emerged during this era of human history. This was a time recorded in story and preserved carefully through the oral tradition. The creative time is both past and present, an unusual concept for non-native historians and other scholars to consider, but one well accepted by native peoples. The creative time occurred at one point in time, but is very much related to the present and future. Events detailed in these stories occurred in the past, but with the retelling occur again and again. In this way they have life and presence in the past and present.

According to Virginia Beavert of the Yakama tribe, "In the Beginning our Creator spoke the word and this earth was created. He spoke the word again. And all living things were put on earth. And then he said the word and we, the (Indian) people, were recreated again."

Thus, "the land where we live and where our ancestors lived was created for the (Indian) people."[4] Coyote, Raccoon, Beaver, and other *Wahtee-tash* created the first law so that Indians could act and deal correctly with each other and with plants, animals, mountains, lakes, and rivers. Through the stories, people learned self-discipline and a belief in the Creative Power. People learned to share, think of others, avoid overindulgence and "bad influences." The Animal People put the laws into motion and established the moral, political, economic, social, and spiritual law that would be the basis of Native American peoples once they arrived on the Columbia Plateau.

As a result of the creation, American Indians of the region are intimately tied to particular places on land and rivers, rock formations, lakes, and mountains. They are tied to plants and animals that once formed the basis of their livelihood. They are tied to the spirits of places, plants, and animals, the spiritual forces that influenced and continue to influence the lives of the people. Lucullus Virgil McWhorter once wrote that "their land was their religion, and their religion was the land."[5] McWhorter was an unusual rancher in the Yakama Valley, a man who collected oral stories and preserved elements of Native American history. He also championed Indian rights, an unpopular position among whites during the early twentieth century on the Columbia Plateau. McWhorter was born in Harrison County, Virginia, on 29 January 1860, and he moved from West Virginia to Ohio in 1897 where he farmed and raised Devon cattle. In 1903 McWhorter moved to North Yakima where he ranched. He brought with him a third grade education and a family tradition of interest in history, literature, and archaeology.[6] McWhorter was self-educated, and he continued his studies throughout his life, specializing in Native American history, literature, and religion.[7]

In the "Time When the Tamaracks Turn Yellow," October 1907, McWhorter met one of the storytellers featured in this collection. His name was Yellow Wolf, an unusual and honorable man who significantly influenced the rancher's life. One fall day, McWhorter greeted an Indian driving a horse in front of him. The horse had a severe wire cut, and the Indian asked if he could leave his horse to mend at McWhorter's ranch. McWhorter agreed. Ten months later the Indian returned to reclaim the horse. When McWhorter released the animal, he did so without asking compensation, "in accordance with tribal ethics."[8] Thus began a lifetime friendship with *Hemene Moxmox*, Yellow Wolf, the nephew of Chief Joseph and warrior-chief of the Nez Perce War of

1877. But even before meeting Yellow Wolf, McWhorter had earned a good reputation as a respected ally of Indians living on the Yakama Reservation.[9] "He hunted and camped with his Indian friends, brought them into his home, shared food with them, attended and finally participated in their ceremonials, and in many ways adopted their point of view." Chief Yoomteebee adopted McWhorter, giving him the name *Hemene Kawan* or Old Wolf.[10]

Although McWhorter was a non-Indian, he became a member of the Indian community. He aided individual Indians in their fight to save their allotments, and he helped secure tribal water rights that legally belonged to Yakama Indians but were threatened to be stolen by local farmers through the Office of Indian Affairs. McWhorter was interested in many aspects of Native American culture, including the old stories which the Indians shared with him openly and freely so that he could preserve them in written form. McWhorter with the intent of publishing them in a book, collected the stories primarily in the 1910s and 1920s, compiled them, but he never completed the book. He had too many other prospects that consumed his time, including his tribal histories of the Nez Perce War. McWhorter died on 10 October 1944 after a long and meaningful life.[11]

McWhorter was acutely aware that the Yakama, Wasco, Nez Perce, Klickitat, Wishom, and others believed that the earth was alive and that every component of the earth was filled with spirit. Spirits of the earth interacted with every other element of the earth, influencing the eternal, unbroken, and sacred circle of life. The laws established during the creations set all of this into motion. In his classic book, *Nch'i-Wana, "The Big River": Mid-Columbia Indians and Their Land*, Eugene S. Hunn writes that "People, animals, plants, and other forces of nature—sun, earth, wind, and rock—are animated by spirit. As such they share with humankind intelligence and will, and thus have moral rights and obligations as PERSONS."[12] This is a basic tenet of Plateau Indian religion, and the spirits of all the *Wah-tee-tash*, who created the laws, manifest themselves in traditional stories. The creation of laws began with the era of the Animal People, and the process continued after the arrival of humans.

The fact that Native American laws were created before and after the arrival of people on the Columbia Plateau was strongly conveyed to me by Palouse Indian elder and holy man Andrew George. At that time Richard D. Scheuerman and I were researching a history of the Palouse

Indians; over the course of four years, we visited several Northwestern reservations. On each reservation, someone told us that we could not do this work without meeting Andrew George, a traditionalist who had grown up on the Snake River and had lived the "old life." We heard from many native people that he was on one reservation or another, but by the time I visited a particular reservation, he was gone. Andrew George was a legend and a phantom. In November 1981, the Yakima Historical Society asked me to discuss the importance of understanding and collecting oral stories and history in my academic research. After the talk, several Indians from the Yakama Reservation told me that we could not write the Palouse Indian book without first speaking to Andrew George. They added that he was staying on the Yakama Reservation at his daughter's house, and they gave us directions to his home.

When Scheuerman, Lee Ann Smith, and I arrived at his daughter's home, I knocked on the door of the third house, hoping this was the right home. Two small girls answered the door and I asked if Andrew George lived there. The girls ran off, leaving the door wide open, allowing the cold north wind to blow into the house. Out of a hall to the left came a short elderly man with long white hair that fell to his waist. He said nothing but reached through the door, taking our arms firmly into his hands, and leading us into the warm home. We walked the short distance into the kitchen to a table where we sat down to talk. All the while, I was attempting to explain why we had come for the visit and the nature of our project, but the old man would have none of it. He heard everything I had said, but ignored my words. When he sat down, Andrew George began telling stories, one right after another. For the next three hours, Andrew George told us stories explaining the history of his family and people. He knew who we were, and he knew what he wanted to tell us. And so he shared those things that he could through words, acts, and stories.[13]

Andrew George was no ordinary elder. He was a teacher, storyteller, spiritual leader, and Indian doctor. He became a friend, and through our meeting and his subsequent letters, he helped me understand the spirit and the law as established by the *Wah-tee-tash*. Born in the heart of the Palouse country of southeastern Washington in the 1890s, George was of mixed Palouse and Nez Perce ancestry. His parents had once lived in Indian Territory—present-day Oklahoma. "They never talked about it much," he told us, "but when they did, they'd cry."[14] His parents had fought alongside Chief Joseph, Ollocott, White Bird, Rainbow, Looking

Glass, Husishusis Kute, Hahtalikin, and all the men, women, and children who had fought in the Nez Perce War of 1877. In 1885 Andrew George's parents, Smith L. George and Julie George, returned to the Northwest. At Wallula Junction on the Columbia River, agents of the Office of Indian Affairs told his parents to accompany Palouse elder Husishusis Kute to the Nez Perce Reservation, but shortly after arriving there, his parents slipped off the reservation and returned to Palus Village on the Snake River.[15]

Andrew George grew up in the old way at Palus Village. He lived at a sacred village site, the place where a Giant Beaver had been slain during the second creation. This Giant Beaver had died during the second creation and left his heart to petrify and mark the site of Palus. The Giant Beaver had once terrorized the people, killing many. Three Warrior Brothers challenged the Giant Beaver, striking their first blow with a powerful lance upstream on Palouse River. The wounded Giant Beaver became so enraged that he chewed a gash in the river. When another lance pierced his body, be chewed the thick basalt more and more, creating Lower Palouse Falls. When the Warrior Brothers struck the Giant Beaver again as the monster moved downriver, thrusting another spear into him, Giant Beaver was so angry that he chewed a huge hole in the river, creating Palouse Falls. Outraged by the attack, the Giant Beaver chewed his way through the dark black basalt, creating a deep canyon that runs from Palouse Falls to Snake River. Giant Beaver died at the junction of the Palouse and Snake Rivers, and his heart remained at this place where Andrew George was born and raised. The entire course of the Palouse River from the lower falls to the confluence of the two rivers is a sacred area to the Palousepum, the Palouse People, but it was destroyed in the mid-twentieth century when whites created a dam, in violation of the "law."[16]

Andrew George never met Leslie Silko, the famous author from Laguna Pueblo, but he would have agreed with her assessment of the importance of stories in tying people to places. "It's story that make this into a community," Silko told Jane B. Katz. "There have to be stories. That's how you know; that's how you belong; that's how you know you belong."[17] Andrew George was from the Palouse country, a region distinguished by sensuous rolling hills that are steep and difficult to traverse. He told us how Coyote had created the Palouse Hills, creating a law so that the hills would be steep and rolling forever. This was the time when Coyote bragged to everyone that he could outrun them in a race.

Coyote told Deer, Grizzly Bear, Salmon, Eagle, Antelope, and others that he could outrun anyone in a race. Coyote bragged so much that the people began to believe the wily one, and no one—not even the fastest runners—would challenge Coyote in a race, except one. Amid the silence came one voice to challenge Coyote and that was Turtle. A great and unified laughter rose up from that place, as all of the people poked fun at Turtle for believing he might beat Coyote in a race. But Turtle was undaunted by the taunts, saying that he would race Coyote on the appointed day. Coyote made the race more difficult by envisioning huge rolling hills and creating the hills with his special power. This was how Coyote created the law that made the Palouse Hills. He put them into being so that they would last forever. This was the law for all times but Coyote had no idea that his own law would work against him.[18]

On the day of the Great Race, Coyote and Turtle looked out over a sea of undulating hills. They lined up beside each other and soon were off up the first hill, down the other side, and up the next. Coyote thought he was far in front of Turtle, but as he started up the grade, he looked ahead to see Turtle rounding the second hill. He raced faster and soon overtook Turtle, but as he was ascending the third hill, he looked forward to see Turtle once again ahead of him. Coyote raced faster and faster, but Turtle was ahead of him on the fourth and fifth hill. Finally, the wily trickster could run no more. He fell to the ground exhausted, panting hard and feeling his heart pound as if it would burst. While Coyote calmed his burning lungs, Turtle descended the fifth hill and crossed the finish line first. Turtle won by using his head, planning ahead in a familial effort by placing members of his family at the top of each hill. They had worked as a team in a communal effort to beat Coyote.[19]

The *Wah-tee-tash* established the first laws of the earth, but other laws developed after the arrival of humans. Indeed, humans helped create and define the laws of creation during their interaction with the Animal People. According to Andrew George, there was a time when humans caught too many Salmon in violation of the law. The Salmon People met in council to discuss what to do, and one person suggested that they should see Rattlesnake, who had great powers to use against humans. So Salmon Chief found Rattlesnake curled up under a shady rock along the river's edge. He asked if Rattlesnake would give the Salmon People some of his power. When Rattlesnake refused, Salmon Chief used his mighty tail to beat the reluctant Rattlesnake on the head. Five times the Salmon Chief asked Rattlesnake for some of his power, beating him on the head each time. Four times Rattlesnake refused. After the fifth beating, however, Rattlesnake grudgingly gave Salmon some of his power. That is why Salmon can bite humans and infect them, using a small portion of Rattlesnake's power. Whenever a human is bitten, it is a reminder of the law. Humans should not take too many Salmon.[20]

The *Wah-tee-tash* shared stories with each other, and when humans arrived, they told the ancient history to humans. The people told stories, shared their knowledge through words, and considered them sacred texts. The people created thought, action, and behavior. They put the laws of creation into action for all time, and they told stories to illustrate and interpret the laws so that they would never be forgotten. Storytelling was an activity common to all native people and was practiced by men, women, and children. Among the Yakama, storytelling always began with the storyteller saying, "*Awacha Nay*" or "This is the way it was." In this way, storytellers conveyed the power of the story and its historical place as a real and definite event that was about to unfold. All of the children and other listeners responded by crying out in a loud and high tone, "*Eeeee!*" This was a way of saying that they were ready to listen and listen with a full heart and clear mind. And after every story, the crowd signaled its approval with the cry, "*Eeeee!*" This procedure remains alive today. Storytelling was and is common among the people living on Northwestern Reservations.

Mourning Dove, the famous writer from the Colville Reservation, once said, "The long evenings were spent in the lodges by Indians telling stories of different incidents of ancient history."[21] She pointed out that for generations, Native American children were taught to "sit down when these Indians are telling stories to save interrupting [sic] the older people in their speech. It is well trained children that will be quiet in a tepee lodge while other people are talking." At one point in her early life, Mourning Dove's mother admonished her children, saying "Have you no ears?" She told her children, "ears are made for people to listen through. You must listen to your elders."[22] Stories were told and heard, a duality of presentation and reception of spoken and heard words. Stories affected both the storyteller and listener in profound ways. "The stories that are heard," says Anishinaabe author Gerald Vizenor, "are the coherent memories of natural reason; the stories that are read are silent landscapes."[23] Stories told by the first humans and *Wah-tee-tash* were heard stories, tales that made mysteries more clear and informed tellers and listeners about the law. Together, the storyteller and listener imagined a past, present, and future that guided future generations, informing them of their identities, relationships, and place. By sharing in the oral stories, they passed down wisdom from grandparents to grandchildren, parents to children. They did this through spoken words, a time-honored educational tradition of Native America.

Stories are songs and lives. They are life and death and life again. Stories are reborn with each telling, explaining laws that bind past and present. Each time the stories are told, they come alive, just as they did at the time of their creation. In this way, told stories are recreations of the first creation, establishing a renewed relationship between storyteller, listener, place, and characters. Stories are alive with spirit, living memories of people, places, and things that are, at their core, sacred bodies of knowledge. Those who share the stories—storytellers—are honored members of native communities because they keep the stories in motion at each telling. Sometimes storytellers are specialists, well respected for their keen minds and playful use of words. More often they are mothers and fathers, aunts and uncles, or grandmothers and grandfathers. Mourning Dove once remarked that "Anything that happened with a humorous event was frequently told over and over by these simple forest people. Since we lived out in one room, any child with any imagination naturally [would] be interested to listen like I use to do."[24] Mourning Dove learned many of her stories from *Tequalt* or Long Woman, a woman adopted by the family who served as a grandmother to the children. Long Woman was a teacher and storyteller who instructed the future writer about the time when "the animals ruled the world a long period of time before the event of creation of man."[25]

Long Woman spent hours with Mourning Dove and other children in the family's tipi, telling tales of Coyote, Bobcat, and Madam Grizzly Bear. She told the children stories about the spirit within the mountains and rivers, how the sun once married five beautiful women—mountains of the Cascade Range. Long Woman told the children how jealousy led four of the women to disfigure the most favorite wife by causing her to erupt in violent volcanic action. Long Woman changed Mourning Dove's life by instilling in her a love of stories that the writer would use in her future works. The stories had such a profound effect on Mourning Dove that she once wrote that she "dreamed of a home of my own where I could have all the grandmothers I wanted to tell me stories."[26] The writer dreamed of that home and all of those grandmothers, just like Long Woman who would spin stories into being, creating a spider's web of plots and characters who played out dramas familiar to the ancient stories of the Northwest. Grandmothers such as Long Woman kept the spirit alive through the old stories, and the words are still moving today. By the light of small fires during winter evenings, storytellers told their stories. Mourning Dove believed that "Indian children of the teepee home love the stories and we always sat quite [quiet] in strict attending while the older people told legends and stories of old." On cold nights the people gathered in their homes to hear stories, and some still do.[27]

Storytellers from the Columbia Plateau had profound voices that are still heard in the echoes of homes, canyons, mountains, rivers, and mountains. Their voices are heard in the warm Chinook wind that blows across the rolling hills and flat plains, melting winter snows that grip the region during the time of the frozen earth. Some of these voices are forgotten today, but their stories are still sung on Northwestern reservations. In October 1993, a traditional storyteller at the Yakama Nation Cultural Center told versions of a few tales provided in this volume. He was careful to share only those parts of the story that he thought were appropriate for his audience, omitting elements of the story that might offend his listeners. Still, he told stories using his own voice, recreating the ancient stories of his people.[28] One of the stories he shared dealt with *Isti-plah*, a monster who once swallowed people traveling on or near the lower Columbia River. Although the story was different in content and sequence from that offered in this collection by Stwire G. Waters of Klickitat and Yakama descent, the themes were identical and the outcome the same.

Unfortunately, some of the stories in this collection are anonymous, and we have no idea who told the stories to L. V. McWhorter. It is likely that McWhorter heard these stories and wrote them down from memory. He often took notes on a small pad of paper or pieces of envelopes, programs, or other remnants. He wrote essential elements of stories on these scraps of paper to remind him of the text and wrote them down as he remembered them at a later date. This is because McWhorter was steeped in native stories that he heard at powwows, ceremonies, rodeos, feasts, and hunting trips. According to Steve Evans, author of a remarkable book, *Voice of the Old Wolf: Lucullus Virgil McWhorter and the Nez Perce Indians*, rancher-scholar McWhorter heard these stories over and over again "because of the fact that he spent so much time with Indians." McWhorter would "hear a story and want to get it right so he'd ask someone else to tell it. That's why there's different versions of stories. He'd hear the same story by different people. He'd hear stories every place he went, because Indians tell stories, all kinds of stories. He was really steeped in it. He'd remember stories and he became a storyteller himself. That's what he did, tell stories through the spoken and written word."[29]

Whenever McWhorter could attribute a story to a particular individual, he did so, but when he could not, he wrote "anonymous" on his typewritten manuscripts. Whenever possible, he attributed the story to a tribe or to several tribes which he felt were most closely affiliated with a particular story. In this collection, McWhorter identified seventeen Native American storytellers. Often he called women grandmothers because they were elderly storytellers who shared their stories with younger people, including McWhorter. For example, he identified *Ana-whoah* (Black Bear) as a "grandmother." In September 1914, she told McWhorter the Wasco Indian version of the "Bridge of the Gods," and at that time she was considered the oldest living Wasco. During this storytelling, *Yes-to-la-lema*, the daughter of *Ana-whoah*, served as interpreter, which raises important points about McWhorter's methods and his ability to represent storytellers accurately. McWhorter knew many Indian words in Sahaptin, Chinook, and Salish. According to Evans, McWhorter "had a good vocabulary of Indian words, but he was not fluent in Yakama, Nez Perce, or Chinook." As a result, McWhorter relied on interpreters, native people who spoke the same Indian language as the storyteller as well as English.[30]

McWhorter did not pay Indians for their stories, but he paid interpreters for their time. McWhorter believed in gift giving, particularly food, and he was known to have given storytellers cans of coffee, fruits, meats, and vegetables as a way of saying thank you. Evans asserted that "McWhorter shared with Indians and they shared with him. That's the Indian way. McWhorter might give Yellow Wolf five dollars. This was friendship money. McWhorter had the money and Yellow Wolf didn't but needed it. Then Yellow Wolf helped McWhorter, telling stories. They both understood that as friends, they helped each other out. It was give and take. The money McWhorter gave Indians was never a 'loan' like in the business sense of the word. It was sharing." In addition to sharing money and stories, McWhorter found work for Indians. When he learned that someone wanted to hire dancers, drummers, or singers, McWhorter arranged to have Yellow Wolf, Many Wounds, or Billie

White Thunder hired. Sometimes McWhorter would "buy feathers and enough material for someone to make four war bonnets." Then, according to Evans, "He'd sell two of them to his connections in Hollywood who wanted authentic headdresses and leave the other two for Yellow Wolf and Peopeo Tholekt to sell and make some money. He helped them out so they could do the kind of work they enjoyed." He helped them find work that they enjoyed such as dancing, drumming, singing, riding, or making bonnets, as opposed to farm work or ranch labor which was dull and always available.[31]

Mourning Dove once reported that she had trouble collecting Okanogan stories about her own people because "James Teit [anthropologist] has collected folklores among the Indians and has been paying five dollars a piece for good Indian legends."[32] Mourning Dove believed the stories should be shared, not sold, particularly to another Okanogan person. Like Mourning Dove, McWhorter "did not pay a certain sum of money for a story." Rather, Indians "gave the stories to him, sometimes remarking that they did so for the sake of preservation and so that non-Indians might understand the history, law, culture, beliefs, and traditions of Indian people. Most likely, many Indians who shared stories with McWhorter were unaware that he was collecting stories for a book, particularly if McWhorter heard the story by chance. Other storytellers knew of McWhorter's work writing about Native American history, and they openly and consciously shared their stories with him. In any case, McWhorter collected the stories out of a sincere interest in the oral tradition, and he always planned on using the stories in a book. According to Steve Evans, McWhorter "never got the manuscript fully prepared." McWhorter never finished the book because of his other work and because he was so deeply "embroiled in defense of Yakama treaty rights."[33] Alanna Brown argued that McWhorter's work in defense of native people "cost him dearly when community leaders thwarted McWhorter's bid to be appointed the government agent for the Yakama Tribe." In addition, it cost him time which he could have devoted to his research and writing.[34]

When I asked Evans if he thought McWhorter had permission to publish the stories, he laughed, explaining that "Indians didn't work that way. They shared stories. No one owned them. When you told a personal story, maybe one about your family and you told it, you shared it and others could tell it. McWhorter could tell it. All of the Indians knew that McWhorter wrote books, told their stories. They kept right on giving him stories. I'd say he had permission to use their stories, publish them."[33] Evans then qualified his statements about the use of stories by stating: "War stories are different. They belong—are owned by the storyteller who lived the tale. They belong to the family. They didn't like younger people telling war stories when they had not lived through the war or participated in a particular action. These are more like owned stories than traditional, communal, tribal stories that are shared." Nevertheless, McWhorter was anxious about recording information correctly. "McWhorter wanted to get the [traditional] stories of the *Wah-tee-tash* right," Evans reported, "be accurate and truthful. The Indians wanted whites to know about the sacredness of places, rivers, lakes, mountains. This was sacred land and should not be disturbed by dams, power plants, and so on." So when McWhorter heard "stories from Indians he met at rodeos," he would attempt to remember them by writing "down notes to refer back to later." Evans reminded me that McWhorter's "collection is filled with scraps of paper, notes, notes on receipts, and all kinds of pieces of paper. Then he'd go back to them to remind himself of the story."[34]

Often McWhorter heard stories when he was with Indians, and he would try to remember them by taking a few notes. McWhorter never worked with a tape recorder, and he did his best to recall the stories as they were told to him. Although he was careful about recording the stories as accurately as possible, he did not take all of them down verbatim or record the names of Indians who had given him particular stories. As a result, the stories often reflect McWhorter's version rather than an exact rendering of the story as given by the native person; these stories are not attributed to particular storytellers or tribes of origin. Moreover, some stories read like composite versions of the same story. When tales are attributed to anonymous storytellers, the voice is that of McWhorter. In addition to voice, these stories are distinguished by McWhorter's choice of words and his run-on sentence structure. I deal with these issues in the notes of each chapter, explaining McWhorter's writings and influences within the text. There is no doubt that McWhorter's reconstruction of the stories is a form of editing or that he is placed into the text through the written presentation of the story. These stories are still traditional, though, and as old as time, but they have been presented in written English by McWhorter, a non-Indian. Nevertheless, the stories were recorded by one who understood, appreciated, and treasured the oral tradition, a man who respected Native Americans.

McWhorter recorded the identity of seventeen native storytellers in this collection. In every case that McWhorter provided the identity of a storyteller, that name appears in the heading. Sometimes McWhorter recorded the person's tribal affiliation as well as his English and Native American names. For example, *Heyoomyummi* (Woman Grizzly Bear) is also identified as Mrs. Susie White, the daughter of *Pe-nah-we-non-mi* and Short In The Head, a man who was a warrior during the Nez Perce War of 1877. *Heyoomyummi* was a Nez Perce elder and her mother, *Pe-nah-we-non-mi*, was by her side when she gave McWhorter the story, "Legend of the Spalding Memorial Rock." *Che-pos To-cos*, or Owl Child, was another storyteller of the Wishom tribe, a tribe whose name is commonly spelled Wishrom today. McWhorter also identifies Owl Child as Columbia River since the Wishom lived in villages along the Columbia River. Whatever information McWhorter provided about the date, place, or circumstances regarding the stories he acquired, I offer in the heading and notes. In addition, I have tried to learn about the storytellers from McWhorter's correspondence, Indians who knew them, Yakama censuses, and authors who have worked in the area. Owl Child, for example, lived many years on the Great Plains with Blackfeet, but he was born at the village of Wishom and knew their stories.

Ik-keep-swah was a Wasco storyteller who told McWhorter about Coyote and the Two Sisters of the Columbia River, while *An-nee-shiat* was an elderly woman whom McWhorter identified as a grandmother. She was not Yakama and did not know the Yakama stories. McWhorter tells us that she grew up and lived her life on the Columbia River, and she was most likely a Klickitat Indian who was never forced to move onto the Yakama Reservation. William Charley was a good friend of McWhorter and a frequent guest at McWhorter's ranch. Charley was Yakama and lived on the reservation adjacent to McWhorter's ranch. He worked with McWhorter on a publication championing Indian rights known as the *Indian Teepee*. Stwire G. Waters was once chief of the Yakama Nation, and he was of mixed Yakama and Klickitat blood. Waters was a Methodist minister, but he was of the old time mind. A respected traditionalist in heart and mind, Waters knew the old ways. Waters also knew the old stories and the power of the spirit and law. He was an old style of leader in that he considered himself a protector and adviser of the people. He was just and kind, well liked on and off the Yakama Reservation.

McWhorter's closest friend among the storytellers was *Hemene Moxmox* or Yellow Wolf. He was a famous Nez Perce warrior and a member of Chief Joseph's family. During the Nez Perce War, Yellow Wolf was a warrior-chief. After the war, he suffered exile in Canada and banishment to *Eekish Pah*, the Hot Place or Indian Territory.[35] First and foremost, Yellow Wolf was a warrior, but he knew the old stories and shared them with McWhorter. His son was Billie White Thunder, who, like his father, had the power of thunder and lightning. Both Billie and his father had tremendous spirit power, but Billie's only contribution to the collection is an Okanogan story about the girl rock formation of Kettle Falls on the Colville Reservation. Yellow Wolf's stories are far superior in content and detail to that of his son's, probably because Yellow Wolf grew up in the Wallowa Valley—Nez Perce country—while his son grew up at Nespelem, Washington, on the Colville Reservation. There is not much information available about the other storytellers, and that which is available is given in the heading and notes of their stories.

On the broad yellow plains, gray mountain slopes, expansive black plateau, thick green woods, and undulating golden hills, storytellers told their stories of the spirit and law. Everywhere on the Columbia Plateau, storytellers told of life's experiences through the stories of the *Wah-tee-tash* and the first people. People listened, not with careless attention but with an attentiveness born of spirit and purpose. Then and now people delight in the words, in telling and retelling stories which recreate life with words from the earth and sky. The stories invite the spirit to come alive, to move from its latent presence to an active one. Storytellers transform listeners, taking them back to another time, making the past part of the present and enlarging the circle into the future. Stories take the listener and storyteller back to the time of the first creation and bring them forward into the present.

Stories are not juvenile literature or fairy tales that grow with the telling.[36] They are facts and truths of Native American cultures and communities. They are at once history and literature, religion and law. This collection contains some of the rich oral texts of Native Americans from the Columbia Plateau, stories that are considered a sacred body of knowledge that set forth doctrines of traditional Indian people. According to Laguna writer Paula Gunn Allen, stories are not the stuff of "Western Civilization," with its "way of segmentation, discontinuity, linearity." They are not the hard evidence sought by "serious" scholars of history, who scoff at the idea that the stories are in truth the first record of the past in the Americas. Stemming from an oral tradition, Native American stories have been written down only recently, and so their validity and usefulness are questioned by those who want their facts on paper. The stories found in this volume are the "way of the Imagination" with their "continuity, circularity, and completeness." American Indian "writers write out of tribal tradition that is at base connected to ritual and beyond that to tribal metaphysics or mysticism." The stories tell us much about native art, thought, and spirit. Without the stories, there is no understanding of American Indian culture, history, or literary tradition.[37]

This certainly is true for Native Americans living on the Great Columbia Plateau of North America. The Sahaptan-, Chinookan-, and Salishan-speaking people of this region believe that their ancient stories tell a great deal about their past and present. Nez Perce, Yakama, Klickitat, Cascade, Wasco, Wishom, and Wenatchi are just a few of the tribes that share the stories presented here.[38] Many elders of these tribes—today living on the Yakama, Colville, Warm Springs, Umatilla, Coeur d'Alene, Spokane, and Nez Perce Reservations—argue convincingly that no one can begin to understand their culture without understanding something of their old stories. The stories provide texts through which outsiders may enter into a native world and become familiar with ideas, values, lessons, characters, places, and knowledge important to specific native peoples. Stories are the cultural foundations of the people, and they are words that brought forth their world at the beginning of time.

Andrew George once looked at me and said, "You come from that university, don't you?" He was asking rhetorically, knowing that I taught at Washington State University. "You have people there who say they know the earth, plants, and animals. Well, I wonder if they really know these things. I have seen things. I have seen things they have never seen. I have heard things they have never heard. I have spoken to these things, and I have heard their words and stories."[39] Andrew George had learned the songs of plants and animals, talked with them intimately. He saw them in a very different way than scientists. He saw them as people, and in the scheme of law and history, it is important for scholars to be aware of this difference which is intimately tied to the spirit and law of traditional people and represented through the old stories. Andrew revealed some truths of his culture through stories. He once wrote that on a trip to the Palouse country, "many things came to my mind as of my father's words as what he told me." These things had been told to Andrew's father by his "uncles, his father's brothers, our beliefs and religion—sounds, dreams, unseen movements, the secrets that should never be revealed."

Grandmothers, grandfathers, and "all creatures" had been given the task by the Creator of "teaching this side of the world, the other side he put his son to teach—the teach was for all the creatures." By sharing his knowledge through stories, Andrew allowed others to enter a way of knowing that is uncommon within the academy. The storytellers in this collection do the same thing, offering stories that are metaphors for those things that can and cannot be known. Significantly, they provided a glimpse into the Native American world of the Columbia Plateau. "I think my traveling is on end," Andrew George wrote in his last letter, "but I have learned many things of my people and will try and pass it on to the next generation, the ones that can look back to know what it was and should be." The stories of Andrew George and other more contemporary storytellers are not offered in this volume because the collection contained herein is confined to those stories collected in the early twentieth century by McWhorter. But George is an example of one link between the storytellers of the past and present, preservers of culture through story. Like other contemporary storytellers, George well understood the spirit and the law, the underlying messages of traditional narratives. During his last days, Andrew George looked to the stories to tell him about the past and future.[40]

The stories found in this volume are part of what the storytellers and McWhorter learned from tribal elders. They constitute an introduction to traditional Native American literature and history, which in turn requires the participation of the storytellers and readers who must patiently consider the meaning of the words. Within each story are important symbols, interpretations, and lessons. They are weighty with thought and spirit. They are fundamental fuels from which we can light the fires of imagination. The stories are meant to be contemplated and used, told and retold. They are masks, exhibiting only part of the meaning and inviting observers to look deeper to find the spirit and law of words and stories. Not all that can be known will be known through the stories, but something of that which can be known will be found in the words. This is the way it is supposed to be for those interested in taking an historical and literary adventure into these Native American texts.

In 1977 I left my teaching position at Navajo Community College to take a professorship in Native American Studies and History at

Washington State University.[41] From the mountains and deserts of northern Arizona I moved to the Columbia Plateau, settling into a house on Military Hill, one of the great Palouse Hills in southeastern Washington. Since I lived in the heart of the Palouse country on a hill overlooking Palouse River, I determined to study the history of Palouse Indians. This was the beginning of a twenty-year journey into a new world, that of Northwestern Indians who had inhabited the area since the time of the second creation. The rural region is marked everywhere by the influence of Palouse Indians, and I began a lifelong interest in the native people of the Columbia Plateau. Manuscripts, Archives, and Special Collections of Holland Library at Washington State University contained a wealth of information pertinent to native people from the Columbia Plateau, including the voluminous papers of L. V. McWhorter, the rancher-scholar from Yakima Valley.

When I moved to the Northwest, I had never heard of McWhorter, but I was quickly introduced to his two classic works, *Yellow Wolf: His Own Story* and *Hear Me, My Chiefs!* [42] McWhorter's use of traditional historical documents and oral histories provide well-balanced accounts that are unique contributions to Native American history. McWhorter wrote the "New Western History" in the 1930s and 1940s, long before recent converts found their way to believing that Native Americans should have a voice in historical accounts. McWhorter's contributions to Northwestern Indian history are significant in themselves, but he also collected Native American oral narratives and preserved numerous stories that deal with the issue of law and spirit. He understood that oral narratives are part of Native American history, as did all the storytellers who gave him stories.

In recent years, some scholars have criticized McWhorter for his work with Mourning Dove, saying that he changed her narrative in her novel. In 1914 McWhorter met Mourning Dove and encouraged her to collect the ancient stories of her people.[43] He also agreed to help her publish her novel, *Co-ge-we-a, The Half Blood: A Depiction of the Great Montana Cattle Range.*[44] McWhorter invited Mourning Dove into his home and worked with her to edit the novel and get it published. McWhorter has been criticized for editing and changing Mourning Dove's work and her voice, but there is no evidence that he intentionally changed the meaning of the stories that appear in this volume. In a few cases, however, he may have editorialized in the narrative, and this possibility is discussed in the appropriate endnote. According to Alanna K. Brown, one of the most accomplished scholars of Mourning Dove's work, "McWhorter understood the importance of keeping the [traditional] stories as close to oral presentation as possible."

It is fair to ask to what extent he changed the stories. This is not an easy question to answer, although several stories that he typed from his notes contained some penciled remarks. For this volume, these have been deleted, placed in "Notes by McWhorter," or placed in brackets. Unquestionably, McWhorter did some editing of the stories as he typed the manuscripts. He may have deleted portions of them or changed the wording, particularly if he thought the words would be offensive to editors or the general public. McWhorter was always concerned that individuals unfamiliar with Naive Americans might consider Indians to be backward, crude, or vulgar. This was apparently not an issue with the stories presented here, for none of the versions of the stories contained information regarding bodily functions or human organs which were deleted in other versions.[45] I feel that McWhorter's representation of the traditional narratives are as accurate as he could present them, although contemporary storytellers may have different versions of these stories that contain more details.

There is no direct evidence that McWhorter significantly altered the voices of the known storytellers presented here. Indeed, the voices of individual storytellers are abundantly apparent in the stories. For example, it is simple to identify the stories of *Hemene Moxmox* (Yellow Wolf) when compared to those of *Ana-whoah* (Black Bear). [The stories of the former are straightforward, direct, and blunt without a great deal of development.] Those of Black Bear are better developed and exciting. The narrative of the latter is a good read. In her story, "Battle of Cold Wind and Chinook Wind," Black Bear states: "The wrestling rule was that the one thrown down must have his head cut off by Coyote. Coyote always came with his flint knife ready. Piles! Great piles of dead lay where Cold Wind had conquered. None could stand before him."[46] Readers can almost hear Black Bear, the "Grandmother," recreate her story. Significantly, McWhorter's transcriptions of the stories attributed to particular storytellers reflect the tone, style, and presentation of the storytellers. The stories by the same storyteller are fairly uniform in style and presentation, indicating that McWhorter respected the individual voice of the storyteller. He did not force their work into a false format created by the recorder. In this way, McWhorter honored the storytellers and their words. The stories attributed to anonymous storytellers, however, contain a good deal of McWhorter's voice, which is discussed in the endnotes.

In editing this collection of stories, I was careful not to change the text significantly in order to maintain its integrity. I did not edit the native storytellers, but I have edited McWhorter. I made changes in punctuation, annotations, and spelling which help the work flow smoothly, but I did not change his spelling of Yakima, a spelling of the tribal name that had become common but was changed in 1994 by the tribe to coincide with the spelling that appears on its treaty. At first, I did not delete the many semicolons and hyphens used by McWhorter, but outside reviewers of the manuscript urged me to correct the punctuation so that the work would be readable. Therefore, I deleted many semicolons and used commas whenever appropriate. McWhorter also hyphenated English words that did not require hyphens. For example, he used hyphens in such words as Grizzly-bear, Bob-cat, and Mountain-goat. Whenever appropriate I deleted the hyphens, except in Native American words. I believe McWhorter overused hyphens in the Sahaptin, Salish, and Chinook words used in the text, but I left them as he had them to demonstrate his presentation of native words. At some point McWhorter wrote to the Bureau of American Ethnology to receive some instructions on how to deal with native words, and he used the phonetic form for these words. But McWhorter was not trained in linguistics, so there are differences between his presentation of Native American words and those of professional linguists. Many of the native words used in these oral narratives are defined in the glossary at the end of the work.

McWhorter's use of hyphens and spelling of Native American words was not consistent and an attempt has been made to standardize both. In the case of *Twee-tash* (Grizzly Bear), for example, McWhorter sometimes spelled the word *Twee-tas*, which may have been his usage and not that of all storytellers. I have heard Sahaptin-speaking people pronounce the name Thomas as Thomash, and I feel that one storyteller from one group or part of the Plateau may have ended the word with the **S** sound, while others pronounced the end of the word with an **SH** sound. McWhorter was also inconsistent with his use of capital letters for the *Wah-tee-tash*, and for this reason, I capitalized such proper nouns as Eagle, Coyote, Salmon, and Raccoon. In addition to this inconsistency, McWhorter used many spellings of *Tah-tah Kleah*, *Queenut*, *Qui-yiah*, *Cle-Elum*, and others, but I feel that this was the result of McWhorter's inattention to spelling details, rather than different voices. I kept most of them as McWhorter presented them, unless I felt that they were simply spelled differently as a result of inattention.

In addition to spelling, capitals, and the use of hyphens, McWhorter's sentences were sometimes cumbersome. McWhorter often created run-on sentences which I broke apart into multiple sentences, using most of the same words but creating a new sentence or two. I did not do this often. Furthermore, I did not change verb tenses because they sometimes change from past to present in oral presentations. This is not uncommon in storytelling as the presenter brings the narrative into the present, acting as if the actions described in the story are happening in the present or about to happen. Furthermore, the issue of time in narratives is not of utmost concern to native storytellers. The variation in verb tenses is revealing, and these were left in the work as first recorded by McWhorter. Within the text, most of the brackets are mine, although McWhorter occasionally used parentheses or brackets to amplify the text. Most of McWhorter's titles have remained the same, although I shortened a few of them, deleting a few words. I also created one new title for a story McWhorter called "Wishom Legend." I changed the title of this story by Owl Child to conform with the more descriptive titles of the collection, calling it "Boy Hero and Cannibal." The changes that I made to the stories are cited in the notes and are intended to enhance the work and illuminate information about Plateau Indian history, culture, and society.

The stories found in this collection are at once universal and unique. They represent a rich collection of Native American oral tradition from the Columbia Plateau, and I have included several versions of the same or similar stories so that readers can see, hear, and feel the differences in the way the various storytellers presented their accounts. For example, there are versions of the stories about the North Wind Brothers, the Five Sisters of *nChe-wana*, and the river monsters that swallowed the people. The notes that I have included compare and contrast the stories, offering insights into people, places, and events described in the text. The stories presented are given by Plateau Indians of the inland Northwest, and they reflect much about the people and the place. They deal with particular mountains, cold winds, and specific rivers of the area. They deal with the animals closely associated with the Columbia Plateau, including Grizzly Bear, Salmon, Black Bear, Frog, Beaver, and Wolf. In these ways, the stories are uniquely Northwestern, but the themes found within the stories are universal. Coyote is a major character in many of these stories, and he is presented alternately as a hero and buffoon. Coyote embodies both the positive and negative powers of creation. At times he is a creator, protector, and dreamer. He sets many things into motion and makes things the way they are today.

Coyote defeated the *Tah-tah Kleah* monsters that once lived along the Columbia River and its tributaries, and he brought Salmon to various people living along the river systems of the inland Northwest. He is continually concerned about the welfare of the new people—Indian people—and he is forever preparing for their coming. In this way, Coyote is a creator. But, he is also a negative force, representing the duality of life with its positive and negative characteristics. According to Andrew George, at the time of creation, "Coyote was present, the symbole [*sic*] of power—teacher of balance, the creator of confusion." Thus, Coyote is creator and destroyer. He is unity and disunity, harmony and conflict.[47]

The stories address many mysteries of life, providing experiences which offer some understanding of life and death. The stories are songs of the earth that teach the listener or reader to submit to those things of the law and spirit. Many Northwestern Indians believe that creative powers manifest themselves within geographic forms and features of the earth. Thus all things are part of the creation. The stories speak of a covenant between the American Indian communities and the creative actors of the Plateau, including Salmon, Coyote, North Wind, Columbia River, Monsters, and Humans. The old stories teach that no one can escape life's joys and sorrows, and no one should try. They explain that all elements of the earth have been thrust into the great journey and that everyone should participate. The stories represent the echoes of the past, the spirit and laws set in motion during the time of the *Wah-tee-tash*, the time before and immediately after humans emerged on earth. The stories live in everyone, and in everyone there are stories. Anishinaabe author Gerald Vizenor once stated that "we can tell stories to ourselves . . . and prevail."[48] In the same way, story is survival is story. Stories are life's experiences, learnings, teachings, and understandings; and experience, as Cherokee humorist Will Rogers once pointed out, is what you get when things do not turn out the way you expect.

Stories demonstrate that humans do not have dominion over plants and animals but that they are on an equal or lower plane than other life. This point is played out yearly throughout the Northwest, as Indians assemble to offer prayers, songs, and stories honoring Salmon, roots, and berries. In familial and communal rituals, the people meet to sing their praises to the first Salmon, first roots, and first berries. They eat these foods in communion with the earth, and the men, women, and children sing their songs of thanksgiving to the foods and creative force that placed these foods on the earth for the people. This is the law and the spirit, the holy instructions given to the people during the time of the creation, and they recreate the spirit and law through song, ceremony, and story. They pray and partake of the foods in holy communion, and they remember their ancestors by fulfilling the law and eating sacred foods. In this way, they reestablish their relationship to the earth and its bounty, remembering the creation that set all of this into motion.

During the first foods ceremony, participants humble themselves and give thanks for Salmon, roots, and berries. They call the ceremony to worship with a metal bell, and they sing songs of thanksgiving. They share by drinking water and eating a small piece of Salmon, giving thanks as prescribed by the law. They sing the ancient songs of the *Washat*, praying for a renewal of life for themselves, the plants, and animals. The ceremony is a story within itself, one that draws the participants into the circle of life by nurturing the body, mind, and spirit.[49] The people of the Columbia Plateau are surrounded by majestic mountains, deep canyons, rolling hills, and channeled scablands—all of which come alive in these narratives. The stories draw people into this special place of enchantment and beauty, a unique place where mountains, rivers, and winds tell their own stories. This place is blessed by the blood and bones of Plateau Indians, and every part of it elicits stories. Many Northwestern Indian people believe that they belong to the earth out of which they came and that their stories open their souls to that which is sacred. Traditional families still believe in *tah* or spirit power, and they know of sacred visions of yellow wolves rising up in front of them, water bugs playing on top of ponds, thunder rising over mountains, birds flying without wings, blue mists floating toward them in song, and singing buffaloes. People know much about *tah* power, personal spirits that emerge with creation and remain with them.

The places where individuals received their power are often on their minds, particularly in times of crisis. Mary Jim, a Palouse Indian elder, often said, "this is my mountain," remembering Steptoe Butte located in the heart of the Palouse Hills in central Washington. Although Mary received her power on this mountain, she often spoke of Badger Mountain and Soap Lake. She said she loved to hear the music of Snake River, the great stream that flowed past *Tasawicks*, the place of her birth. She once cried thinking of Snake River, taking me outside her home on the Yakama Reservation and pointing to an irrigation ditch. "This is not my Snake River," Mary Jim announced, "I want to hear my Snake River make music, sing." Her voice vibrated and tears formed in her eyes. The river is sacred to Mary Jim as are other elements of the Columbia Plateau, places she visited as a child to race horses, dig roots, pick berries, fish, and meet boys. In the spring of the year—The Moving Out Time—Mary Jim used to leave her home at *Tasawicks* with her mother and father, and on horseback they traveled across the Columbia Plateau, camping with family and friends.[50] Like Andrew George, Emily Peone, Arthur Kamiakin, Annie Owhi, James Selam, and a host of other elders, Mary Jim understands the earth, plants, and animals. She knows the rocks and mountains, rivers and lakes, and sky and stars. She knows Coyote and she can tell stories about the *Wah-tee-tash*.

Although Mary Jim has never met N. Scott Momaday or read one of his books, she shares with him a great love of place.[51] For her the special places are found on the expansive Columbia Plateau. The elder has spent every year of her life listening to Coyote's howl, the cry of Redtail Hawk, songs of Snake River, and voices in the wind. She knows the power of the sun and moon as they follow their trail across the sky. Mary understands the clear daylight reflecting off rolling hills, black canyons, and sheer mountain cliffs. She has heard the songs of camas and couse, seen life within the huckleberries, and touched the spirit of Salmon People. The land and people are one for Mary Jim, and both are filled with timeless stories of transformation. The native spirit and law are mirrored throughout these stories, first told by the *Wah-tee-tash* to each other, then to mountains, rivers, roots, berries, and trees. They in turn told stories to humans, as generation after generation shared stories through spoken words. Only recently have non-Indians written them down, creating paper spirits filled with stories. L. V. McWhorter was one of the first to record stories of Northwestern peoples, and the result of his work appears in this volume.

The stories are magical and historical, unlike historical texts generally used by scholars. They are offered by a number of different storytellers—some known, some unknown—all of whom felt themselves one with the earth, plants, and animals. They invite readers into the circle to hear the sounds and stories, feel the creation and emotion of the first history of this land. All the Grandmothers and Grandfathers of the past join Old Wolf in asking you to listen to the words, to read the stories aloud, to imagine, delight, and wonder.

1

Alo-Quat and *Twee-tash* Contend over the Division of Light and Darkness
Anonymous

ALO-QUAT [FROG] WERE five brothers, who came with *Twee-tash* [Grizzly Bear] down the Yakima River from the big lake, *Kecheless*.[1] They stopped at *Pah-qy-ti-koot* [now Union Gap], where *Alo-quat* went up to the rocky point on the West side of the Gap, while *Twee-tash* climbed to the top of the mountain on the East side of the Gap. *Alo-quat* was saying fast, never stopping to rest:

> *Lux-i!*
> [One Night!]
> *Lux-i!*
> [One Night!]
> *Lux-i!*
> [One Night!]
> *Lux-i!*
> [One Night!]
> *Lux-i!*
> [One Night!]

Twee-tash on the opposite side of the pass, heard this song of *Alo-quat*. He listened! Then he said:

"No! One night will not do. People will have too short breath. They will not live long enough. Time will not be long enough."

Twee-tash liked to sleep long at one time going to bed. He began to say:

> *Put-um an-wikt, yah-hi at-ta!*
> [Ten years night, come daylight!]
> *Put-um an-wikt, yah-hi at-ta!*
> [Ten years night, come daylight!]
> *Put-um an-wikt, yah-hi at-ta!*
> [Ten years night, come daylight!]
> *Put-um an-wikt, yah-hi at-ta!*
> [Ten years night, come daylight!]
> *Put-um an-wikt, yah-hi at-ta!*
> [Ten years night, come daylight!]

But *Alo-quat* could speak too fast for *Twee-tash*. He could say his song many times while *Twee-tash* said his once. Five *Alo-quat* mah, all singing at once:

> *Lux-i!*
> [One Night!]
> *Lux-i!*
> [One Night!]
> *Lux-i!*
> [One Night!]
> *Lux-i!*
> [One Night!]
> *Lux-i!*
> [One Night!]

Twee-tash grew tired, but he kept on singing:

> *Put-um an-wikt, yah-hi at-ta!*
> [Ten years night, come daylight!]
> *Put-um an-wikt, yah-hi at-ta!*
> [Ten years night, come daylight!]
> *Put-um an-wikt, yah-hi at-ta!*
> [Ten years night, come daylight!]
> *Put-um an-wikt, yah-hi at-ta!*
> [Ten years night, come daylight!]
> *Put-um an-wikt, yah-hi at-ta!*
> [Ten years night, come daylight!]

Twee-tash was now very tired. He could not speak fast enough. He heard *Alo-quat* still singing, never resting:

> *Lux-i!*
> [One Night!]
> *Lux-i!*
> [One Night!]
> *Lux-i!*
> [One Night!]
> *Lux-i!*
> [One Night!]
> *Lux-i!*
> [One Night!]

Twee-tash tried hard to talk fast like *Alo-quat* to keep up with him but could not. He was mad! He jumped down the mountain, making a flap place where he landed about half way down the bluff. From there he slid to the bottom, swam the river and ran up where *Alo-quat* was to kill him. But *Alo-quat* was too wise. He hopped down the north side of the mountain and hid in the mud of the Ahtanum Creek.[2] *Twee-tash* followed, reached in the mud, but could not find him. *Twee-tash* went back to his place on the mountain and again began his song:

> *Put-um an-wikt, yah-hi at-ta!*
> [Ten years night, come daylight!]
> *Put-um an-wikt, yah-hi at-ta!*
> [Ten years night, come daylight!]
> *Put-um an-wikt, yah-hi at-ta!*
> [Ten years night, come daylight!]
> *Put-um an-wikt, yah-hi at-ta!*
> [Ten years night, come daylight!]
> *Put-um an-wikt, yah-hi at-ta!*
> [Ten years night, come daylight!]

Twee-tash heard *Alo-quat* up on the other mountain:

> *Lux-i!*
> [One Night!]
> *Lux-i!*
> [One Night!]

> *Lux-i!*
> [One Night!]
> *Lux-i!*
> [One Night!]
> *Lux-i!*
> [One Night!]

Twee-tash was now awfully mad. He sprang down the mountain again and chased *Alo-quat* back to the mud. But he could not catch *Alo-quat* who dived deep in the mud and water. *Twee-tash* wanted to kill-drown *Alo-quat*. *Twee-tash*, all wet and muddy, went back to his place on the mountain. He began anew his song for ten years night and ten years day. *Alo-quat* was back on his mountain singing for the shorter night. This was kept up a long time, each singing, *Twee-tash* chasing *Alo-quat* from the rock place, *Alo-quat* hiding in the mud. Finally *Twee-tash* got so tired he came down to the flat place in the side of the mountain and said:

"I am tired! I will make it five years night, then comes day."

Twee-tash sat on the flat place and sang:

> *Pah-ha an-wikt, yah-hi at-ta!*
> [Five years night, comes day light!]
> *Pah-ha an-wikt, yah-hi at-ta!*
> [Five years night, comes day light!]
> *Pah-ha an-wikt, yah-hi at-ta!*
> [Five years night, comes day light!]
> *Pah-ha an-wikt, yah-hi at-ta!*
> [Five years night, comes day light!]
> *Pah-ha an-wikt, yah-hi at-ta!*
> [Five years night, comes daylight!]

Alo-quat was not tired, never got tired. He kept up his song:

> *Lux-i!*
> *Lux-i!*
> *Lux-i!*
> *Lux-i!*
> *Lux-i!*

Twee-tash heard the continual voice of *Alo-quat*, singing for the shorter night. He sang against him for a time, then slid down the bluff, swam the river and hurried up to the rocky point. *Alo-quat* had left, was nearly down to the Ahtanum Creek. Before *Twee-tash* could follow, *Alo-quat* was hid in the mud. *Twee-tash* could not find him, and all wet with mud, he went back to his seat on the bluff. As he sang for the five years of night, he heard *Alo-quat* back at his place singing for the short night. Thus they opposed for five suns and five nights, singing.[3] *Twee-tash* chasing, *Alo-quat* hiding in the mud. Then *Twee-tash* was so tired he quit, let it go as *Alo-quat* wanted. He was beaten, could not talk as fast as *Alo-quat* who was five. Had *Twee-tash* won, he could have slept ten years or five years as was his song. People would have had longer breath, longer to live than now. *Alo-quat* won, and *Twee-tash* can only sleep extra during the winter moons. When *Twee-tash* quit, he said:

"All right! let it be one night. A people are coming, a new people. Salmon will come up the *nChe-wana* for them every year. There will be a good time for every one. All will have as much salmon as they want."[4]

Notes by McWhorter

Some versions of this legend have it that *Twee-tash* never ascended the mountain farther than the "flat place" in question, and that this "seat" of Grizzly Bear was always in existence.

There are several places where *Alo-quat* and *Twee-tash* disputed about what should constitute the length of the night. One such is in Klickitat County, a small lake or pond called by the Klickitat Indians: *Alo-quat tow-wow-now wu-kus* [meaning] "loud speech" or "loud talk of the frogs." Frogs are so plentiful that their noise during the spring days is continuous and unbroken. The solitary Grizzly, with his slow speech, has no show with the many and fast-speaking *bractrachians*.

2

How Coyote Killed Sun
Hemene Moxmox, Yellow Wolf (Nez Perce)
14 September 1924

EVERY OLD STORY is Coyote.[1] Coyote and Fox, two brothers, lived in the same lodge. They know that Sun is over someplace, killing people. Coyote makes a law, all by himself.[2] He said:

"I am going down there to stop him killing so many people."[3]

Coyote went. Sun is on a high peak, by the river watching for the people. Coyote peeps over a ridge from behind! Yes, there it is, the Sun.

Coyote snakes [sneaks] up on him. Stood right behind Sun. Coyote coughs loud. Sun is scared! Jumps up quick. Turns around. Coyote told him:

"What is matter with you? You almost run away! My father and your father never looked for people from here. Right over there is where they looked for people. Come over here! I will show you where my father and your father cashed [cached] arrowheads, where they put them in a hole."

Sun thought:

"I have been here since the earth was first. I do not know when my father and his father were here."

Coyote said:

"Your father used to stand over there, and my father stood right here. The people traveled around [them]."

They stood there for a very short time. Saw about ten people going. Coyote said:

"Look there! A bunch of people are going. You were in wrong place. You always go wrong way. We will go down this ridge. Good spring! We will take a drink and lay [in wait] for them. We will club them there."

They get to the spring. Coyote said:

"Go ahead! Let me have your *cop-plux* [warclub or tomahawk]. You will get it dirty. Let me hold it for you."

Sun lay down and drank. As he raised up, Coyote struck him in the head with his own tomahawk. Coyote killed Sun. Coyote has an old style knife [flint]. Coyote skinned Sun.

The people made to pass were Coyote's own droppings. Coyote made them to appear as his own children. Coyote had tricked Sun. Coyote said to the children:

"You better go inside and do not get dried out."

Coyote knows where Sun's father is. He is going to take the body of dead Sun to his father. So he packs him and goes there. When Coyote got there it was nearly dark. The old man jumped up when he carried that thing inside the lodge. The old man cut off one of his dead son's [testicles] and ate it. He said:

"I never eat anything so strong. Must be something wrong with it."

It was not very dark when the old man went to sleep. Coyote sleeps too. Hears the old man snoring. Hears him snoring and gets up. He sees the old man rubbing his eyes, looking at him. Coyote thinks:

"What is the matter with him? He is asleep, but eyes are open."

Coyote thought:

"I am going to leave him."

Coyote took the old man's shield, spear and *cop-plux* and left. He thought:

"No use for me to stay here. He is looking at me. I cannot kill him."

The old man snored. That was why Coyote was leaving him. Coyote left, traveling over five big mountains. He thought:

"I will sleep! I have gone far enough."

Coyote [thought he had] gone quite a ways. The old man awakened him. He said:

"Son, why don't you get up? You are sleeping in the dirt. Why don't you sleep in the bed?"

Coyote awoke. He is right in the doorway of the lodge. He said:

"My father, I am dead now. I dreamed! That is why I lay outside."

That shield, spear and tomahawk. The old man said:

"We do not want them to get dirty."

The old man grabs them. Hangs them up. Coyote thought:

"I go quite a ways, go over five big mountains, and I wake up right in the doorway."

Coyote looks at the old man. He is snoring with eyes wide open. Coyote must have lots of bunch grass; as the Indians build fire. He calls:

"Father, you are burning up!"

The old man is still snoring. Coyote thinks to sleep. Coyote looks at him for a long time. Motions with club to see if he bats eye. Coyote watches for some time. Examines eye, see flint there, just like opening of eye. Coyote thought to kill him by knocking him on the head. Coyote said:

"I will kill you now! You will not be that way very long. There will be a different people coming. You are a chief, but you will not be this way any more, killing people. You will go up in the sky and stay there. You will be up in the sky all the time."[4]

Coyote killed the old man and left him. He traveled about for maybe two days. Was going on the trail. Hears Indian singing, coming towards him. Coyote thought:

"I meet a pretty bad man coming."

Coyote looks and sees a man coming. He is one legged. Is carrying one of his legs. He has a Grizzly Bear Dog. Coyote cut off one of his legs and carries it, too. He makes himself a dog out of *Cah-hapt* [Wild Cat]. He puts sharp flint on his dog, from nose to tail along its back. He meets *Sach-us* [quills], Porcupine. *Sach-us* said:

"I am going slow. I am cleaning the Indians up. Nothing but dogs are going over this country."

Sach-us had one horn on front of his head. Coyote made himself a same kind of horn. He said to *Sach-us*:

"I am going on the trail. I am cleaning up Indians, dogs and all."

Coyote and *Sach-us* bumped heads, came together. Pulled horns out when they came apart. Coyote said:

"We ought not do that."

Sach-us took off his lunch bundle, dried human meat. Coyote unpacked his lunch of dried deer meat.[5] *Sach-us* gave some of his lunch to Coyote. Coyote tricked *Sach-us* by slipping it back to him. Coyote kept his own lunch of dried deer meat. After through eating, *Sach-us* said:

"You better stop your dog. *Hoy-hots* [Grizzly Bear Dog] will kill him for chasing Coyotes around."

Coyote laughed and made answer:

"Better stop your dog. He brings back ten or more people. Better keep him to chase porcupines."

Hoy-hots chased Coyote's dog. *Cah-hapt* ran under *Hoy-hots'* belly and ripped it open all across. He ripped *Hoy-hots'* belly open from front to back with his flint-knife back. He ripped *Hoy-hots* in two; killed him. Coyote said:

"I told you to stop your dog; that my dog would kill him. He is pretty mean."

Coyote said:

"There are lot of people over the hill. We will go kill them and dry meat over there."

Coyote "framed" up on *Sach-us*. Coyote imagined:

"We got good spring over the hill. We will take drink over there."

Coyote and *Sach-us* went. They came to the spring. They used to have Indian tomahawks, stone-headed. Coyote said to *Sach-us*:

"Let me hold your tomahawk for you."

Sach-us did so, and then lay down to drink first. As he raised up, Coyote struck him on the head. Killed *Sach-us*. He said to him:

"You will not [now] be that way, killing people off. A new people are coming close now. When these people come and see you, they will say: 'Well, that is a porcupine!'"[6]

Coyote said:

"Humans will be here soon. They will see your quills, will make things out of them."

"This," concluded the narrator, "is all." On the end of the story now. Coyote was good, pretty good. If hungry, he prayed for certain things and got it. If Coyote was crippled or blind, he would say:

"Get up. Open your eyes!"

And Coyote would do so. *Hoy-hots* felt himself smart. He sometimes traveled along the *pe-cooh* [river].

3

Legend of the Great Dipper
Ik-keep-swsah (Wasco)
October 1921

THERE WERE FIVE persons, five brothers. They were the Wolves.[1] They ran all over the country every day, hunting. Coyote watched them all the time. He ate with them, ate what they brought from their hunting. Deer meat, elk, all kinds of meat.

Every evening the Wolves talk about seeing something in the sky. One evening Coyote asked the oldest Wolf brother:

"What do you talk about? What is it you see in the sky?"

The Wolf would not tell. The old Wolf was sly, always afraid. Wise with years, the old wolf of today is hard to trap. The next evening Coyote asked the next oldest Wolf the same question. The Wolf would not answer him. The next evening Coyote asked the third oldest Wolf what it was that they talked about, what it was they saw in the sky. The Wolf would not tell him. The next evening Coyote asked the fourth Wolf brother the same question. The fourth Wolf said to Coyote:

"Maybe if I tell you, you would tell my brothers. They would be mad at me."

One morning the five Wolves all got together. The fourth Wolf spoke:

"Coyote asked me what we are talking about. What it is that we see in the sky. I said to Coyote: 'Maybe if I tell you, you will tell my brothers. They would be mad at me.' What do you think? Are we going to tell him what we see in the sky?"

The Wolves have one little dog. The youngest Wolf said:

"We will go tell Coyote what he asks about. We can do nothing with it! It is away up in the sky, those two things. What you think, my brothers! Will we go tell Coyote?"

The brothers answered:

"Yes! We will tell Coyote all about it."

The Wolves were all satisfied to tell Coyote. One day Coyote came in and they said:

"We saw two animals in the sky. We do not know how we can get at them. They are away up high."

Coyote said:

"All right! We will go see! We will go up and see."

The youngest Wolf asked:

"How will we go up?"

Coyote answered him:

"It is well! I will show you how we can go up without trouble."

It was middle winter time. Coyote got five quivers filled with arrows. He shot one arrow towards the sky. The arrows struck the sky, stuck there. Coyote shot a second arrow. It struck the end of the first arrow, struck and held fast. Coyote shot all of his arrows. They reached the ground, a shaft from the sky to the earth. Coyote had cut rings [spirals] around the arrow shafts so he and the Wolves could hold good with their hands. The oldest brother Wolf always carried the dog. There were no stars in the sky at that time.[2]

The next sun all go up the arrow-way. Coyote goes first, followed by the five brother Wolves. Many suns, many nights they climb. They all arrive at the sky, reach there safely. They see those two animals plainly. They are Grizzly Bears! Coyote says to the Wolves:

"No one go near them! They will tear you to pieces."

The two youngest Wolves go up close. They are not afraid. The two next youngest Wolves follow. Oldest Wolf stays behind with the Dog. He is always behind, always careful, always afraid. The two youngest go up closer. The Grizzlies do not get mad at them. They all stand there just like a good show. Coyote stands back. He looks at them. All is a picture to him. Coyote smiles. He walks about, looking. He is thinking about it, thinking what he will do. He thinks:

"I am going to picture this for the different people who are to come. They will look at it. They will think: 'There is a story about it.'"[3]

Coyote pictures them there. He made them stay there in the sky, Five Wolves and the Dog. The two Grizzly Bears had always been there.

When Coyote came down, he took the arrow from the sky, took it away. When he had passed the second arrow, he took it off and so on till he came to the ground. The Wolves cannot come down. When night time comes, Coyote goes out and looks at the nice picture in the sky. There they are: two Grizzlies, five Wolves, and the little Dog.

Coyote said to the bird *Whoch-whoch* [Meadow Lark]:

"Maybe I will die! You tell the new people what I have done. Pretty soon there will be many stars growing in the sky. It is my work."

Whoch-whoch got the story from Coyote to tell to us. From this sun, now we know. You see this bird, *Whoch-whoch*, when he flies up singing. He is telling you this story, how Coyote pictured the sky. It is good to know the *Whoch-whoch*. From there, from the Grizzlies and the Wolves, came the stars, as Coyote pictured them.[4]

Coyote came this way from the sunrise. He traveled a long distance to this country. One night he looked up and saw many young stars. They were pretty thick, all growing rapidly. In the meantime he had made *Whoch-whoch* to tell it all everywhere, scatter all around the news, what he had done. He asked *Whoch-whoch*:

"What is wrong with those stars up there? Too many of them!"

Whoch-whoch answered:

"Oh! Those stars are growing pretty full in the sky. They are growing fast. If they grow too thick in the sky, they may fall down. This earth will become all frost."

Coyote gets scared about his work! Coyote took [made up] his mind:

"I will go up again! That is my work! I will go up again."

Coyote took his five quivers of arrows. He shot them upwards, making a trail as before. He climbed again to the sky. He rounded up the stars, like war-parties in camp, all different places. You see sometimes, stars pointed together, maybe squares [Orion's Belt]. That was Coyote's work. He placed them that way. The Big White Road [Milky Way] across the sky. Coyote made that trail. Coyote said to the stars:

"You must not grow too fast. You must keep together! If you want to go somewhere, fly as the lightning, speed like the light! You do that! Never grow too fast."

Coyote put up a knife of stars. Watch that! Coyote put up a bunch of stars [Pleiades]. Watch them! Sometimes this bunch comes up in the evening over the mountain as trails the sun. These stars give luck, when the bow and arrow-woods are in bloom. This luck is for gambling, horse-racing or any thing where you may gain.

Notes by McWhorter

Several tribes on the Columbia Plateau have stories relating to Coyote and the arrow trail to the sky. The "picture" described by Coyote is the group of seven bright stars in the constellation, Ursa Major, known as the Great Dipper. The three older of the Wolf Brothers constitute the handle, while the two younger brothers form the contiguous half of the bowl, Delta and Gama. The oldest brother is the second star from the tip of the handle, Zeta. The small star in close proximity is the Dog which the old Wolf is leading. The two Grizzly Bears comprise the farther extremity of the bowl, known as the Pointers.

A Yakima-Klickitat version of this legend has it that the extreme "pointer," Alpha, is a Black Bear; the lower "pointer," Beta, is a Grizzly Bear. A great battle took place between the youngest Wolf (Gama) and the Grizzly Bear (Beta) in which the Wolf came off victor. Ever since that time the wolf has been the master of the Grizzly Bear.

Whoch-whoch was the friendly Meadowlark. It was this bird that piloted Coyote when in quest of the people-devouring monster of the Nez Perce. The "bunch of stars," *Schy-que* [meaning uncertain], is the source from which the gambler receives his winning power. They are the Pleiades or Seven Stars in the constellation Taurus. The "Knife," described as a line of six stars in close proximity to the Pleiades, has not been identified.

On a spur-flat at the eastern base of the highest point of the desert [near] Ahtanum Ridge, Yakima Indian Reservation, are to be seen several crude stone heaps, memorials left by *tah*-seeking gamblers, the devotees of *Schy-que*. Some of the "testimonials" are in ruins, the work of a recent vandal [1921].

4

How Beaver Stole the Fire
Listening Coyote
November 1921

THERE WAS NO fire on this earth. The people were always cold. Fire belonged to the Upper World people. It could be seen darting across the sky, flashing among the clouds when the storms grew heavy. The people wondered how they could get some of this fire.[1]

Eagle, who could fly higher than any other bird, soared into the Upper World. Coming back, he reported:

"I have been where the Fire People live. I found a country very much like our own. A river is there, and I saw where the people have a fish-trap. They were catching salmon. A big fire was in the open. I was afraid to steal any of the fire."

A big council was called to consider Eagle's announcement. A way might be found to bring some of the fire to earth. Eagle was not a coward. He had no tricks for getting the fire. Coyote [a trickster and hero] said:

"We could get the fire if we had a way to climb to the sky. I will make an arrow-trail to the sky. I can shoot an arrow straighter than any one else."

Coyote then shot an arrow upwards through the air. It went out of sight, but it came back to earth. Five times he shot the arrow. Five times he failed to make it stick to the sky. Then Coyote quit.

Wolf thought he could fasten an arrow to the sky. Five times Wolf failed.

Grizzly Bear, the strong, shot with a mighty bow. Five times he shot, five times he failed.

Cougar, the long, shot five arrows upwards. Five times the arrows fell back to earth.

One by one the men tried their skill, their strength.[2] One by one they failed to fasten an arrow to the blue. They gave it up. No fire could be had.

Only *Cis-chel*, [Winter Wren], the small, had not bent his bow. He had said nothing. Just sat watching, listening. When the men all quit the trial, *Cis-chel* stood up and spoke:

"I will make a trail for climbing to the Fire Country. I can shoot an arrow farther than anybody."

Grizzly Bear, the strong, laughed. The people said to *Cis-chel*:

"No! You cannot do it. You are too small a man. You are only half finished! No use you trying."

Four times *Cis-chel* asked to try; four times the people refused. Then when he asked the fifth time, they told him:

"All right! Go ahead and show us what you can do."

Cis-chel, the small, now stepped forth, armed for shooting.[3] Straight upwards, he sent an arrow. It went out of sight and did not return to earth. It struck the blue [land of Fine People] and held fast. *Cis-chel* shot a second arrow, a third, a fourth, a fifth arrow, and so on, not one of them falling back to earth. Each arrow striking the end of the former, held fast.

After a time, the people watching, saw the feathered end of the last arrow far up towards the sky. As *Cis-chel* kept shooting, the hanging arrows came closer to the earth, ever growing down from the sky. At last the trail was completed. It stood unbroken from earth to sky.

The people again counseled. A brave man must be found to climb the arrow-trail and steal the fire. Coyote spoke:

"I am the most cunning of all. I can trick the Fire People and escape with the spark. I will climb up the arrow-trail and steal the fire."

But the Council knew Coyote and made reply:

"No! You cannot go. You are always getting in trouble, always making mistakes. You would be caught in your tricks."

Grizzly Bear, the strong, said:

"I am strongest of all animals. I will go! I will kill the Fire People. None will escape me! I will come away with the fire."

The Council considered, and then replied:

"No! You are too big, too heavy. We would like you to kill the Fire People. That would be good. But you could not get away. You could not hide from them."

Wolf stood up and told his plan:

"I am the best fighter of all. My jaws are strong, my legs are active. I will rush in, kill the people, and grab the fire. I am a long runner. I will go!"

But the people said that Wolf would not do. Deer stood up and said:

"I am the swiftest runner among animals. I can leap in, catch the fire-spark and escape. I will go!"

But the people knew that Deer could never escape with the fire. His only trick was running. When tired, he would be caught.

Different Animal People showed their minds, their plans for stealing the fire. Buffalo, the largest of all, talked to go.[4] But Buffalo brought no good power to cheat the Fire People. Elk was the same way. Cougar, Fox, Martin, Lynx, Porcupine, Squirrel, Weasel, Whistler, Raccoon and Muskrat. None of them could bring good showing for the work. Kingsnake, and every kind of *puch-mah* [snake], were refused by the Council. Birds, all colors. None of them were suited. Salmon said:

"I will go! I will swallow the fire in my belly and swim in the river. The Fire People cannot find me in the water."

When the people heard Salmon's words, they talked this way:

"If Salmon goes into the river, he cannot get away. He will be unable to escape back to earth with the fire. He would have to stay in the water. Salmon cannot go."

Frog stood up and told his power. He made promise:

"I will steal the fire-spark and hide it in my mouth. I will jump in the water and stir up the mud. They cannot see me. I will bury in mud so they cannot find me. I will go!"

That was Frog's talk, but the people answered:

"You will not do. The Fire People will know when you come from the mud."

Finally, every kind of people had talked their plans, all but Beaver. Beaver sat silent, saying nothing. He heard everybody talk, but gave no words of his own. When asked his turn, Beaver stood up and said:

"I am the hardest of all animals to skin. My hide is tough to take off. My home is the water, but I can live on the land. I travel by day, I travel by night. I will go steal the fire. See, I have constructed pockets in my finger nails where I can hide two sparks of fire. I can trick the Fire People."

The Council agreed that Beaver was best man for the work. He was asked:

"What is your plan, your idea to manage stealing the fire?"

Beaver told the assembly:

"I have plans laid, how I will get the fire. I will lay on the water and float down against the fish-trap as dead. The people will see me and take me from the water. I have the nicest fur, and they will want my hide. I am tough to skin! It will take the Fire People a long time to peel off my hide. If they get it entirely off, then I am done. I can do nothing. It will kill me! But if they get my hide only part way off, I can roll over and it will grow fast again. I can then steal the fire and escape. But I must have protection. Who is the brave man to protect me in this business?"

Eagle, who knew the way, spoke:

"I am strong of wing and can fly higher than any other bird. I will protect you."

Beaver asked Eagle:

"How will you protect me? What is your plan, your idea?"

Eagle made answer:

"I will fly up while the Fire People are skinning you. I will drop down near you. I will flutter and tumble about as hurt. They will try to catch me. Then you can steal the fire and escape down the hazel-vine rope which I will bring and fasten to the sky ready for you."[5]

Beaver was pleased. He said:

"That is good. I will climb the arrow trail during the night. I will reach the Fire Country just before the light breaks. The people there cannot skin me fast. You must be on time. What is your plan to start?"

Eagle answered:

"I will be flying while the morning is yet young, when the sun first looks on the land. I will arrive at the fish-trap, from where the sun will stand half on the downward trail. I will be there in time to protect you."

Beaver was now satisfied. Dark came and he climbed up the arrow-way. After going some distance, he became afraid. He could not hold to the smooth shafts. His hands slipped and he came down. *Cis-chel* said:

"I will fix it so Beaver can climb. I have a plan."

Cis-chel then fastened crosspieces to the arrow-trail, making an Indian ladder. Beaver now climbed without trouble. Long into the night he climbed. When he arrived in the Fire Country, he freed the arrow from the sky, and *Cis-chel*, from below, took all his arrows down. Beaver found the river Eagle had described. There was the fish-trap, but no people.

They were in their lodges sleeping. Beaver studied hard how to work the business before him. At last he thought:

"I will follow my plan. I will go up the river and swim on the water. I will float down against the fish-trap just as the darkness leaves. I will pretend that I am dead."

Beaver went up the river and got on the water. He floated with the current, striking the fish-trap as morning came. There he lay on the water as dead. Soon the people came from their lodges to attend the trap. They built a fire and then came on to their trap. One of them spied Beaver. Eh! He called to his friends:

"A strange bird is on the water. Come see it!"

The people came close, all of them. One is wise, he speaks:

"No bird. That is an animal! See how soft its hair. It is dead! We will take it from the water."

They took Beaver and carried him close to the fire. This was what Beaver wanted. All the people stood looking at him. He was a strange being to them. The Chief ordered him skinned. He wanted the fur.

Laying him near the fire, three men began skinning Beaver. They work, taking off his hide. The people are watching them. Beaver is tough to skin. The sun reaches the middle sky. Beaver thinks:

"Where is Eagle? If Eagle is late, if they get my hide all off, then I am done. I will be killed!"

The sun is now on the downward trail. Eagle has not come! Beaver is uneasy. He might be killed, might die right now. The sun has reached the middle of the downward trail. Still Eagle does not come! Where is he? Beaver is uneasy. If protection is longer delayed, he cannot get the fire. Suddenly he heard someone say:

"Eh! There is a strange bird. It is hurt!"

Beaver is now glad. He knows that Eagle has arrived, is there to help him. Eagle knows the trick for protecting him. He hears the chief say to three of his men:

"Catch the bird for me. I never saw one like it. I want it for myself."

Beaver hears the men trying to get hold of Eagle. They cannot catch him! He is leading them away from the fire. Beaver hears the chief telling others to help. Eagle is too smart for them all. The chief now calls:

"Everybody help catch the strange bird. Surround it! That is the only plan to get it. Do not let it escape! There is no other like it. I want that bird!"

Everyone now went after Eagle, the three men skinning Beaver joining in the chase. Eagle was shaking his wings, all the time tumbling farther and farther from Beaver and the fire. The people surround Eagle, but he limps over their heads, dropping again to the ground. He is still crippling away from Beaver. It is now that Beaver acts quickly. Jumping up, he looks around. The chief and all his people are away after Eagle. Beaver's thoughts are swift. He thinks:

"Now is my chance! I will get the fire."

Beaver flops over on his loosened hide. It becomes fast to him again. Running to the fire, he hides two sparks in his finger nail pockets. He runs for the rope of twisted hazel-vines which Eagle had fastened for him. Hurrying, he goes down the rope, sliding; holding fast with his hands.

Eagle now rose from the ground, soaring into the air. He looked around for Beaver, where they had been skinning him. Beaver was not there. He had vanished. Eagle knew that he had escaped, gone with the stolen fire. Eagle was satisfied. With a glad scream, he flew away.

The Upper World people ran back to where they had left Beaver. He was gone; the fire was gone. They now knew that they had been tricked, cheated by their two strange visitors.

Beaver reached the earth safely, bringing the sparks of fire with him. Eagle also returned unharmed.

This was the way that fire was stolen from the Upper World people, how it was brought to this earth. After that time, there was always plenty of fire. The people could keep warm and cook their food.

This fire was for the new people, the Indians, who were yet to come.

Notes by McWhorter

Cis-chel or *Cihs-chl* is named from its song-notes. This is the "snow" or "winter" wren of the Pacific Northwest. A brush bird, it resembles very much its eastern cousin in both habits and general appearances, minus length of tail. It is the "*Chic-adee*" of the Okanogan legends. The unusual muscular development of this active though diminutive bird is suggestive of great arm strength, an essential in the bending of the powerful hunting and war bow.

Beaver's curious "pocket" is found in a peculiar double formation of the claw next to the outside toe of the hindmost foot. Among other qualifications, this secret receptacle was Beaver's greatest asset in being chosen for the heroic task of procuring fire from the Upper World for the comfort of the Animal People and for the Indians who were yet to come.

5

Boy Hero and Cannibal
Che-pos To-cos, Owl Child (Wishom)
7 June 1926

A BOY MADE five quivers of arrows.[1] He said to his parents:

"I am going now."

He went towards the sunrise. He travels so far and sticks an arrow in the ground. He travels on, and places another arrow. Thus he continued until all the arrows of one quiver were used. He did the same thing with his second quiver of arrows, and then the third quiver was used. Then the fourth quiver of arrows was placed at distances apart as had been the arrows from the other three quivers.

Now he had reached where the sun comes up. He still had the fifth quiver of arrows, the last one. He started beyond the sunrise, placing arrows as he went. He came to a lodge where he found a young woman. She was the daughter, but her father was not there. He was a bad man. Always traveling about, bringing people to his lodge to eat them.[2] The girl said to the boy:

"My father is a bad man. He will kill you and eat you. But I will hide you some way."

The boy answered:

"All right! You can hide me somewhere."

The girl covered the boy with skins, placing them all over him. Soon they heard a great noise. It was a roaring like a big storm in the forest, a terrible thing to hear. The girl said:

"My father is coming! He is bringing people with him to eat them."

44

The man entered the lodge. He said:

"Daughter, somebody is here."

She answered him:

"No! You smell the people you have killed and brought here."

He answered:

"No, I smell somebody."

"No, you smell your own dead people," his daughter answered him.

"No, I smell somebody here," replied the bad father.

"No, you smell those you have brought here and killed," was the answer.

"No, it is a different person I smell," he continued.

"No, it is the same people you have killed," his daughter said.

"No, I smell one different from the others," he answered.

"No, it is not different. You smell those you have brought with you after killing them for food."

This was the fifth time that he had spoken thus, and five times his daughter had answered him "No." This ended the talk. The bad father did not find the boy hidden under the skins.

The next day the bad father again went hunting for people to eat. The girl said to the boy:

"You now see! This is the way my father does every day. I will help you if I can."

The girl knew that the boy was good. They talked five times what to do, repeated five times what they thought was best. The boy said:

"I will go bring all kinds of food. I will have everything cooked ready when he comes. He will kill people no more."

The girl listened and then answered:

"He is coming! I hear his coming in the distance."

The boy had everything cooked. All kinds of birds and animals. The father entered the lodge. He spoke to the girl:

"Daughter, I smell something nice!"

The girl made reply:

"Yes, your son-in-law has brought all kinds of food."

Then the boy showed up. He said to the man:

"When we eat we will be through."

They ate of what had been cooked. The boy said to his father-in-law:

"Come outside."

They went outside the lodge. Deer, buffalo, elk, and every kind of animals good for food were seen, like *moos-moos* [cattle] in pasture. The man killed no more people for food. He said to the boy:

"This is well, my son-in-law! I am glad you have come."

In time the young man became father of a boy and a girl. He now thought to go back to his own people, taking his wife and children. The old man gave his son-in-law a suit of buckskins. Gave one each for himself, his wife, and the two children. He gave his son-in-law the entire country, so when he got back home he would have the whole country to give to his people. When he arrived home he told the people everything. The gifts and the land were given away among his people.[3]

(This story is incomplete. Owl Child said at this point:

"I do not remember just right. This story ends nice, has a nice ending. I will ask Sallie [his wife] about it and will tell it to you some other time. It is a fine ending story." 7 June 1926.)

6

Iques and *Twee-tash* Gamble for Control of the Weather
Simon Goudy (Yakama-Klickitat)

ONE TIME THERE was a *Twee-tash* [Grizzly Bear] going around eating people, killing and eating them.[1] He went from camp to camp, locating all kinds of people, making food of them. The people who knew that he was coming would get out of the way, would hide from him. In one place he came to a small village by a river. He knew that many people lived there. But when he arrived at this place, he found only *Iques* [Cotton Tail Rabbit] who was up in the foot-hills, among the rocks. *Twee-tash* looked around good. Looked every where, but he found no one but *Iques*. He was hungry, had had nothing to eat for a long time. Whenever he came near *Iques*, *Iques* would run into the brush, dodge into the rocks and hide. *Twee-tash* could find no way of killing him. He finally thought:

"I better gamble the *Pa-loute* [bone game] with *Iques*. I better shake the bone game with him to see who will win."[2]

Twee-tash knew that *Iques* could not hurt him. He wanted to get hold of *Iques*, but *Iques* was wise. He would not go near *Twee-tash*, would not let *Twee-tash* get near him. *Twee-tash* said:

"Do not be afraid! I will not hurt you! I will not harm you."

Iques replied:

"You look awful! You look terrible! A little boy like me is nothing to you."

Twee-tash spoke:

47

"No! I will not harm you. I will play the *Pa-loute* with you. We will play to make the weather, to see which of us will have the kind of weather he likes."

Twee-tash wanted to play for the ruling of the storm, ruling of the cold. *Twee-tash* likes snow and rain, likes mixed snow and rain. He wants it that way all the time. *Iques* likes it cold and dry. Cold! Cold! Cold! He does not like the rain and wet snow. *Iques* thought the idea of *Twee-tash* good. He said:

"It will be well for us to try the *Pa-loute*. We will gamble with the bones. We will see whose power is strongest, who will have the kind of weather he likes."

Iques started the game, guessed the correct bone the first time. Cold started as he wished it. *Iques* sang as he juggled the bones, calling the cold, calling the blue ice to cover the water. He sang:

> *Ooh-qohl-li-mah!*
> [Blue Ice]
> *Ooh-qohl-li-mah!*
> [Blue Ice]
> *Ooh-qohl-li-mah!*
> [Blue Ice]
> *Ooh-qohl-li-mah!*
> [Blue Ice]
> *Ooh-qohl-li-mah!*
> [Blue Ice]

As *Iques* sang, it grew colder! Colder. The east wind came, causing the ice to thicken. *Twee-tash* shivered with the cold. *Iques* held the two bones, the one white, the other with the black stripes. *Twee-tash* guessed. He missed the white bone. *Iques* juggled the bones anew. He sang:

> *Ooh-qohl-li-mah!*
> *Ooh-qohl-li-mah!*
> *Ooh-qohl-li-mah!*
> *Ooh-qohl-li-mah!*
> *Ooh-qohl-li-mah!*

Colder grew the wind! Thicker grew the ice. The cold blue ice over the river. *Iques* held up the bones to be guessed. *Twee-tash* called on his *tah* for help, called and then guessed.[3] He missed the white bone. The cold came swifter, came more deadly. *Iques* was feeling good, feeling strong. He swung the bones more rapidly. He pitched them in the air, caught them as they came down. He juggled them, singing as he juggled:

> *Ooh-qohl-li-mah!*
> *Ooh-qohl-li-mah!*
> *Ooh-qohl-li-mah!*
> *Ooh-qohl-li-mah!*
> *Ooh-qohl-li-mah!*

Twee-tash shivered with the cold. *Iques* was warm in his fur. Cold could not hurt him. He held still his hands for *Twee-tash* to guess. *Twee-tash* lost again. *Iques* was winning. He shook the bones faster, still faster he shook them. *Iques* passed the bones from one hand to the other, passed them so fast that *Twee-tash* could not see them. *Iques* sang louder, still louder he sang his *tah* song:

> *Ooh-qohl-li-mah!*
> *Ooh-qohl-li-mah!*
> *Ooh-qohl-li-mah!*
> *Ooh-qohl-li-mah!*
> *Ooh-qohl-li-mah!*

Iques held the bones hidden in his hands. *Twee-tash* studied, studied hard which hand held the white bone. Then he guessed. He struck his arm fiercely in guessing. *Twee-tash* missed for the fourth time. *Twee-tash* shivered, shivered with the growing cold. He trembled with the cold which grew at the calling of *Iques*, at the song of *Iques*. If he missed the next time, he would lose the game. Five times missing would lose the game. Five times guessing the white bone would win the game.[4] *Iques* sang:

> *Ooh-qohl-li-mah!*
> *Ooh-qohl-li-mah!*
> *Ooh-qohl-li-mah!*
> *Ooh-qohl-li-mah!*
> *Ooh-qohl-li-mah!*

Iques held the bones for *Twee-tash* to guess. *Twee-tash* studied which hand hid the white bone. He called on his *tah* to help him. He fixed his mind hard which way to guess. Then he struck his arm heavy. That was his guess, to strike the left or the right arm. The arm struck, meant that hand guessed. *Twee-tash* got the bones. The cold loosened. *Twee-tash* was glad. He juggled the bones. He passed them behind him. He threw them from hand to hand. *Twee-tash* sang:

> *tChlum!*
> [Snow rain!]
> *tChlum!*
> [Snow rain!]
> *tChlum!*
> [Snow rain!]
> *tChlum!*
> [Snow rain!]
> *tChlum!*
> [Snow rain!]

Twee-tash held the bones ready for *Iques* to guess. *Iques* studied which hand was the white bone, the bone without the black stripes. Then he struck his arm. He won the right bone. The cold grew. *Twee-tash* threw the bones to *Iques*. *Iques* sang. He passed the bones back of him from hand to hand. *Twee-tash* guessed. Eh! He missed. Cold began getting stronger. *Iques* sang the song of this *tah*, sang loud his power song. Again he was ready for *Twee-tash* to try his luck, to guess the white bone. *Twee-tash* missed. Three times more he misses as he sat shivering with the frosty cold. *Iques* likes the cold, the still, deadly cold. He is growing fat. Cold is what he likes. *Iques* tosses the bones in air. He catches them, swings them hard. He changes them fast from hand to hand. Now he is ready for *Twee-tash* to try his power at guessing. *Twee-tash* studies to find the white bone. He makes the good guess. He gets the bones. The cold stops.

Twee-tash sings his song, sings loud his song. He must win the game. He juggles the bones. He holds for *Iques* to guess. *Iques* wins the bones. The cold tightens. *Twee-tash* is mad. He thinks:

"I will grab *Iques*! I will throw one bone only a little ways, the other one half-way. When he reaches over to get them, I will grab him. He cannot hurt me."

Then *Twee-tash* threw the bones towards *Iques*. Threw one about fourth distance, the other one half-way. *Twee-tash* is trembling; it is so cold. The river by the village is almost covered with ice. Frozen from both sides to near center. *Iques* picks up one bone. He reaches for the other bone. *Twee-tash* is watching. He grabs for him. *Iques* is wise. He jumps for the brush, escapes in the brush. *Twee-tash* calls to him:

"Do not run away! I was only fooling. Only playing with you. I did not mean it. Come back! We will gamble all over again."

Iques came out of the brush, out from his hiding. They began to play the *Pa-loute* again. Five times *Twee-tash* lost his guess. Five times he missed the white bone. *Iques* had won. The weather would now be as he wanted. It would be cold, no rain with snow. *Iques* was glad. He jumped! Frisking about among the rocks. *Twee-tash* was shivering hard. The cold was going to his insides. He said:

"I am cold! I am hungry! There is not much to eat on this side the river. I want to cross to the other side. Where is a place to cross with wading?"

Iques answered him:

"Yes! I know where you do not wade in the water. Where you cross without wading."

Twee-tash wanted to cross. It might change his luck. He might find food over there. He had it about cleaned out where he was. He said:

"Yes! That is what I want. I do not like to wade."

They both go to the river. It is nearly frozen over. Ice from each side almost meet in the middle of the river. *Iques* is feeling fine. He is leaping! Racing around. *Twee-tash* is trembling, shaking with cold. It is evening, nearly getting dark. *Iques* said to the shivering *Twee-tash*:

"Can you wait till the morning to cross?"

Twee-tash answered:

"Yes! I am cold! I will wait till the morning to cross. I will find a place to sleep."

Iques said:

"I will show you where to cross when the sun is up."

Twee-tash sheltered for the night. *Iques* traveled all night, locating a place to cross the river. When morning came, he had everything fixed as he wanted. He had found a riffle where ice was thin. A deep hole was below, at foot of the riffle. Ice was clear across, but it could not hold *Twee-tash* up. It was thin out in the middle of the river. *Iques* went back. He meets *Twee-tash*. He spoke:

"Yes! I have found the place. Ice is all good, is strong for walking. I have been across; it is strong."

Iques took *Twee-tash* to the place. During the night *Iques* had dropped pills on the ice. Dropped them all the way across. He made piles of them, changed as stone. He made them to look like stone, but they were not stone. He showed them to *Twee-tash*. He said:

"Ice is solid all across the river. See how strong it is! How it holds up the rocks."

Twee-tash steps on the first rock pile. Ice cracks! *Twee-tash* draws back! He said:

"Eh! Ice is breaking!"

Iques laughed. He answered:

"No! Do not be afraid! See!"

Iques threw a rock out on the ice. It struck, bounding away. That rock was only a pill. *Twee-tash* said:

"Take the rocks away. They are too heavy. Take all away."

Iques took all the stones off the ice. They were not stones, only looked like stones. *Twee-tash* stepped on the ice. It bore him till he got to middle of river. There it was weak, was very thin. It caved with *Twee-tash* who drifted under the ice. Drifted down into the deep water where he drowned. *Iques* laughed as *Twee-tash* went down into the cold water, laughed to see him perish. He said to *Twee-tash*:

"You are not great! You are not to kill everybody as you have been doing. There are people coming, another kind of people. You can kill once in a while, kill a few, but not all the time."

That is how *Iques* was too much for *Twee-tash* in the *Pa-loute* game for control of the weather. That is how he drowned *Twee-tash* in the icy water. Had *Twee-tash* won in the game, it would be wet snow. Snow with rain all the time. That is the kind of weather he likes. He would now be the main animal, the chief animal. He would be going from village to village killing people. But that was the end of *Twee-tash*'s great power. He was killed by *Iques*, the timid, the cunning.

Notes by McWhorter

Pa-loute or *Pi-loote* is "gambling" or "betting." It is the great "Bone Game" of the Northwestern tribes, described in various works. An exciting game, success depends wholly upon the skill and dexterity of the "juggler" to conceal the identity of the winning or "white" bone, as pitted against the intuitive ability of his opponent in "guessing" the hand wherein is concealed the determining talisman. Any number may engage in the game, the opposing factions seated facing each other, with the stakes occupying the intervening space. The advantage of starting the game is determined by "guess." The "points" are tallied by means of a number of pointed sticks, ofttimes numbering as high as twelve to the side. The full possession of the tally sticks determines the winner. Usually the "juggling" and "guessing" is left to professionals on either side, while the body of participants aid by song, keeping time with pounding-sticks on a resonant board or slab of timber. The Puget Sound Indians excel at the game.

Ooh-qohl-li-i-mah is literally "blue ice"; an invocation for "blue ice to cover the water." *Iques*, the "cotton-tail," revels in the dry, frosty cold so conducive to the formation of the solid, glassy blue ice. It is to be noted that there are five "calls" or repetitions to the stanza, and these in turn are repeated five times before the achievement of victory.

tChlum! repeated five times as in the text, with "e" intervening between the third and fourth repetition. Literally it means: "snow-rain." *Twee-tash* or Grizzly Bear delights in such weather conditions, so disagreeable to the rabbit and other fur-bearing animals.

7

The *Qui-yiah*, Five Brothers
Simon Goudy (Yakama-Klickitat)
No Date

IT WAS THE first morning that five brothers, the *Qui-yiah* [Spears from Deer Horn], came along the Cascade Mountains bordering the Kittitas country where Ellensburg [Washington] now stands.[1] They saw a big lake. The water covered all the valley, flooded all the level land. This was bad. The *Qui-yiah* went on the highest peak to see which way to draw the water. They wandered around all over to discover which way it would draw. Then oldest said to his four brothers:

"Let us look around these big high mountains and see what we can find."

Then they travel from mountain to mountain. One place they found was *Mo-kehl mo-kehl* [house built by animals]. They sat on top of this *Mo-kehl mo-kehl*, look all over. They watch what was in the mountains, what they could find. The four oldest brothers say:

"We do not know what we can do."

Then they ask the younger brother what he thinks. He answered:

"I know how to manage this thing if I were you fellows."

They look at him wise. Then they ask:

"What would you do if you were us?"

They left it with the youngest brother, said to him:

"You know how to manage this thing. We will help you out. What is your mind, how to handle this thing?"[2]

The youngest brother then said:

"Cut a long, big pole."

The oldest brother asked:

"What for?"

Youngest brother replied:

"I know what for. I will show you when we get pole cut."

After pole was cut, they took it to top of *Mo-kehl mo-kehl*, the high mountain where they had sat. The oldest brother again asked:

"What next?"

The youngest brother now told them:[3]

"We are on [at] the lodge of the *Wah-nun-pace-ye Yeh-kah* [Red Cheeked Beaver], chief of all beavers. He it is who has flooded all the level land with water."

The four older brothers now knew. They did not know this before that hour. The youngest brother now said to next to oldest brother:

"Raise the pole! Shove it into the *Yeh-kah*'s [Beaver's] lodge, into the doorway as far as it will go. Shove it far in and scare the beavers out."

He said to the oldest brother:

"Now get your spear ready."

This was before mid-day. The oldest brother gets ready his spear to strike. The one brother handles the pole and the other three look on. One gets tired and another takes his place at the pole; the older brother stood for a long time with spear raised, watching for beaver to come out of doorway. All kinds of beaver came out, but they watch for the main one—the biggest one. It is the chief they want. Then next oldest brother said:

"Let me have the spear! I will try! You are tired holding it up."

The older brother let him take the spear while he sat down to rest. The youngest brother sat talking all the time, instructing them:

"Wait! Do not strike the big beaver! That is not the one! Wait till I tell you to strike! I know which one!"

Every time a beaver came out, the other brothers would say:

"That is the one! He is the big chief of all. Spear him!"

But the youngest brother would not let him throw the spear. Until weary did the second brother stand with spear uplifted. Then he gave it up and said:

"Take the spear! I am tired!"

The third brother took the spear. The other brother sat down and watched, urging:

"Strike the big beaver! That is the chief!"

But the youngest brother would instruct:

"No! Do not throw the spear! I will tell you which is the one!"

Until weary did the third brother stand with spear uplifted over the door-way of the beaver house. Then he said to next younger brother:

"You take the spear! I cannot get the big beaver!"

The fourth brother took the spear. He stood with it lifted ready to strike. The older brothers kept telling him:

"There is the big chief! Spear him before he gets away!"

The younger brother sat silent, only instructing:

"Wait! I will tell you which one to spear!"

The beavers grew scarce. Only at long intervals did one come out. At first they had come fast, hurrying one after another. It was fast nearing sun-down. It had taken most of the day to route the beavers from their lodge. The brother with the spear was tired. He said to his youngest brother:

"Try your luck! I cannot get him!"

The young brother answered:

"That is just what I will do!"

The brother gave him the spear and said:

"You know best! Go ahead!"

The young brother stood over the door-way with spear raised high. The other brothers were making fun of him. They would call:

"Spear that one! He is the right one! He is the big chief! Spear him now!"

But the younger brother did not listen. He said:

"No! I am looking for the right one."

When the sun was almost down, the largest beaver yet came out. He was next to the chief beaver, the one for which the young brother was watching. The older brothers called:

"Hurry! Spear him! He is the big chief! Do not let him go!"

No! The boy would not do it, would not strike this biggest beaver. All the brothers yell at him:

"Go on! Spear him! Strike quick! Do not let him get away!"

The boy did not reply. He was waiting for another one. After trying to scare others, nothing came out of the doorway.

Just as the sun went into the ground, when the west sky grew red like a forest fire, then a small beaver came out the doorway, small like a frog. The boy braced with foot to throw the spear.[4] The brothers laugh:

"*Caw!* He is trying to spear the little baby! He let the big chief go!"

The beaver was pulling out into the water. Pulling away from the lodge. The boy, hard braced, threw his spear at the swimming beaver.

The brothers were laughing at him. They made a big noise as he hurled the spear. Before the beaver was struck they could hardly see him he was so small. When the spear hit him, he became so large that nothing could hold him. He was the *Wah-nun-pace-ye*, chief of all the *Yeh-kah*, greatest of all in the lake, greatest in the world. He leaped from the water, jerking the boy in, carried him from the shore out into the deep lake.

The spear was made from the *Qui-yiah*'s [deer's] rib. He [the Spear] could not get loose from the *Wah-nun-pace-ye*. When the *Wah-nun-pace-ye* leaped, the water was thrown high up the mountain. Great waves rolled to the far side of the lake. The mighty chief now knew that he was going to die unless he could reach the *nChe-wana*. He rushed across the big lake to break the *we-hon-me wah-chesh* [beaver dam], which he had built at the canyon of the Yakima River, covering all the Kittitas Valley with water. He reached the *wah-chesh*, carrying the young *Qui-yiah* [Spear made of deer rib] with him. He broke the dam, swam on the roaring flood, to the Selah Gap. There he had another *wah-chesh*. This he burst, running through it, letting all the water free. He now swam to *Pah-qy-ti-koot* [Union Gap, Washington] where he had his last *wah-chesh*. All the level land was under water, the Moxee and Ahtanum valleys. The *Wah-nun-pace-ye* tore away this last dam, letting all the water through. He hurried on. The boy now knew that he was getting near the *nChe-wana*, and he tried to stop the beaver. He grabbed at anything which might stop his course but nothing could hold him. He began crying. He would be killed if the *Wah-nun-pace-ye* reached the *nChe-wana*. Thousands of beaver following on the rushing waters. The boy continued to catch hold of anything in reach, to hold him. The Cottonwood called:

"Catch to me, nephew! I will hold you!"

He did so, but the tree broke off. Then the Willow called:

"Catch hold of me, my child! I will save you!"

But the Willow was torn out by its roots. Nothing could [hold] the weight. The boy was crying for help. Below *Cee-cee* [Toppenish, Washington], he saw the jointed weed. You call it the bull-rush. The Rush called to him:

"If you want help, catch me! I will hold you, my poor child!"

He did not heed. Nothing he had tried could help him. Four times the Joint-Weed called:

"Try me! I will save you!"

But he would not try the weed. He was dying, because he would not again see his brothers. By this time the beaver was not very strong, was nearly paralyzed. At last the Rush called the fifth time:

"My grandchild![5] Try the Old-man! I will wiggle my little seat and hold fast in the ground. Nothing can tear me out from my hold. I will save you!"

The boy caught hold of the Old-man. The weeds began making noise, breaking from the ground. The boy cried:

"You said that you would hold me back! Now is the time for you to hold me back!"

The weeds said:

"That is nothing! Do not be afraid! I am an old man. Nothing can pull me from the ground."

The boy held tight. The great *Wah-nun-pace-ye* began to turn on his side, belly up. This was below the mouth of Satus River. Big force of water was on top of them. The flood backed up. Filled all the plain, all the desert to the hills above *Mool-Mool* [Ft. Simcoe]. Filled the valley above *Pah-qy-ti-koot* [Union Gap]. It was such big force that it broke through to the *nChe-wana*, below *Top-tut* [near Prosser, Washington]. After all the water had drained from the lakes, after all the land went dry, the boy was saved. He was still hanging to the beaver and to the Old-man. Then he wondered where his brothers were. The brothers were coming, following around the mountains above the water, crying and looking for their young brother.[6] They thought that he was killed. Afterwards they found him. They were glad. They said:

"Our brother! We thought you were dead! We were crying for you!"

The younger brother said to them:

"No! I am not dead! I am alive! The Old-man saved me!"

Then they skinned the *Wah-nun-pace-ye Yeh-kah*. They took all his ribs. The brothers asked the boy:

"What you do with the ribs?"

He replied:

"I know what to do with the ribs."[7]

He took shortest rib, threw it toward the coast and said:

"Here is the rib! Certain people will grow, Puget Sound Indians. All short and squatty."

Next smallest rib he threw toward the mountains, to the Kittitas country, which had been drained. He said:

"Here is the rib! Indians will grow, called *Pish-wan-a-pums*.[8]

The third rib he threw toward *Thappanish* [near head waters of the Toppenish River]. And said:

"Here is the rib!" and the Thappanish Indians grew.

The fourth rib he threw toward Wenatchee, and said:

"Here is the rib!" and the Wenatchee Indians grew.

The fifth rib he threw toward the Okanogan country and said:

"Here is the rib!" and the Okanogans, Nespelems and kindred tribes grew.

Then turned to the south and threw the sixth rib toward the Dalles, and said:

"Here is the rib!" and the Wasco Indians grew.

The longest rib he threw to Pendleton [Oregon] and said:

"Here is the rib!" and the Nez Perce Indians and Umatillas grew. Tall people and large.

Then came other tribes and different languages, for there were ribs not yet used. From other parts of the beaver, he made all the animals and birds. The tail he threw toward the *nChe-wana*, and the salmon and the sturgeon grew.

Then the brothers were all glad. The youngest brother now said:

"Let us go back to Cascade Mountains and hunt for deepest lake."

They all came back where the *Wah-nun-pace-ye Yeh-kah* had been found. The water was gone. They said to each other:

"This is what we wanted! We now have country fixed ready for the Indians. It is best for us to hide before the Indians grow up."[9]

The *Qui-yiah* now counselled how best to hide. The youngest brother knew how they would hide. They conferred with him. He planned to hide in the water. The brothers asked:

"What way can we hide in the water?"

He said:

"Let us look for deepest lake we can find."

They went to Lake Cle Elum first. Four of them got in center of lake. The youngest stay out from the water. He climbed up a hill to look if he could see his brothers in the lake. He saw them and told them:

"Lake not deep enough. Better come out and go to another lake."

They came out and went to lake called *Kachess*. The four brothers went again to center of this lake, while the youngest stay out to see. He went up on the mountain side to look. He called to them:

"Water not quite deep enough! Better come out and move to another lake."

They came out and went to lake called *Keechelus*. The four brothers went into the center of the water. The younger brother climbed the mountain, *Mo-kehl*, and looked. He said to himself:

"This is a deep lake! We should stay here."

This was the third lake. The young brother came back from the mountain and said to his brothers:

"I could not see you! We will stay here."[10]

All the brothers then made up their minds to stay in this lake.

Notes by McWhorter

Mo-kehl mo-kehl is a "house built by animals" or "animal built house." It was the name of the lodge of the Chief of beavers. It is the high, sharp mountain peak north of the Yakima River and between the mouths of the Squawk and Teanawa rivers, in closer proximity to the last named stream. It is in Kittitas County, Washington. The doorway to the "lodge" is a small lake, about midway up the mountain, west side. This lake contains fish. A smaller lake on the summit of the peak is where the pole was "churned" by the *Qui-yiah* for the purpose of routing the great chief from hiding. *Wah-nun-pace-ye Yeh-kah* is a "red cheeked beaver," or "red over the eyes," the chief of all beavers. *Yeh-kah* or *uy-hi* is the common beaver.

Dr. G.P. Kuykendall, a former agency physician for the Yakamas, and who devoted considerable time to their folklore, gives as the name of this great beaver, *Wish-poosh*. This monster dwelt in Lake Cle Elum, and was destroyed by Coyote. The battle lasted until the mouth of the Columbia River was reached. Coyote had secured the spear to his own wrist with stout thongs. "*Wish-poosh*" does not appear to be Yakima, but belongs to the Umatilla. One version of the legend has it that "*Wish-poosh*" was killed in the Columbia, near the Umatilla Reservation. The Columbia River was called by the Yakamas and kindred tribes, *nChe-wana*: "big river."

Qui-yiah means "fish spear of deerhorn." The spear used in the combat with the beaver chief was formed from the *Qui-yiah*'s own rib, from which he [the Beaver] could not become detached. This is the only legend that I have found among the various tribes comprising the Yakima Nation, wherein Coyote does not appear as the primal sub-creator, or finisher of the earth, fitting it for a "different people" who were soon to appear. But it must not be overlooked that there was a Supreme or Higher Power, often referred to as "The Man Above," from whom Coyote received his potential strength. Coyote was NOT the Primal Creator, as some writers contend. His superior wisdom and consummate cunning placed him at the head of the animal world, the big chief over all. He was not a deity [I disagree].

The elevation, or hill on which the Ellensburg Cemetery is located, resulted from the bursting of the first great dam built by the *Wah-nun-pace-ye Yeh-kah*. Originally a depression of the ground, the receding waters left a lake. The beavers stranded there built a lodge, a second *Mo-kehl mo-kehl* , as preserved in the present eminence. The Yakima River was formed by the various mountain springs which originally fed the great bodies of water confined by the dams built by the chief of beavers.

Pah-qy-ti-koot is the Indian name for Union Gap where the Yakima River breaks through the solitary mountain ridge, northern boundary of the Yakima Indian Reservation. The name has various interpretations;those generally accepted signify "two buttes" or "two [mountain] heads." One intelligent tribesman contends that the name, as pronounced, denotes any number of "buttes" or mountain "heads" above two, and that the proper name of the Gap is *Pah-koot!* as descriptive of the two "bluff-heads" guarding the pass. Still another definition of the accepted name by an educated Yakima is suggestive of "two bunches of horsemen running meeting" or "two bunches of horsemen running together from opposite directions."

Cee-cee means "sand that breaks under foot." *Cee-cee* is the name of the country in and about where the town of Toppenish, Washington, on the Yakama Indian Reservation.

Top-tut is where Prosser, Washington, now stands, on the Yakima River. *Pish-wan-a pums* is the Yakimas proper. The seat of government of the tribe was in the Kittitas Valley, of the upper Yakima River. Various bands of the tribe were scattered throughout the lower Yakima and tributary streams, and were designated as *Mam-a-chets* or *Mom-a-chets*, with local distinguishing appellations. The upper villagers, as divided by Selah Gap, were the more warlike.

Thappanish means "sloping down." The name pertains to the upper desert reaches near the head of Toppenish River, Yakama Indian Reservation. It is descriptive of the topography of the locality in question and does not apply to the entire stream. "Toppenish" is a corruption of the Indian name. The *Thappanish* Indians were of the *Mam-a-chets* who, more than any of the bands, have retained their native tribal traits. Their peculiar conversational accent, while not generally marked by the white man, distinguishes them from the other tribesmen. *Mo-kehl* is a distinct mountain not to be confused with *Mo-kehl mo-kehl* proper.

8

Battle of Cold Wind and Chinook Wind
Ana-whoa, Black Bear (Wasco)
1917

AT ONE TIME there were five brothers and one little sister, *Tah-mat-tox-lee*.[1] They lived at *Taman-towl-lat* on the *nChe-wana*. Their father and mother lived not far from there in a cave. From that cave the five sons came to stay at *Taman-towl-lat*; to wrestle with anyone who would meet them. Cold Wind called to anybody; called from sunrise to sundown; to anyone to come and wrestle with him. *Tah-mat-tox-lee* was lame. When her brothers were wrestling, she would throw water from five baskets; one at a time, on the ground. This formed ice so the one wrestling with her brothers could not stand. The wrestling rule was that the one thrown down must have his head cut off by Coyote. Coyote always came with his flint knife ready. Piles! Great piles of dead lay where Cold Wind had conquered. None could stand before him.[2]

Eagle and his wife lived at a spring, *Taman-towl-lat*; across the *nChe-wana* opposite *Taman-towl-lat*, where Cold Wind stayed. Eagle's son had married the daughter of *Nihs-lah*. He had brought her from *Sko-lus*.

Chinook Wind was five brothers who lived with Eagle.[3] Nine were in that lodge of Eagle. Although Eagle's son lived so near Cold Wind, he never answered when called to wrestle. He stayed away. But at last he went to wrestle and was killed. *Tah-mat-tox-lee* poured water on the ground; making ice. Eagle's son could not stand. He fell; and Coyote cut off his head. Cold Wind now boasted the more.

Chinook Wind, the five brothers, now went out to wrestle. Cold Wind killed them all. *Tah-mat-tox-lee* was there with her five baskets of

62

water. She poured them, one at a time, over the wrestling ground. The ice threw Chinook Wind brothers down. Coyote cut off their heads with his flint knife. Cold Wind was more boastful than ever.

The wife of Eagle's son was with child. She went back to *Sko-lus*. She said to her father-in-law and mother-in-law:

"I will leave two feathers; one red, one white. I will leave them standing here over my bed. Watch them. If the red feather falls down, the child is a girl. If the white feather falls, the child is a boy. Then you can rejoice, for he will come and wrestle with Cold Wind."[4]

The girl went back to *Sko-lus*, leaving the two old people alone in the lodge. She left them alone near the boastful Cold Wind, just across the *nChe-wana*. Finally the feather fell. The old man said to his wife:

"You threw the feather down?"

His wife answered:

"No! It is a son born. In five days he will come to see us."

The old man cried. He did not believe her. He cried; for his heart was lonely. Cold Wind was growing more cruel each day. Eagle's wife said:

"If it is a boy, we will live. If it is a girl, Cold Wind will kill us. But if it is a boy! We will live!"

The old man stopped crying.

Every day *Tah-mat-tox-lee*, the lame girl, would come. She would pour cold water on them, to make fun of them. All but the two old people were dead at the lodge. She laughed at them. There were none to answer to the call of Cold Wind to come and wrestle.

When the son was born [at *Sko-lus*] his mother told him how his father and the five Chinook brothers were killed by Cold Wind. How the two old grandparents were still living lonely in their lodge at *Taman-towl-lat*. How *Tah-mat-tox-lee* came and poured cold water on them every day. They would soon be killed. His mother said:

"You stay here at *Sko-lus* five days, then go see the old people. It will take you five days to go. You will grow to be a young man as you travel. You must practice your strength while going. Pull up pine trees, throw them about. Pick up big rocks, cast them from you. Leap! grow strong. Build the *whe-acht*, take sweats. Go in the cold water. If you do not do this, if you do not practice, you will be killed as was your father. You will fall before Cold Wind as did the five Chinook brothers."

The boy stayed five days at *Sko-lus*. Then he started to go see his grandparents at *Taman-towl-lat*. His mother said to him:

"When you come to your grandmother, catch the biggest salmon [sturgeon].[5] Have her get all the oil out of it; roasted at the fire. Get all the oil. Save it in five baskets."

As the boy traveled, he practiced his strength; doing as his mother had told him. He tore up pine trees, threw them about. Some he pitched across the *nChe-wana*. He picked up big stones, hurling them far from him. Before he arrived at *Taman-towl-lat*, he could pitch great rocks to a long distance. He grew big and strong. He was a man.[6]

When the boy reached the old people, they were in their earth-lodge, hovering over their little fire. He stood outside the door-way. He heard them crying; shivering with cold. He stepped inside the lodge. The dim light revealed his form; a strong man. The old people were glad; glad to see their grandson. The grandmother said to the boy:

"One more night and we would be dead. Killed by *Tah-mat-tox-lee*; pouring cold water on us. We are glad you have come."

Early next morning, the boy stripped. He dived into the *nChe-wana*, where the water was deep. He caught the biggest sturgeon, as his mother had told him. He brought it to the shore, laid it on the rocks by his robe, where Cold Wind could see it. Cold Wind looked across the *nChe-wana*; saw the big fish lying there. He saw the boy putting on his robe. He knew that a strange man had come to wrestle with him. The boy caught up the great sturgeon by the head with one hand. He held it out at arm's length, so Cold Wind brothers could see how strong he was. He carried it to the lodge. The sturgeon's tail dragging the ground, cut a deep line in the earth. You can see that mark today. It is called *Taman-towl-lat* [place cut in the ground]. Soon as the boy reached the lodge, the grandmother took the sturgeon and cut it into small pieces. She took the oil out of it by the fire. Cold Wind was all the time calling:

"Hurry up! Come out and wrestle now! Do not stay in the lodge like an old woman."

The next morning the old man, his wife and the boy, went out from the lodge. They had the [sturgeon] oil in five baskets. They got in their canoe, covered the baskets so Cold Wind could not see them. They crossed the *nChe-wana* to wrestle. While crossing, they saw the oldest Cold Wind brother standing stripped for wrestling. *Tah-mat-tox-lee* had poured water on the ground to form ice. It was already ice. The boy said to his grandmother:

"Let them pour water first. Then you pour oil over the water [ice] quick. They cannot stand. I will throw them sure."

He told her over many times how to do. They reached the other side of the *nChe-wana*. The boy, and the grandmother with the five baskets hid under her robe, got out from the canoe. The boy went up to Cold

Wind, all stripped for wrestling. They began wrestling hard. Coyote was there with his flint-knife. He said to them:

"I will be on the side of the one who whips. I will cut off the head of the one who is thrown down."

The boy was matched. The lame girl had made ice. He called to his grandmother:

"Now! Throw the oil quick!"

The old grandmother threw the oil from one basket. Cold Wind could not stand. He was thrown down. Coyote cut off his head and carried it to the old man in the canoe.

Second Cold Wind brother came to join in the wrestle. The lame girl made ice, but the grandmother poured a basket of oil. Second Cold Wind could not stand; he was thrown as was his brother. Coyote cut off his head; gave it to the old man in the canoe.

The third brother came; then the fourth brother came. They were both thrown by the boy; their heads cut off by Coyote. They stood strong; *Tah-mat-tox-lee* pouring water; bringing ice. But the boy would call to his grandmother:

"Pour the sturgeon oil quick!"

She would do this, and they could not stand. The lame girl was crying; four of her brothers had been killed.

Then the fifth, the youngest Cold Wind brother wrestled. *Tah-mat-tox-lee* poured water, forming new ice.. The grandmother threw the fifth basket of oil making the ice slick. This youngest Cold Wind brother asked Chinook Wind if he could not live.[7] He did not want to die. Chinook Wind did not answer. Three times Cold Wind asked if he could not live. Chinook Wind kept silent. He asked the fourth time, the fifth time if he could not live. Then Chinook Wind answered:

"No! You killed all my people. You cannot live."

He then threw Cold Wind to the ground. Coyote cut off his head, as he had the four older brothers. Coyote carried it to the canoe, to be taken across the *nChe-wana* with the other heads.

Tah-mat-tox-lee ran away crying. Coyote ran after her, laughing at her. He said to the lame girl:

"Are you sure Chinook Wind whipped?"

Five times Coyote asked this, then the lame girl answered:

"Yes! I will be cold only a few days. Then Chinook Wind can come. I will have to stop."

Coyote said:

"All right! You stay there where you now are. I will stay here and watch you."

They are there yet. You can see *Tah-mat-tox-lee*, the lame sister of Cold Wind Brothers, where Coyote placed her. You can see Coyote near by watching her, laughing at her. They are both rocks, big rocks. The place is where lots of *his-to mah* [mussels] are to be found.

Notes by McWhorter

An aged woman of the Wan-a-pums, or Sokults of Priests Rapids, on the *nChe-wana*, averred that there were ten Cold Wind brothers, which is the only instance coming to my notice of a claim that there were more than five. This last is the mystic numeral pervading the philosophy of the Yakamas and kindred tribes, embracing the Sokults. Very rarely, the number seven appears, as where *We-now-y-yi* kills the youngest and last of the five *At-te-yi-yi* brothers, at the seventh turn or whirling. At the funeral of Chief *Sluskin We-owikt*, the cortege circled the residence three times, and the cemetery seven times, making ten all told.

Taman-towl-lat is a noted spring, location not determined. The name means, literally, a "place cut in the ground," as explained in the text. The scene of the legend is laid about the Tumwater, above The Dalles.

Sko-lus, *Skoo-lus*, or *Sco-lus* is an edible root. The name is applied to a "rim-rock" on the lower *nChe-wana* between Lone Rock and Rooster Rock, as pointed out by *Ana-whoa*, while steaming up the river in September 1911. It is nearly opposite Multnomah Falls. *Ana-whoa* refers to the five laws.

The salmon and the sturgeon are often refered to as one and the same fish. In the *Battle of At-te-yi-yi* and *Qee-nut*, salmon oil was poured on the ice by the old aunt, so *Qee-nut* might be enabled to stand. It is notable that not until this point of the story was reached did the narrator refer to the hero as Chinook Wind. Emphasis apparently was placed on the fact that he was a mere boy, although endowed with supernatural strength.

His-to mah is "place of mussels." The exact location, while not definitely determined, is in close proximity to Tumwater, Washington. The name applies also to both the clam and the oyster.

To be added to *Legend of Battle of Cold Wind and Warm Wind*

The Nez Perce version of this legend has it that the Cold Wind people powdered the snow, and in the battle this snow was used on the ground for purpose of making it too slippery for Warm Wind or Chinook Wind to stand. In the big snow storms you see a bare place on the mountain where the snow is melted. There is the work of Warm Wind.

The young Chinook Wind, in his practicing and exercising, pulled up great trees, carried them on his shoulder to his mother's tepee, or lodge, and cast them on the ground with such force as to shatter them into firewood.

The great sturgeon from which the oil was made to be cast on the ice so as to prevent the feet of Chinook Wind from slipping was caught by the old grandparents.

Chinook was lying in the bottom of the canoe, and when they were pursued by Cold Wind who had always robbed them of their fish, coming near the boat, Chinook shook himself and the boat darted away from the pursuers. Cold Wind said:

"Eh! That was never done before."

This happened five times and then Cold Wind gave up the chase, saying:

"Let them go with this fish. Just this one time they can go."

Taman-towl-lat, "dragging," is near the mouth of the Yakima River. The scar in the earth from the sturgeon's tail dragging is to be seen just above the mouth of the Yakima.

All of Cold Wind's five brothers were killed but the youngest. He begged to be let live, promising that when he was lonely he would make it cold only five years. Chinook would not agree. The period was shortened to three years, two years, one year, five months, and finally to one moon. This is the generally prevailing condition now ruling. Formerly it was cold ALL the time.

9

Coyote and *Lalawish*
Simon Goudy (Yakama-Klickitat)
No Date

THE *QUI-YIAH* REMAINED in Lake Keechelus five days and five nights.[1] In the meantime, during these five days and five nights, Coyote found himself where he had grown from the *Wah-nun-pace-ye* [Beaver]. He came to the high mountain, *Mo-kehl*, where the younger brother had last stood to look into the lake. He saw the five brothers lying deep on the bottom of the lake. He called to them:

"It is a shame! You are plain! You are not hiding enough!"

The *Qui-yiah* heard Coyote making fun of them. They were ashamed and left the lake that night. They started out toward *Klum-tah* [a mountain north of Tahoma, Mt. Ranier]. They struck a lake [*Enum-Klah-Pah*, place of hunger] along the Rocky Cascades. The five brothers went into this lake and are there today. It is a bad lake. You see rainbows in this lake and it gets foggy right away. Nobody troubles there much. The *Qui-yiah* was bluffed out of Lake Keechelus. This was Coyote's first trick. He did not want them in this lake. It would be dangerous for Indians.[2] Coyote now came down from the mountain and said to himself:

"I am going to look around. I will see what the *Qui-yiah* were doing about here."

He went back to the Kittitas Valley. When he got there, he saw that it was a beautiful country. Water was all gone. He came down the Yakima River, then a small stream. He followed it to the *nChe-wana*. He found the big river, with all kinds of fish coming up. Salmon, sturgeon and many others. He looked at the river. He said to himself:

"Those five brothers were not smart. I will make a layout for the new people, the Indians."

He then studied:

"It will be best to send some salmon up along this river [Yakima]."

This he did. He over-powered the salmon with his spirit.[3] They followed him as he walked along the shore. He came to the Satus River and sent salmon up that stream. He was hungry. He wanted salmon for dinner. He called for the largest salmon to come from the water. When Coyote called there was a splashing in the river. A great salmon rushed forth, floundering on the smooth boulders of the sloping shore. Coyote sprang on the big fish, sought to carry it away from the water. The salmon was wet and slippery, and although very strong, Coyote could not overcome the mighty *Wy-con-nis* [King Salmon]. It went out of his hands, gliding over the slick stones back into the water.

Poor Coyote knew not what to do. He was hungry. He passed his hand over his stomach. Yes! He was very hungry. What should he do? Coyote had five sisters, the Huckleberries.[4] These sisters, he carried in his stomach. They were his advisors in all big troubles. He brought them out and asked them to tell him how to catch the salmon. Always when they gave him advice Coyote would say:

"That is what I thought."

The sisters did not like this and they refused to give him advice. They said to him:

"You are so wise. We will not tell you. You always say: That is what I thought!"

Coyote threatened them with rain and hail, which would destroy them. They saw a great storm coming and got afraid. They agreed to tell him how to catch the salmon if he would stop the storm. He did so.[5] They made fun of his stupidity. They said:

"You are Coyote! Coyote who knows so much. You, who are wiser than all other people. You are starving because you do not know how to catch the big salmon, because you cannot hold him on the smooth rocks. Go to a sandy place. Call the salmon and when he comes out of the water you can hold him good."

Coyote replied:

"That is what I thought!"

Then he went to the river, finding a sloping bar of clean fine sand. He called again to the great salmon to come out of the water. With splashing, the chief of salmon rushed out upon the shore. Coyote, springing on him, had no trouble in holding him, all coated with gritty sand. Coyote laughed. He clubbed him and baked him by the fire, baked him on a stick and ate him. Now Coyote was happy. He was not hungry.[6]

After dinner, he told the fish to stay there. He went up Thappanish Creek to see what he could find. When he came up half way he found Indians there. They had started to grow. He said to himself:

"Now is time for me to get a woman."

He found love for the best girl there. He was ugly in face and parents of girl did not want Coyote. They told him:

"You better not come around here any more. Go back where you belong! We do not want you."

Coyote was willing to do so. He said:

"I am going right back. When you people learn news of me, do not feel bad about me. I was going to bring salmon, bring fish along this stream, if I was to marry this girl. But now I will not bring the salmon. They are coming but I will not let them stop. I will send them all past you."

Parents then wanted him to marry the girl. It would be good thing to have fish along Thappanish Creek. This would be like paying for the girl. That was the way Coyote had figured it. He was giving plenty salmon for a wife. They said to Coyote:

"Better take the girl!"

Coyote was angry. He said:

"No! There will be no salmon, no good fish along Thappanish Creek. I will take all my fish up Yakima River toward Kittitas Valley."

This is why there are no salmon in Thappanish Creek to this day.[7]

Then Coyote came up through *Pah-qy-ti-koot* [Union Gap] with his fish, came to Naches River. Here he called another big salmon to land and had dinner. After dinner, he drove salmon up the Naches. He knew there were Indians up there; they should have fish. He went up the Yakima River into Kittitas Valley, driving the salmon with him. It was now morning. He was tired and hungry. He wanted another dinner. He thought:

"I am hungry! I better take two salmons." He found a nice sandy place along the water. He called the salmon to come out. A big one came. He caught it and clubbed it. Then he called another one, which he clubbed. Coyote laughed. He was happy. Soon he would have a big feast. He carried the salmon to a secret place and dressed them. He made splints and stiffened the salmon. It must stand spread out to the fire when stuck on a stick planted in the ground. He built a fire, and set the salmon up before it. It began to bake and smell good. Coyote was feeling fine. He laughed when he thought how good it would taste.

In the meantime, five brothers, the *Lalawish* [Wolves] are prowling around. They are also very hungry. They see the smoke from Coyote's fire. They slip up to investigate. They smell the broiling salmon. They get up close, spy through the bushes. Coyote is sitting with his back to them, watching and tending his salmon. It is nearly done on inside, nearly ready to turn and bake skin side. The five brothers hold council. They will trick the wise Coyote, cheat him of his dinner. They blow their breath toward Coyote. This breath contains sleep medicine. Coyote feels this sleep coming to him. He yawns, grows drowsy. He says to himself:

"What is wrong with me? I am sleepy."

The brothers continue sending their breath to Coyote. He again says to himself:

"Yes! I am sleepy." [Coyote nods.] "Yes! I must sleep!"

He looks at his salmon. He thinks:

"It is nearly done. I will turn it, let it roast on other side while I sleep a little. When I wake up, I will have good feast."

Coyote turns the salmon. The *Lalawish* breath is strong, has power.

"Yes! I am sleepy, I am hungry. I will sleep and then eat."

Coyote fell over by the fire in sound sleep. The five brothers watch him. He will not wake. Then they come out from hiding, sneak up to the fire. The salmon is cooked, looks ripe. It smells good. The five brothers are very hungry. They say:

"Let us steal salmon from Coyote. He is wise, but we will trick him."

They took poor Coyote's nice salmon and sat down by the fire. They eat it all. They rub the greasy splints over the palms of Coyote's hands. They rub his lips with the oily bones, grease his mouth well. Then they pile the splints, the bones, all in a heap close at knees of sleeping Coyote. Then the *Lalawish* go silently away, sneak into the woods. They feel fine. They had good dinner, had tricked the wise Coyote. They laugh as they think what Coyote will do when he wakes up.

After the *Lalawish* goes from sight, Coyote comes from sleep. He yawns, stretches himself. He will now eat. He turns to the fire. It is burned out. He looks for the salmon; all is gone. The two sticks where salmon was stuck are still standing. It looks suspicious. He did not eat. What is wrong? Then he saw the bones, the splints lying heaped in front of him. Had he eaten it? He looked at his hands. They are greasy. He placed them to his nostrils; there is the odor of salmon. He licked his lips. Yes! he must have eaten the salmon. He could taste it on his lips. But he feels hungry. If he had eaten both those big salmon, he would feel good, feel happy. He cannot understand. Maybe somebody stole it? He did not know. He thinks:

"I better start up! I better drive my salmon up farther."

He starts up the river, goes a little ways, feels weak, is hungry. He stopped and said to himself:

"I better get salmon and eat some more."

He found a sandy place, called a big salmon out and killed it. He built fire and put salmon up on stick to bake. The five brothers came on following him, making fun of him. Soon they saw smoke along the river. They made a spy on him, found him sitting by the fire watching his salmon roast. They again make him sleep with their breath, then eat his salmon. They rubbed his lips with the oily splints and bones. Rubbed his hands the same, left bones in his hands; like he had eaten salmon himself.

The *Lalawish* now went to a high place, watched Coyote when he woke up. He found the bones in his hands. He licked his lips, tasted salmon. He thought:

"Yes! I have eaten alright! But I feel hungry. What is wrong? I do not eat enough. I will counsel with my sisters."

He called his five sisters, the Huckleberries, and said:

"Sisters! What is wrong? I eat plenty salmon but I am still hungry. I ate twice, but I am weak with hunger."

They laughed at him and said:

"We know about what is wrong, but you are smart. Find out yourself. We will not tell you."

Coyote threatened them with rain and hail. A black cloud came out of the west. The sisters were scared, they said:

"Yes! We will tell you about it. The five *Lalawish* have been following you, eating your salmon when you cook it. They have tricked you. They brought sleep to you with their breath. Then they eat your nice salmon, rubbed the bones, the greasy sticks on your hands, on your mouth to make fun of you. They are now laughing at you."

Coyote said:

"I know it! I knew something was wrong, and now I find it out. How will I manage it? How will I get even with the *Lalawish*?"

"Do not bake any more salmon. You watch for smoke. Go up the river, watch for smoke. The *Lalawish* will soon get hungry, will cook something as you did."

Coyote said:

"That is what I thought! I will fix them."

The *Lalawish* had gone towards *Wenatchee*. Coyote took his sisters' advice and followed them [to the Wenatchee River]. One day he saw a little smoke, not much smoke. Coyote made a good look. He said to himself:

"Now I will catch the wise *Lalawish*."

The smoke was up in the brush. Coyote scouted, got up close. All the *Lalawish* were sitting around the fire. They were cooking something. Coyote waited in the thicket awhile. It was about noon, very hot sun. Coyote got a little closer, blew his breath toward them. The *Lalawish* felt sleepy. They opened their mouths and yawned. One, two of them lay down; then all lay down and go to sleep. Coyote knew that they were all dead asleep. He went up to the fire. He took his time. He smoked. The *Lalawish* had lots of roasted venison on sticks about the fire. Coyote ate all he wanted, carried away the rest and hid it. Then he went back, rubbed the hands and lips of the sleepers with the greasy sticks and bones.

The *Lalawish* were all fine looking men. Handsome faces, small mouths, small ears, fine noses. Had small hands and feet. They were proud. Coyote studied. He said to himself:

"I will fix you wise minds! I will play a good trick on you."

Then he thrust his hand into their mouths, stretching them far back toward their ears. He pulled their noses till they became long snouts. He pulled their ears, made them sharp, standing up straight from the side of their heads. He then squeezed their hands and feet, shrinking them like a dog's foot. He piled the bones and splints from the roasted meat near their knees. Then he left the five brothers still sleeping by their dead camp fire.

Not long until the *Lalawish* awoke. They looked to their fire, to their meat. The fire was dead, the meat gone. They looked again, saw the picked bones, the splints all laid at their knees. What did it mean? Had they eaten all? Yes! Their hands were greasy with handling the meat. Their lips were still oily from eating. But they were hungry! What was wrong? If they had eaten all the meat roasted, they would not be hungry. They would feel good, feel rested. They could not understand.

Then the *Lalawish* saw how they were changed. They felt ashamed. They recognized the work of Coyote. They uttered yells of rage and defiance. These were only long drawn howls of lamentation. Ashamed, they slunk away to the prairies, where they wandered for several days. Finding no hiding place, they fled to the thick woods. There they have ever since wandered, hungry, fierce and savage amid the darkest tangle of the wild forests. Coyote had changed the five handsome brothers to the ever dreaded timber-wolf, the *Lalawish*.

When Coyote left the sleeping, transformed *Lalawish*, he returned to his salmon waiting in the Yakima. He continued driving them up the river. He got up this side where the town of Cle Elum now stands. He saw smoke in the bushes. He thought:

"Here are Indians, I will stop."

He headed off his salmon and went to see about the smoke. He found Indians, stayed there and got acquainted. He took salmon every day to the camp. The Indians thought he was a smart man. They knew he was from somewhere, but did not know he was Coyote. They gave Coyote a woman, they liked him. They looked upon him as a wise man, who knew how to catch fish without trouble. He stayed quite awhile. Then he said:

"I am leaving you. I am going back toward the sunrise, but I leave salmon for you. Every year they will come up this river."[8]

The Indians did not want him to go. They asked:

"When will you come back?"

Coyote answered:

"I will never come back. I learn there is a big time going on towards the sunrise."

They did not want him to leave them. They asked him to show them how to catch salmon. The Indians had tried to catch them but could not. Coyote went with two men to show them how to get salmon. He got down on the rocks where there was no sand and called:

"Come out!"

A dog-salmon came out and Coyote told Indian to catch him with his hands. Indian caught hold of salmon, but it was slippery. It got back into the water. Coyote stood laughing at them. They tried three times, then gave it up. Fish was too strong for them. They went back to camp. Then Coyote went to a sandy place and called the fish out of the water, where he could hold them. He took five big salmon back to camp to show the Indians what he could do. The Indians liked him and asked him to show them how he caught them. The next day he did so. He showed them how to make fish nets. He made different falls and rapids, traps where they could catch fish. In order that the salmon might not all escape into Fish Lake, he made the high waterfalls [*Wi-pe-na-tash*] above where Roslin, Washington, now stands. It is the best salmon trap of all.[9] Coyote said:

"As long as you live, you will have salmon along this river. I am going to the sunrise. I leave my wife here. I have other work to do."

The Indians have since lived at that place. Salmon have always come, every year they have come, according to the rules of Coyote. This is one story. Where he went back to the sunrise, another story begins.

Notes by McWhorter

Klum-tah means "head." This is the Klickitat name for a mountain north of Tahoma, the "big white mountain (Mt. Rainier)." Lake *Enum-Klah Pah*, "place of hunger," is situated on the summit of the Cascade Mountains, between Lake Keechelus and Tahoma [Rainier], the "big white mountain." Indians describe it as located in a rocky basin, circular in form and about one fourth of a mile wide. From its unknown depths in former times, deep thunder-like rumblings were heard, hence its name. The hiding place of the *Qui-yiah*, the lake is bad [dangerous]. Game goes into its water to die when old, for no aged animals are ever found in its vicinity. Tribesmen no longer hunt there.

"Toppenish" is the name conferred on the lower reaches of this stream by the white man. But few, if any, of the important water courses were known to the Yakimas by the same name for their full length. A place-name would be given with no relation to the stream on which it was located. A minor river might be known by a score of names, at as many different points. Mouth of the Toppenish was called: *Pis-co*.

One version of this story is that the wolves transformed Coyote into his present form, after first devouring his salmon. Coyote went to the river to drink and saw his reflection in the water. Surprised, he sprang back with a startled ejaculation, believing that it was someone else, perhaps an enemy. Investigation revealed to him the terrible truth, and the vengeful Coyote inflicted on the five handsome brothers the same treatment that they had accorded him. Discovering their predicament, and seeing the wily Coyote standing at a distance laughing at them, the wolves gave chase for the purpose of punishing him, but were unable to overtake their fleet-footed tormentor. For this reason the wolf and the coyote have been enemies to this day.

The falls, *Wi-pe-na-tash*, "drifting down," are on the Teansway River, below what is known to the Indians as Fish Lake. It was here that *Qah-steeh*, the famous fisherman of the Yakimas, had his trap. So great was his reputation as a salmon fisherman that it won for him a distinctive appellation. One day he met a white man who asked his name. The old Indian had a salmon in a gunny sack strapped to his saddle, and supposing that the inquiry was relative to same, he replied in very imperfect English that it was a salmon in the sack. He was ever afterwards known as *Sam-a-lee Sack*, the name that his interrogator understood him to pronounce. *Qah-steeh* was also a great bear hunter, which, coupled with his skill as a fisherman, made him a favorite among the women. He was a good provider. Versed in the lore of his tribe, he was an instructor, a professional storyteller, and a trainer of children. He ofttimes amused the young people during the winter days with the jaw of a jack rabbit or beaver, in "wishing" games.

10

Battle of the *Atteyiyi* and *Toqeenut*
(Klickitat, Cascade, Wishom, and Wasco)
July 1918

IN THAT DAY the *Lalawish*, the Wolves were five brothers.[1] They talked against *Toqeenut*, the Chief of Salmons, chief of all fishes. The *Qeenut* talked against the *Lalawish*. The *Lalawish* prepared to fight the *Qeenut*. *Speel-yi* was a great Chief.[2] He said:

"I cannot stop the people from fighting, but I will be there too. I will fight for the *Lalawish*."

So the news go to all the people that the *Lalawish* will fight against the *Qeenut* [Chinook Salmon] people, fight the Chinook people.

There came the *Atteyiyi*, the five brothers, the icy, the strong Cold Northeast Wind before whom none could stand. These five brothers said:

"All right! We will be there to fight for the *Lalawish*."

So they get together, the five *Lalawish* and the five *Atteyiyi*. They talk this way:

"What will we do with the *Qeenut*?"

The *Atteyiyi* said:

"We think this way. We will wrestle with the *Qeenut*. If we throw him down, ice will be all over the *nChe-wana*. Ice and cold over all the water, cold everywhere."

The *Lalawish* said:

"All right! When you throw him down, we will fight and kill all his children. None will be left."

They sent word to the *Qeenut*:

"You come! Bring all your children and have a big time on the ice of the *nChe-wana*. Bring all your people."

Toqeenut, the Salmon Chief said:

"I cannot help this! My people. I cannot refuse this fight. We will all go! My people. We will all go to meet this boaster."[3]

So all the people went, lined up on each side to fight or wrestle. The *Lalawish* spoke:

"All ready for the big trial of strength. *Toqeenut*, you wrestle with oldest *Atteyiyi* brother. Wrestle with him first."

Toqeenut went to wrestle with the oldest *Atteyiyi* who was not strong. *Toqeenut* said to his wife and children:

"I am afraid! I am afraid of the *Atteyiyi*. Be careful! If you see they are going to beat us, you run away. Run quick and hide."[4]

Both sides are looking on, watching to see the great wrestling match. The *Lalawish* calls:

"Now ready! Now go!"

The big man of the *Qeenut*s and the oldest brother of the *Atteyiyi*, both stripped for wrestling, walk out on the ice, out on the *nChe-wana* covered with ice. The *Atteyiyi* can stand on the ice, but *Toqeenut* cannot stand. They go out a short distance, out on the ice. All the people are looking at the big men wrestling. *Toqeenut* throws the *Atteyiyi* down, and from the *Qeenut* side comes the victory [cry]:

"Ow-ow-ow-ow-ow-ow-ow-ow-o-oo!"

The *Atteyiyi* say nothing. They cannot say anything. They keep still.

Then the second *Atteyiyi* steps out on the ice to wrestle with *Toqeenut*. He is a little stronger than his brother, but *Toqeenut* throws him. Then his people again set up the long shout of triumph. The *Atteyiyi* keep still. They cannot say anything. But all the time *Toqeenut* kept thinking:

"I will die! I will die! They are five against one. They are too many for me. I will die! The *Atteyiyi* are too many for me."

Then the third *Atteyiyi* brother steps forth to wrestle with *Toqeenut*. He is a little stronger than either of the older brothers. He stands strong on the ice and throws *Toqeenut* down hard. Throws him quick. He is dragged and killed on the shore of the frozen *nChe-wana*. The *Atteyiyi* yell:

"Ow-ow-ow-ow-ow-ow-ow-ow-o-oo!"

The five *Lalawish* run against all the young *Qeenut*, all the young children. There are lots of *Lalawish*, Coyotes and Foxes. All fight the *Qeenut* people. They had first killed the Chief, *Toqeenut*, then his wife. She has lots of *Qeenut* eggs, salmon eggs in her belly. They throw her down, burst her open. The eggs spill out. It was on a flat rock, the eggs are scattered all about. All the *Queenut* people are killed, children and all. The *Atteyiyi*, all the people on their side now set up:

"*Ow-ow-ow-ow-ow-ow-ow-ow-o-oo!* The *Qeenut* are no more! We will now all the time have it cold. Ice all over the *nChe-wana*. Cold all the time, ice."

All the *Atteyiyi* side yell that it will be cold, no warm. *Speel-yi* thought:

"I did wrong helping the *Lalawish*. They killed a good man, a good people."[5]

The *Lalawish* call loud to their people, to their side:

"Come! Help kill eggs on the rocks! We do not want one left to grow."

They came and scattered the eggs, destroyed them. That time *Speel-yi* stood away back, far back. *Speel-yi* did not help destroy the eggs. He said:

"We killed a good man, a good chief. I am sorry."

He talked that way. *Speel-yi* was sorry. He nearly cried. The *Lalawish* yell loud:

"We have killed all! Killed all the *Qeenut*! We have done a great work! Now it will be cold all the time!"

The rock where *Toqeenut*'s wife was killed, is cracked deep. The eggs were there, lots of eggs. One egg was deep down. One *Lalawish* called:

"One egg I cannot get it. It is too deep in the rock."

Other *Lalawish* came and tried to lick the egg from the crevice. They lick once, twice! Once, twice! They cannot get it. They said:

"If we don't get it, it will come to life. There will be other."

The *Lalawish* all tried to lick the egg from the rock, but they failed. All stood with their front feet in the same place, making but two tracks. These tracks can be seen to this day, there in the rock where they stood. It is near the Tumwater, on the *nChe-wana*, at Wishom. Finally they gave it up. They said:

"Let it go! It is dry, it is dead now. It will not grow."

They quit. All gave the long:

"*Ow-ow-ow-ow-ow-ow-ow-ow-o-oo!*"

They had killed all the *Qeenut*s, all fishes; and it would now be cold all the time. The five brothers, the *Lalawish*, went to the mountains. They said:

"We quit now."

The *Atteyiyi*, five brothers, stayed on the *nChe-wana*, had a cave where they stayed. It is a rock cave at *Wah-pe-us* [meaning "catching fish with a dip net" located near Celilo], and was cold, cold and icy. They talked, talked together.

"We killed him now! We killed the *Qeenut*! We killed him! His wife and all his children are dead, killed by the *Lalawish*. It will now be cold all the time. It was our work, our big work to do this."

All the *Atteyiyi* people went off the next day, left that place. Clouds came up, came up fast. The clouds grew darker and darker. It rained, rained and the Spirit which rules helped the one *Qeenut* egg. The egg began to swell. It rained! Water went there where the egg was in the split rock. Clouds stayed, and it rained, rained more and more. The egg swelled bigger, still bigger. The Spirit still helped, helped that egg to come to life. It rained five days and five nights, when a little fish came out from that egg. On the sixth day it went into the river, went with the water from the rock. The little fish grew. It went down to the mouth of the *nChe-wana* near the ocean. At the mouth of the *nChe-wana*, it found its grandmother, an old woman. From a little salmon he grew and found his grandmother, found her far down where the *nChe-wana* enters the ocean.[6]

The grandmother knew from away-off, knew from where she was that her son had been killed by the *Atteyiyi*, thrown on the ice and killed by the *Lalawish*. She told the little boy:

"My son, your father was killed, killed by the *Atteyiyi*. His wife and all his children were killed, all but you. I knew it before you came. I am glad, glad that you have come, my little grandchild. I am glad you have come back."

The grandmother caresses her little grandchild, talking to him all the time, telling him how glad she is to see him. She knew, knew when the fight was going on, although she was far away and near the sea. The little *Qeenut* boy said:

"Tell me how my father was killed. Yes, tell me how I saved myself alone, how I am alive today."

She told him all, knew all and told it to him. Then she worked to make the boy grow, to make him grow fast and strong. She had Indian medicine to rub on him. She made him bathe every morning. It was to make him grow, to make him strong. She said:

"You prepare. Bathe in cold water all winter. Practice! Try your strength, grow strong, and in the spring, go fight the *Atteyiyi*. I am going to fix it, fix five baskets of oil [oil of eel or dog salmon], *Qeenut* oil for your feet to stand strong on the ice. There are five brothers of the *Atteyiyi*, against my grandchild. I will help you to stand strong before them."

All winter the boy bathed in cold water, bathed, took hard exercise all winter. When spring came he was big! Tall! Strong! His grandmother said to him, told him often:

"I am glad, my grandchild! I am glad! You will be strong, stronger than my son, your father. You will not fall down before the *Atteyiyi*."

Early spring came. The boy went outside of the tepee.[7] He looked around, all around. He said to his grandmother:

"Now look at me."

She had a small mat lodge, lived there. She went out to look at him. She watched him to see what he would do. He was big, tall, strong. He went a short distance to a thicket and pulled up small trees. Pulled them easily, threw them on the ground. His grandmother was glad, glad that he was so strong. She said:

"That is right, my grandchild. You will be strong enough in two moons more."

That is the way the Indians used to be. They did those things to make them strong in the hunt, strong in the battle. The boy twisted trees the size of his arm, twisted them to their roots. He would say:

"Look at me! See how strong I am, how I can twist and pull up trees."

The grandmother was pleased. She would watch her grandchild and say:

"Yes! You are strong, my grandchild. You are now stronger than was your father. You will not fall before the *Atteyiyi*."

These things he did for five days, then he pulled up trees that fifty men could not shake. The grandmother said:

"That is right! You will beat those people, the boastful *Atteyiyi*. You will not be thrown, will not be killed by them like your father."

The boy is now stronger than ever. He goes outside and says:

"Look at me! See what I will now do, my grandmother."

There are big rocks lying around. One is bigger than the others, a great rock like a tepee, like the mat lodges of the people who are gone.[8] He walks to that rock, picks it up. Throws it to the middle of the *nChewana*. He threw it easily, was not hard for him to throw it. The old grandmother was glad, glad that her grandchild was so strong. She said:

"Oh my grandchild! You are strong! You are brave. The *Atteyiyi*, the cold, bad people cannot stand before you. You will beat them. You will not fall before them. I will help you. I will give you the five baskets of oil for your feet."

In this way, *Wenowyyi* [Young Chinook Wind], the son of *Toqeenut*, grew up, the way he prepared himself to fight the cold *Atteyiyi*. He said: "I will fix it! I will fix it about this boastful *Atteyiyi*."

The old woman was sorry because her son had been killed. She cried, but she was now glad that her grandchild was so strong. He would stand and fight the *Atteyiyi*, stand on the ice at *Wah-pe-us* [near Celilo] on the *nChe-wana*.

For six moons did *Wenowyyi* prepare for the battle. For six moons, until the salmon would run in the spring. Every day he practiced at everything. Lifting, to get strong feet. Throwing, to get strong arms. Running, jumping to get strong legs. Pulling up trees to get strong back; strong shoulders. He thought to get a strong mind, strong head. He said to his grandmother:

"They cannot beat me! The *Atteyiyi* cannot stand before me. Five days more and I will go fight the five brothers, the *Atteyiyi*. Get ready the five baskets of oil."

The grandmother answered:

"Yes, my grandchild. I will fix the five baskets of oil for you, for your feet to stand strong on the ice. You will not fall."

The *Atteyiyi* had a slave woman, a sister to the old grandmother.

They watched her close, would not let her go anywhere. They treated her badly.

The *Atteyiyi* had a sister, *Atsteyiyi*, a cripple, a sister to the Chief *Atteyiyi*. Every morning this *Atsteyiyi* would go out, then come and befoul the old slave-woman's hair. It was all bad. The grandmother told *Wenowyyi* [another sister also called Young Chinook Wind] all about this. How her sister was nearly starved; no food, no robes. Cold all the time with icicles hanging to her hair. She was nearly dead.

Wenowyyi [the male Young Chinook Wind] finished the five days. Finished practicing, finished preparing for the battle. He said:

"Goodbye, my grandmother. I am now going to meet the *Atteyiyi* on the ice of the *nChe-wana*. I will kill the *Atteyiyi*, the five brothers who killed my father. Goodbye! I will go now."

The grandmother put her arms around him, carressed him. She said:

"All right! Go! Be strong before the *Atteyiyi*. Take these five baskets of oil. When you get to my sister, she will tell you all about this oil, how to use it. She knows and will fix it for you. Go! Goodbye, my grandchild. You will not fall before the *Atteyiyi*. You will beat them on the ice, beat them in the wrestling match."

Wenowyyi answered:

"All right!"

Wenowyyi came on foot. He came to the Cascades. There he threw trees, threw rocks far out into the river. Pulled up big trees, threw them into the *nChe-wana*. Tore big rocks from the ground, hurled them far out into the water. He felt strong. He practiced his strength on everything, in every way as he came. He kept saying:

"Nothing can beat me! Nothing can stand before me. I am *Wenowyyi*, the *Toqeenut*'s son. I am stronger than was my father. The *Atteyiyi*, the five brothers, the cold wind cannot stand before my breath. I will beat them! I will throw them on the ice of the *nChe-wana*. I will kill this cold. It cannot stay everywhere all the time."

Thus *Wenowyyi* traveled up the *nChe-wana*. He came close to Celilo, where the *Atteyiyi* lived in the rock cave. The *nChe-wana* is covered with ice, cold all the time. *Qeenut* was the warm wind, the Chinook wind. *Wenowyyi* was his son. He got close to the *Atteyiyi*. He thought:

"These people will know that I am coming."

Thoughts, like breath, go ahead. The old aunt, covered with ice, cold, starving, sat in her little mat lodge. The breath of *Wenowyyi* broke the icicles in her hair. They fell to the ground. She groaned:

"*Ah-h-n-nn!* He is coming back!"

She knew all. Then *Wenowyyi* walked slowly. He saw the little mat hut, this side of the *Atteyiyi*'s cave-house. He goes in. She can only whisper:

"I am poorly! They are treating me bad! Every morning the sister of *Atteyiyi* comes and filths my hair. Every morning you will hear a noise at the door. It is her. She comes but does not look at me."

Wenowyyi answered:

"All right! I will fix her! I feel sorry they make slave of you. Go out and cut rose bush with thorns.[9] Tomorrow I will fix this girl, this lame sister of *Atteyiyi*."

The old aunt went out and brought back the rose bush with all its thorns. Then they slept a little. In the morning they get up. The aunt said:

"Sit near the door, hide your rose bush near the door. She will come. She will not look around; she will not see you."

Wenowyyi sat by the door. Soon he hears a noise coming. Yes! It is *Atsteyiyi*! She comes in! She does not look around, does not look at the old woman. When she backs near the old aunt, *Wenowyyi* strikes her on the neck with the thorny rose bush. Strikes her hard. *Atsteyiyi* cries:

"*Owo!*"

Atsteyiyi ran out of the house, blood running down her legs. She hurried back to her brothers, the *Atteyiyi*, and said:

"Our enemy has come to life! I do not know how he is alive, but he is there in the mat lodge with the old woman. I do not think that the old woman did this to me! I do not think that she struck me with the rose bush thorns."

Atsteyiyi told her brothers this, how she had been struck. They answered:

"Yes! Last night we were a little afraid. Last night the warm wind came a little and we were afraid. It is he! It is *Qeenut* come to life again. He has come to meet us on the ice, to wrestle with us on the ice of the *nChe-wana*."

Then the *Atteyiyi* sent word to all the people, to everybody to come and see the great wrestling match, see it again that day. The five *Lalawish* came from the mountains. The big chiefs came, all the chiefs of the foxes, the birds, all came bringing their people. Word was sent out:

"*Qeenut* has grown up! *Qeenut* wants to wrestle, has come to wrestle with *Atteyiyi*."

Wenowyyi had his five baskets of oil. The old aunt fixes them, makes everything ready. That means five baskets of oil against the five *Atteyiyi* and against the five *Lalawish*. The old woman puts oil on his feet, on the feet of *Wenowyyi*, the strong. The *Atteyiyi* sees him. They called to him friendly:

"Is that you, our friend? Have you come to wrestle with us?"

Wenowyyi makes answer same way:

"Yes! I have come to do this thing. I have come to wrestle with you, my friends. Wrestle on the ice of the *nChe-wana*."

The *Atteyiyi* thought:

"He is only one, he is not strong. We are five, we are strong. We will kill him, this boasting *Qeenut*."

It is near mid-sun. All go to see the wrestling, go near the bank of the *nChe-wana*, all covered with ice. Ice made by the *Atteyiyi*. The five *Atteyiyi* laugh at *Wenowyyi*. Laugh loud! Laugh long! *Wenowyyi* answers:

"I will be there! I will meet you on the ice of the *nChe-wana*."

Atsteyiyi, the lame sister, is there. The people all want to see. *Speel-yi*, the big chief, said:

"Yes! We will beat! We will beat the *Atteyiyi*. *Wenowyyi* is stronger than was his father. He will stand strong to wrestle."

All five of the *Atteyiyi* are to wrestle against *Wenowyyi*, the *Qeenut*. He said to his aunt, the old woman:

"Soon as I get to the place on the ice, pour one basket of oil at my feet. Pour it on the ice at my feet."

She answered him:

"All right! I will pour the oil.[10] It will make you stand strong."

Wenowyyi stood in his place. The old aunt pours the oil at his feet, pours it on his feet on the ice. All the people are looking at him. All the people are anxious to see him. He looks big! Looks strong! All stripped on the ice for wrestling. The *Lalawish* are a little afraid. The oldest brother, the oldest *Atteyiyi*, steps out to wrestle with *Wenowyyi*. He is not so strong-looking. They try strength four times when *Atteyiyi* is thrown on the ice. Killed. Head cut! Bursted on the ice. *Speel-yi* gives a long:

"*Ow-ow-ow-ow-ow-ow-ow-ow-o-oo!*"

It is the cry of the victor. The *Atteyiyi* and their people cannot say anything. They must keep still.

The second brother of the *Atteyiyi* steps out to wrestle with the *Qeenut*. He is a little stronger.[11] They stand to wrestle, stripped naked on the ice. The old aunt pours oil at the feet of *Wenowyyi*. All is ready! Right away they wrestle. It is the same way as with the first brother, only a little longer, a little harder struggling. Three times *Wenowyyi* swings the *Atteyiyi*. Three times they swing and bend hard. Then the fourth time the *Atteyiyi* is whirled, thrown on the ice, his head bursted, killed. *Speel-yi* again calls the long yell of the victor, calls it long and loud. The five *Lalawish* stand mad. They say to each other:

"They will beat us! *Speel-yi*! *Speel-yi*, the big chief, is against us."

The third *Atteyiyi* comes out to match his skill and strength with that of the mighty *Wenowyyi*. They stand. The old woman pours the third basket of oil at the feet of *Qeenut*. *Wenowyyi*, the *Qeenut*, stands strong on the ice. They wrestle. *Wenowyyi* turns the *Atteyiyi* three times, turns him slowly. Then he whirls him fast, throws him on the ice, bursting his head.[12] The other two *Atteyiyi* brothers are scared. *Speel-yi* gives louder the cry of victory. His side calls to the *Atteyiyi*:

"Hurry up! Hurry up and wrestle! We cannot stand here so long!"

The fourth brother walks out on the ice. The old aunt comes and pours the fourth basket of oil at the feet of *Wenowyyi*, pours it on the ice at his feet. He stands strong, a big man. They begin to wrestle. The

Atteyiyi is stronger than were any of his three brothers killed. He stands and wrestles strong. Four times he is swung by *Wenowyyi*, four times slowly swung. Then *Wenowyyi* whirls him quick, throws him and his head is bursted on the ice.

Speel-yi cries the long call of the victor, of the best man. The last *Atteyiyi* brother stands afraid. He says to himself over and over:

"He will kill me! Kill me sure. All my brothers are dead! Killed by this strong *Qeenut*. He will kill me! But I cannot run. It is the law that I must fight, must wrestle and die."

Speel-yi's side calls:

"Hurry up! Hurry up! Wrestle with *Qeenut*. Do not be afraid!"

Slowly he comes, comes slowly out on the ice. He stands where his brothers stood, where all four of his brothers were killed. The last basket of oil is poured by the old aunt at the feet of *Wenowyyi*. *Wenowyyi* places his feet. He said to himself:

"I am going to stand strong, this, the last time."

Then they wrestle. Wrestle harder, faster. The match is closer than the last two. The last and younger *Atteyiyi* is strong, struggles hard. Six times does *Wenowyyi* turn him, six times slowly. Six times he has turned him, then the seventh whirls him fast, throws him on the ice. His head is bursted like those of his four older brothers. The last of the *Atteyiyi* lies dead at the feet of *Wenowyyi*, the son of *Toqeenut*, Chief of Chinooks. It was then that *Atsteyiyi*, the lame sister of the *Atteyiyi*, ran crying to the *nChe-wana*, all after her to kill her. She went into the water through a hole in the ice. She escaped.

Speel-yi yelled louder, louder the cry of the strongest sides. All the people shouted, were glad. *Speel-yi* called:

"We beat them! We beat them, those bad people. Now it will be warm. We will have nice rich food. The salmon will come, all the salmon we want to eat. Now we will all stand, all run against the five *Lalawish*."

Speel-yi said this. He ran against the *Lalawish*, heading all the people fighting against them. The *Lalawish* fled to the Cascade Mountains, are there yet. The *Lalawish* said:

"*Speel-yi* is chief! We cannot beat him! We cannot stand before him."

Speel-yi was then the big chief. He commanded. He said:

"*Atsteyiyi* has escaped into the water. For this reason it will be a little cold, but not cold as it has been. It cannot remain cold all the time."

The ice at that moment melted in the *nChe-wana*, ran down to the ocean. There is now only a little ice in the winter, a little ice during a few moons only. This was many thousand snows ago. There is no record, but that is the talk.[13] That time *Speel-yi* said to *Wenowyyi*, the big Salmon Chief:

"I am going to fore-tell! From here, from *Wah-pe-us*, from *Skein*, people will live to the mouth of the *nChe-wana*, to the ocean. They will be different people, different from all kinds of bird and animal-people, and all will eat freely by and by. Nothing will be to pay. Food is for all kinds of people, free."

The Salmon Chief said to *Speel-yi*, said when they were together:

"Yes! You put it down that way, put the law that way.[14] All will be friendly and good. We killed the *Atteyiyi*. They were strong but we killed them. Those bad people are now dead. No more war at this time."

It was that way. And now, from that time, *Speel-yi* said:

"Other people will come, and when they meet and have a big time, when they play games of any kind, the Coyote call by the victors will be given:

'*Ow-ow-ow-ow-ow-ow-ow-ow-o-oo!*'

The beaten party must keep still, cannot say anything."

That is the law, given by *Speel-yi* at that time.[15] It stands today, in games and in war. That cry is the cry of the victor only

Notes by McWhorter

Atteyiyi is the "cold northeast wind," most deadly of all winds. It is sometimes called *Tayea*. *Wahpeus* means "catching fish with a dip net" is located at or near *Skein* [cradle board] along the *nChe-wana*; not far from Celilo. Salmon jumping out of falls were also gaffed at *Wahpeus*.

The oils of the dog salmon and of the eel possess the properties of non-slipping on the ice. Either of these oils applied to the sole of the moccasin insures the wearer a secure footing on the smoothest of ice. The dog-salmon is the *Qeenut* or royal chinook salmon at a certain period.

The *umtoli*, or *mtola*, is the *qeenut* at spawning.

Wenowyyi means "young chinook-wind," and it is a powerful, warm wind from a distance. In the legend, young Chinook-wind is personified as *Qeenut*, the chinook-salmon, and the son of *Toqeenut*, chief of salmons, chief of all fishes.

In some versions of this legend, even in the same tribe, as with the Klickitats, this slave-woman held by the *Atteyiyi* was *Wenowyyi*, a sister to *Wenowyyi*, young Chinook Wind.

In this legend, it is noticeable that *Atsteyiyi*, the crippled sister, does not pour water for the purpose of forming ice that the enemy of her brothers might not stand. Such service is rendered by a like sister in other versions.

The peculiar cry or call is rendered by placing the hand over the mouth and by rapid vibrations of the palm, break into sharp staccato, a long drawn quavering yell. It is a signal of triumph; of victory and defiance and is never used by the vanquished in either games or in war. Such was Coyote's law or "ruling" when the world was yet young, when Animal People held sway.

11

How Coyote Destroyed the Fish Dam at the Cascades: Distributing Salmon in the Rivers
Che-pos To-cos, Owl Child (Wishom)

October 1916

THE FIVE SISTERS [*Yuka-mah* or Beaver] lived at the Cascades of the *nChe-wana.*[1] The youngest sister was smartest of them all. They had a dam [Celilo Falls] in the river and headed off the salmon from the upper waters. This was bad. Coyote said:

"This must not be done! Fish must be free for all the people."

Coyote sat and studied a long time. He would go see the Five Sisters. But if he went as a man, they would not have him, would not let him come there. Coyote knew what he would do. He would be as a baby. He took tulies, same the old women use in weaving mats, and made matting. He made a basket. Coyote said:

"I will be a baby in the basket!"

He put the basket in the *nChe-wana,* got in the basket, crying like a baby every evening. One of the girls went down to the river to get water where she heard the baby crying. She called to her sisters:

"Little baby has come down the river! Somebody has drowned!"

All the women but the youngest came and saw the baby. They said:

"We must take the baby and care for it!"

The youngest sister knew something was wrong.[2] She did not go. The other sisters rushed and got the baby, took him in the lodge. They gave him a little fish to eat. He liked it. The sisters said:

"He will grow quick! Grow big quick!"

The youngest sister told them:

"Yes! Your baby will grow big quick!"

The next morning the sisters all went to dig roots. They left the baby in the lodge, tied about the waist to a stake. They gave him a fish to eat, a small fish. He ate it. The youngest sister knew all about it, what was going to be done.

Soon as the sisters left him alone, Coyote untied himself. He commenced making wooden hats. He made five wooden hats. He also made five root-digging sticks. He made all these in one day, preparing for a big work.[3] Coyote thought:

"This will not do. I must open the dam and let fish go by for all people."[4]

Coyote now commenced to dig open the big dam so the fish could get through. He knew when the sisters would be home, when he must be back in the lodge again, a baby, only a little stronger. He stayed that night in the lodge. Next morning when the sisters went to dig roots, he worked at tearing out the dam. For three days he did this, going back to be a baby in the lodge each night. Every day he was growing a little bigger, a little stronger.[5] The oldest sisters would say:

"Our baby gets stronger every day."

Coyote worked again on the fourth day. He worked all the time with the root-digging sticks. The baby appeared stronger, and the sisters were glad. But the youngest sister knew what would happen.

On the fifth day the sisters again went to dig roots, leaving the baby in the lodge tied to the stake. On this last day Coyote unhitched himself and put the five wooden hats on his head. On this day he had the dam nearly opened when the sisters returned home. They said:

"Eh! Our baby is gone!"

The youngest sister told them:

"Yes! Your baby has the dam nearly out."

They ran to the river, saw Coyote working. They fought him with clubs. They struck him on the head. The first wooden hat broke. They stuck him again; the second hat is broken. They struck him again; the third hat is broken. They struck him again; the fourth hat is broken. The fifth time they struck him on the head; the fifth wooden hat was broken. All the time Coyote was digging hard. When the fifth hat broke, the dam gave way. The water rushes by, and the fish go upstream in big herds. The *nChe-wana* is alive with them. Coyote is glad. He yells:

"*Ha-a-a-a-aha!* The new people will come and all will have fish. You cannot keep the salmon this way. Salmon must be free for all."

The sisters could not say any thing. Coyote had destroyed the great dam, he said:

"I will make this a big fishing place. Indians will camp here and have good times. They will study out all about high water and low water. How the best way to catch fish."[6]

Coyote made a good fishing place at the ruined dam of the Cascades.

Coyote brought the salmon up the *nChe-wana*. He traveled along, got hungry. He wanted salmon, but did not know how to catch it. He asked his five sisters [Huckleberry Sisters who lived in his stomach] how to get salmon. They said:

"We will not tell you. You always say: 'Yes, that is as I thought.'"

Coyote said:

"You better do it."

The sisters answered:

"No! We will not tell you."

The sisters were afraid of rain, and Coyote said:

"*A-ow!* I will make it rain."

He threw back his head, blew rain from his mouth:

"*Ch-ch-ch-ch-chu.*"

The sisters were scared, they said:

"Oh quit! We will tell you."

Coyote quit making rain and the sisters said:

"You go to the edge of the river and call: 'Come up, my make.[7] I am hungry.'"

Coyote said:

"Yes, Yes! I thought so."

He did as they told him. The fish came up on the rocks, *c-c-c-r-ca !*[8]

Coyote grabbed a fish, but it got back in the water. He could not hold it. He did not know how to catch the salmon. Coyote said:

"Well sisters! How is this? I called, 'Come up my work, [Salmon],' but they go back again."

The sisters would not tell him. Coyote said:

"All right! I will make it rain."

He threw back his head and blew the rain:

"*Ch-ch-ch-ch-chu.*"

The sisters were scared and said:

"Quit! We will tell you. Go call the fish out on the sand. You can hold them there."

Coyote said:

"Yes! That is what I thought."

He went to a sandy place and called:

"Come up, my make! I am hungry."

The fish came up on the sand: *c-c-c-r-c!*[9] This time Coyote caught a salmon and held him [this occurred on the Columbia River at the former site of Wallula, Washington]. He hit him on the head with a club, killed him.

Coyote made a fire. Split the salmon, stuck it on sticks to roast before the fire. It smelled good, for Coyote was hungry. It was about roasted. Coyote had his salmon nearly done. He soon would eat it. He watched it and felt good.

There were five wolves living away off from the river. They said:

"Coyote is roasting his fish. We better make him sleep. We better go eat his fish now."

Coyote went to sleep, just as his salmon was done.[10] The wolves came. They took his salmon, ate it all up. They greased Coyote's face and fingers good, while he was sleeping. The wolves then went away. Coyote woke up and looked for his fish. It was gone. He said:

"I roasted him! When did I eat him? My fingers, my face are greasy. I am hungry, but I ate my fish."

He went on again, still hungry. He could not stand the hunger. He stopped at a sandy place and called:

"My make, come up! I am hungry."

The fish came up on the sand *c-c-c-r-c!* Coyote caught one and clubbed it on the head, killed it. [Coyote clubbed the salmon at a place on the Columbia River where he caused seven choke cherries to grow, declaring, "Here will grow the largest and the best cherries for the New People who are coming."][11] He cleaned it, put it on sticks to roast by a fire he built. It was about done when the wolves put him to sleep again. They took the hot salmon. They ate it all up. They greased Coyote's mouth and fingers good, then ran away.

Coyote woke up to find his salmon gone. He said:

"I ate him. My fingers and face are greasy. I am hungry, but I ate my fish. I cannot understand."

Coyote then went on a distance up the river. He was too hungry. He came to a sandy place at the water's edge and called:

"Come up, my make. I am hungry."

The salmon came up *c-c-c-r-c!* Coyote caught a fish, cleaned him, split him. He built a fire, put his salmon on sticks to roast. It was about done.

The wolves put him to sleep. They came and ate all the roasted salmon. They greased Coyote's fingers, his face, then went back home. Coyote woke up. He looked for his salmon; it was gone. He felt hungry. He found his face and fingers all greasy and said:

"I ate my fish, but I am hungry. I cannot understand why I am so hungry when I ate my fish. I am awfully hungry."

Coyote went on again, suffering with hunger. Soon he came to a sandy place and called:

"Come up, my make! I am hungry!"

The fish came up: *c-c-c-r-c!* Coyote caught one, hit it on the head with a club, killed it. He cleaned it, split it open and put it on sticks to roast at a fire he built. It was about done when the wolves put a sleep on him, took his fish and ate it all up. They greased his mouth good, then went back home. Coyote woke up. He looked for his fish, but it was not there. He felt his fingers, his face. All greasy. He said:

"How is this! I ate my fish but I am still hungry. I will ask my sisters [Huckleberry]."[12]

He called:

"How is this, my sisters? I ate my salmon but I am still hungry. Five times I have ate a whole salmon. I am more hungry than at first. I am awfully hungry. Tell me about it."

But the sisters said:

"No, we will not tell you. You always know anyhow."

Coyote said:

"All right! I will make it rain."

He threw back his head, he blew rain from his mouth:

"*Ch-ch-ch-ch-chu.*"

The sisters did not want to get wet. They cried:

"Oh wait! Do not make it rain. We will tell you all about when you roast fish."

Coyote then quit making rain. The sisters said:

"Five wolves live in the mountains. They put sleep on you, came and ate your salmon. They greased your mouth, your fingers. They do this five times."

Coyote said:

"Oh yes! yes! That is what I thought."

The sisters said:

"We will tell you now what you do. The wolves gather all kinds of eggs and roast them. They get duck eggs, pheasant eggs, any kind they

find. You go over there where they are now roasting their eggs. You put
them on sleep and eat their eggs. When you are through, put egg on their
mouths, their fingers. They will think that they ate the eggs."[13]

Coyote said:

"Yes! That is what I thought to do."

Coyote then went to where the wolves were roasting eggs. He put
sleep on them and ate all their eggs. He rubbed egg on their fingers,
about their mouths, then went away. Soon the wolves woke up. They see
their eggs are all gone, but they are hungry. They look at each other, see
egg on their faces. They said:

"You eat the eggs."

"No, you eat all the eggs, it is on your mouth."

The wolves gathered more eggs, built fire and began roasting them.
Coyote sneaking up, came near. He put a sleep on the wolves, ate their
eggs. He stuck egg on their fingers; on their mouths. He placed shells
near each of them. Then he hurried away. The wolves woke up, found
eggs all gone. They think:

"How is this? Eggs gone, but I am hungry."

They see egg on each others faces. They get mad and quarrel about it.

"You ate the eggs. Most shells are with you!"

"No! You ate all the eggs. It is on your mouth and I am hungry. I did
not get any eggs!"

This was a big quarrel among themselves.

The wolves hunted more eggs after awhile, built a fire to roast them.
Coyote was watching. He put a sleep on them, then came and ate all the
eggs. He played a trick on them again, rubbing egg on their fingers and
mouths. The wolves woke up, found no eggs. The shells were with them;
egg on hands, on mouth, but they were hungry. They look around, then
look at each other. They began to quarrel:

"You ate all the eggs! It is on your mouth! Most shells are with you."

"No! You ate them! I am hungry! I got no eggs! You ate them all!
There are shells near you."

The wolves quarreled like that, then went to hunt more eggs. When
they had a lot of eggs, they built a fire and began roasting them. Coyote
came. He put a big sleep on them. Then he ate all their eggs again. He put
egg on their fingers and mouths, then ran away. The wolves woke up and
found no eggs. They were awfully hungry this time. They got mad, because
they thought the other one was tricking them. They quarreled hard:

"You ate all the eggs! There are the shells with you."

"You ate the eggs! It is on your mouth. I got no eggs! I am hungry!"

They quarreled long time and then went hunting more eggs. When they found many, they came and built a fire to roast them. When nearly cooked, Coyote made a sleep to come over the wolves, then came and began eating their eggs. He smeared egg on their mouths, on their fingers. They woke up, saw Coyote eating the last of their eggs. There was nobody to tell them this. Only way to know it, was seeing him eating the eggs. They saw him getting even on them. They now knew who had eaten all their eggs. They sneaked away ashamed. Coyote laughed at them.

Coyote came to The Dalles. Here Wishoms would be. The falls would be heard far away. Coyote put the rocks in place and made a great fishing grounds.[14]

Coyote then came to *Y-yum* ["Fish Tail" or Celilo, Oregon]. Here would be different Indians, different language. But they could understand each other. They would be not far apart. The fishing would be good. Coyote ruled that they make different net, different spear.[15]

Coyote came above Celilo making different fishing grounds. Here he fixed for canoes, for different nets.

He came on again, making for fishing the same way, all different kinds. He came to the Yakima River. He reached *Top-tut*. Coyote said:

"This is far from *Y-yum*. I will make a good fishing place. Catch fish from both sides the river. The people will come from above to fish here."

Coyote made the *Top-tut Falls*, good fishing. He made three holes [triangular] clear across the river below the falls. In these, posts can be set and tied together for scaffolding. These posts can be worked in high water. Make them from both sides.

Coyote came on up where Mabton now is. He was going to make a fishing place there, but it was too close to one he made at Prosser [Washington]. He made the *Tom-man-cha-tah-nee-kohpt* [falls of the fish trap] in the Satus River. He made a rule that salmon must be caught certain way at this trap. He ruled that salmon could not go above there. They could go up the other way, up Dry Creek, *Pawen-kute-copa* [tule or swamp tule], but not to the head of Satus. No salmon could go up Toppenish Creek. Coyote wanted a wife from the Yakimas. They would not give him a woman, so he let no fish go up that stream. The water in it is too bad for salmon.[16]

Coyote came on up and started to make a fishing place near [now] Chief Sluskin's below *Pah-qy-ti-koot*, but it was too close to *Top-tut*. He tore it out. It shows some. He left it so a few fish can be caught there.

Coyote then went to Wenatchee. He made the fishing grounds there. They are good. He then went to Spokane, made the falls in that river for other people. He stopped there and said:

"Salmon can go on up above these falls. People can catch them anywhere."

Here Coyote was tired. He quit.

Notes by McWhorter

Some Indians say that the five head coverings used by Coyote on this [when he broke the fish dam] occasion, were large bivalve shells of an unidentified variety. Others speak of them as five horn spoons. *Y-yum* means "fish tail" and the place is Celilo, Oregon. *Top-tut* is located where the diversion dam of the Sunnyside Canal is built on the Yakima River. During the construction of this fish trap, Coyote's ear caught the sound of water pouring over *Top-tut*. He stopped work, listening! Oo-oo-o-m-m! came the distant rumble of the cataract. Coyote said:

"This is too close; too close to *Top-tut*."

He then tore the trap out, leaving only a trace of it where a few fish may be caught. It was called *Koop*. Another version of this legend has it that there were five brothers of Coyote, and that one of them continued directly up the *nChe-wana* rather than the Spokane River, while one went up each of the following tributaries, constructing the various fisheries to be found along these streams. The Snake, the Yakima, and the Wenatchee rivers, while one of the brothers in some way reached the Clear Water and Salmon Lake, in Montana, in the region where Chief Joseph made his last stand during the Nez Perce War, 1877.

12

Speel-yi and the Five Sisters of the *nChe-wana*
An-nee-shiat (Klickitat)
May 1918

IT WAS ON a stream entering the *nChe-wana* [Columbia River], somewhere in the upper country, that *Speel-yi* [Coyote] had his residence.
There were several people in the lodge, some of them young. One young
man was mightiest of *yahmas* [mule deer] hunters. No one could equal
him as a hunter of the deer.[1] One day this young hunter killed a deer. He
dressed it there in the woods where he killed it. He decided to play a trick
on *Speel-yi* who was greatest of all tricksters. He would make a good trick
on *Speel-yi*.

The hunter fixed everything ready for *Speel-yi* to carry the deer home.
He took out the entrails, made rope of them and tied deer into a pack for
carrying. He then left it, going to the lodge without any game. He said
to *Speel-yi*:

"I left the deer there for you! You better go bring it home. It is all tied
ready for packing."

Speel-yi went for the deer where the hunter told him. He found it and
started home with it on his back. Why the young man tied it with guts
was to bother *Speel-yi* for a time. The rope broke. *Speel-yi* did not know
that this rope was guts. It might be buckskin!

In the meantime the young man made the rain to come.[2] He possessed the same power over rain as did *Speel-yi*.[3] The rain fell fast. It
raised and made high the streams. It kept on raining hard. The gut-rope,

now wet, broke often. Soon *Speel-yi* could hardly cross the creeks in places. The hunter was watching. He thought:

"*Speel-yi* will go down and drown!"

He wanted to get rid of him. *Speel-yi* crossed in several places, but at last he came where he could not cross. He tried but the water took him down stream. Rain was still falling, pouring down on all the earth. *Speel-yi* floated into the *nChe-wana*. He floated quite a ways, when he thought:

"I may as well go on down and see what I can find."[4]

He went still further. Then he got ashore and gathered some tulies. He gathered enough to make a baby basket, a cradle-basket. After making the cradle, he got on it, packed in like a baby. He could get in and out of it as he pleased.[5]

Speel-yi fixed himself, a baby in the basket, and shoved from the shore, pushed out on the water. He floated down the river, down the n-Che-wana and out onto the ocean. Then he floated towards the South.[6]

There were five sisters [*Weet-weet yah*, Cliff Swallows] living at the ocean side. These girls had control of all kinds of fish. No other person could catch fish. They had all the fish stored in a lake.[7] Any time they wanted fish, they could get them, only themselves get fish. *Speel-yi* in his basket floated round to these five sisters. The sisters happened to be at the ocean side and heard the child crying in the cradle. The oldest sister said:

"Somebody got drowned! A child has floated down this way! We better catch him and raise him as our brother."[8]

The youngest sister said:

"No! It is not a baby! It is *Speel-yi*! We better not have any thing to do with him!"[9]

One of the sisters said:

"We better raise him up! He will be a help to us!"

The youngest sister said no more. She let them have their way.[10]

The oldest girl took the child from the cradle. He was small and the sisters thought:

"Maybe we cannot raise him!"

After they took him into their lodge, they put the tail of the eel to his mouth. He began nursing at it. This is why the eel's tail is pointed to this day. It has no tail like other fish.[11] The older sisters thought:

"He is old enough to eat! We can raise him! He will grow up to be our brother."

They cared for the baby, for *Speel-yi*, keeping him in their lodge.

Every morning the sisters went to dig roots, be gone all day. Then *Speel-yi* would leave his cradle to look where the fish were kept. He studied how to get them loose. The girls had five horn spoons or bowls. *Speel-yi* sized up every thing. He made five wooden diggers. He would make a canal, draw the lake and let the fish go. It took five days to get things ready to begin work.[12] At night there was a baby in the cradle for the sisters to care for. In the daytime, this baby was a man, working at the canal. On the day to draw the lake, *Speel-yi* took the five horn spoons. He fitted them over his head. He thought:

"I will not be able to complete this work before the sisters come home and find me."[13]

Everything was ready to dig the last of the canal. *Speel-yi* dug all day, dug hard. He had about finished, when one of the women broke her digging stick. She said to her sisters:

"Something wrong at home! We must go see about it right now!"[14]

They started home, hurried all the way. They found the baby was not in the cradle basket, was not in the lodge. They did not know where he had gone. The youngest sister said:

"We better go to the lake! It may be *Speel-yi*! I told you not to have anything to do with him! Better [to have] let him alone!"

The sisters hurried fast to the lake. Yes! *Speel-yi* was there. He was digging hard to draw all the water out. The sisters said:

"We will have to club him!"

Each of the sisters had a club, the kind used in clubbing the salmon when caught. *Speel-yi* had the five horn spoons with him. He saw the sisters coming. He knew that they would kill him if they could. He had the five horn spoons ready! He put them on his head. The oldest girl struck him on the head and broke one of the spoons. She did not hurt *Speel-yi*. He kept on working hard. The next oldest sister struck him; another spoon broke. *Speel-yi* paid no attention, kept on digging. The next oldest sister struck him and broke another spoon. *Speel-yi* was not hurt in the least. He kept digging, digging fast. The fourth sister struck him, struck him on the head and the fourth spoon was broken. *Speel-yi* now had but one spoon left to protect his head. There was also but one club still unused, held by the youngest sister. She struck hard, broke the last spoon just as *Speel-yi* finished his work. The water and the fish went into the ocean. *Speel-yi* hallooed, called loud:

"All little fish go up streams! Big fish stay in ocean!"

The fish began to do as told. *Speel-yi* called again:

"I made mistake! All big fish go up streams! Little fish stay in ocean!"

But it was too late. The first order could not be changed. All small fish, salmon, sturgeon, eels and others went up the streams, while larger fish and whales remained in the ocean. Had *Speel-yi* made no mistake, big fish and whales would now be in the streams for use of Indians, while fish now in streams would be in the ocean.[15] After *Speel-yi* had given these orders, he hurried to leave. He first said to the sisters:

"No use for you to keep and kill all the fish. Other people are coming. We might as well have fish for them. This is why I came, why I drew the water from your lake. Here is the rule, the law I now make.

"You [Cliff Swallows] can go with the fish only as they travel up the *nChe-wana*. Go along the shore, a little ahead of the salmon as they travel. When people see you, they will know that salmon is coming in the river. Soon they will learn to watch for you, to know when fish are coming. You shall no more control the fish, only as I am telling you. I will make fishing grounds up the *nChe-wana* and other streams. Indians can always find plenty of these fishing places."[16]

Speel-yi now left, followed his fish up the *nChe-wana*. After going for a time, he got hungry. He said to himself:

"I have fish in the ocean and in the *wana* [river], traveling for every body. No use for me to go hungry. I will make a fishery here on the ocean side."

Speel-yi looked, saw smooth water every where. He studied how he could make a good fishery there. He then made this rule, this law:

"When people come to this place and are hungry, this they must do! Call these words, halloo loud: 'Fish must come ashore as my make [creation]!'"

Speel-yi then called out the command of his own ruling. The fish came ashore, but *Speel-yi* had made a mistake. It was a gravelly place at the water's edge, too slippery for him to hold.[17] The big salmon got back in the water. Then *Speel-yi* said:

"I will counsel with my five sisters."[18]

He did so but his sisters said:

"We will not help you! Whenever we tell you what to do, you always say: 'I made mistake! I knew that before!'"

Speel-yi threatened to bring rain to destroy the sisters. This scared them. They agreed to instruct him what to do.[19] They said:

"You have club ready to kill the fish. Hit him on head! You must call the salmon out of the water where there is sand. You can then hold him. You cannot hold him on the rocks. Too slippery."

Speel-yi made reply:

"Yes! I knew that, but I forgot. I made mistake."

Speel-yi traveled on. He found a sandy place sloping down to the water. He hallooed:

"Fish must come to ashore as my make!"

A big fish came out of the water, rolling in the sand. *Speel-yi* could hold him good. He had club ready as his sisters had directed. He struck the salmon on the head, killed him. He carried the fish away from the water; cut him open. He placed him on a stick to bake before the fire. While the fish was roasting, *Speel-yi* was very tired. He laid down to rest.

There were five wolves who knew that *Speel-yi* was cooking fish. They wished him asleep.[20] While he was sleeping, they sneaked up and ate nearly all the fish. Left only a little end of the tail for *Speel-yi*. They oiled his lips, his hands, rubbing bones of the salmon over them. Then they left him sound sleeping.

Speel-yi awoke, stretched himself. He thought:

"Well! I must have slept! My fish is all gone! I must have ate it."

He found the oil on his lips, on his hands. The bones and split-stick lying by his knee. He said:

"Yes! I must have ate the fish, but I am hungry! I left only a little piece of the tail. I will finish that."

Then *Speel-yi* ate the rest of the salmon, the small tail-end left by the wolves. He was still hungry! He wondered how it was [that he ate the fish and was still hungry] and decided to again consult his five sisters. He said to them:

"What became of the salmon? It is gone and I am still hungry."

The sisters replied:

"We will not tell you! You would say: 'I know all about the salmon!'"

But when *Speel-yi* was bringing the rain, they told him:

"The five wolves ate the salmon while you slept. But you can do the same to them some time. They catch all kind duck and waterfowl eggs."

Speel-yi was cunning. He said:

"I know all about that salmon. I know all about the wolves, how they cook eggs with hot rocks, baked on the ground."

Speel-yi had the same power as the wolves. He could wish them asleep while eggs were cooking. He found where they were cooking eggs in the brush. He wished them asleep, then ate all their eggs but five, one for each wolf. He rubbed egg on their mouths, ruffled up the hair on their necks to make them ugly. Then he placed one egg by the side of each wolf as he slept.[21]

After completing this work, *Speel-yi* left the wolves and followed on up the river. At every stream entering the *nChe-wana* he made some kind of fishery. He ordered certain kinds of fish for each stream, certain way to fish in each stream. In some streams, fish would only run when about ready to spawn, would then run up from the *nChe-wana*. In some, Chinook salmon would run before being ready to spawn. *Speel-yi* went up each stream and made fisheries, made falls or some kind of trap. He came to top of Cascade Falls. He said:

"No Chinook will run up *Ho-ho-lah-me* ["River of Crows" known as Wind River in Skamanis Country, Washington]. Only *um-to-li*."

Speel-yi came on up the *nChe-wana*. It was between—[place and incident forgotten by narrator]. He came to the Little White Salmon River and said:

"Nothing but *to-las* will come to this place. I will drive the *to-las* to this place. It will take a good man to spear them."

This is so. You see the salmon's back in the water, but you miss him. You cannot spear him. But there is a way to catch the salmon. It takes two men to catch them, two of all men to be there. Traps of sticks must be placed. The two men must stop there all night. No other men must go there at night. Salmon only run here at night, go into the lake in daytime. All the salmon come down the stream. The men close the trap with sticks and the fish cannot get back up stream to the lake. Clubs only must be used. Indians kill with these clubs and divide the salmon among themselves. In drying at this place, salmon never spoils. It can be dried either by fire or no fire. Hang it on bushes or trees and it dries without tainting. This was the law made by *Speel-yi* to rule this and fisheries on *Ho-ho-lah-me*.

Speel-yi fixed all these fisheries there, and again traveled up the *nChe-wana*. He came to the *Lou-le-pol-me* [Klickitat for White Salmon River]. Nothing but *um-to-li* to come up this stream. No trapping. Only spearing in the *Lou-le-pol-me*. Not much fancy fishing. All the salmon here to be dried by fire. This was the law made by *Speel-yi* to rule the fisheries of *Lou-le-pol-me*.

Speel-yi came on up the Big River where he ran among some women he was afraid of. They were Fleas. Fleas got all over him, nearly ate him up.[22] *Speel-yi* said:

"I cannot go through here!" [Part of story forgotten by narrator.]

Speel-yi came a ways and made a place in rocks to hand his robes, his clothing. This place can still be seen in a bluff. You hang your clothes there in the sun and fleas all jump off and leave them. *Speel-yi* got rid of all the Flea women and came on up to *Why-phoht* [Klickitat for mouth of Klickitat River]. He said:

"This river [Klickitat] will belong to one big tribe. I will make Chinook salmon and eels to go up its waters. I will make good fishing grounds for the people who will live here."

Speel-yi made the *Klah-ti-hut* ["dropping over" the falls of the Big Klickitat River]. He made everything nice at this place. He made a place to sit, a place to brace the foot. He made a place a short ways above the falls where the salmon was to be ground, a solid rock hollowed out. *Speel-yi* tried the grinding, to see how it would work. There is a great smooth rock where the half-cooked salmon was to be spread to dry, to become brittle in the sun so it could be ground. He tried it once then gave it up and did not finish it good. He gave up the grinding. Salmon would come but could not be ground, could only be dried. *Speel-yi* did this for the Klickitat Indians, a big tribe that was to come.

Below [present-day] Fort Casteel on the *Klah-ti-hut*, *Speel-yi* created a fishery where salmon are to be speared only. If a fish escapes the spear-man, there is no use trying more that day. If he does wait, it will be a long time before another fish comes for him to try his spear. That was a rule laid down by *Speel-yi* when he made the fishery. He also formed a "basket" in the rocks where the salmon can be placed when caught.

Finishing up on the *Klah-ti-hut*, *Speel-yi* continued up the *nChe-wana*. He made another fishery at *Soom-me* [big-eddies], below The Dalles. Here the fish could be seined only.

Speel-yi came and made the *Wishom-mah* [Wishom place]. This Wishom Falls, the Tumwater, is fine fishery. Here they can grind the salmon good. The rule of *Speel-yi* is that the fish must be dried in the wind. It does not spoil in drying. *Speel-yi* was satisfied with his work here. He made this fishery for the *Wishom* Indians.

Speel-yi continued up the *nChe-wana*, and made a fishery between Tumwater and Celilo. Then up to *Y-yum* [east of The Dalles]. There he made all kinds of fisheries. Made *Skein* Island. *Speel-yi* said:

"There will be an island fishery here. Any time the people want good fishing, if they work it as I make the rule, they will have best of fishing. When the fish begin to come up the *nChe-wana*, one man, only one must go to the [*Skein*] island. He must strip naked, roll in the sand, run about and do all sorts of fun-tricks. He must do this one whole day. If this is not done, then there will be no good fishing. Fish will not come. But if he does my ruling, fish will come. After the man has done this thing, the people can go to the island, stay there catching and drying fish. This fishery is for all people."[23]

Completing his work at *Skein*, *Speel-yi* traveled on up the *nChe-wana*, making various fisheries for the tribes that were to come. Made them [fisheries] up the many streams, fisheries of different rulings. Everywhere he fixed fish traps for the use of the tribes. Somewhere in the Umatilla country he made a place where, if the person stands in exactly the right place on bank of the *nChe-wana* and calls this command loud—.

"Salmon must come to shore as my make!"—the salmon will have to come out for the use of the caller. One salmon only will come. This was the rule of *Speel-yi*.

Speel-yi made fisheries up Snake River and all its streams. Many of these are unknown to the Yakimas. He made seining and spearing fisheries all along the *nChe-wana*, above the mouth of Snake River, and above [now] Pasco, Washington. For these fisheries, he made a north wind to blow. Dry and cooling, this wind blows during all the fishing season that the people may dry their catch. No fire is needed. This wind begins about mid-sun and continues during the afternoon and evening. It always comes as ordered by *Speel-yi*.

When *Speel-yi* passed a certain gap in the hills above White Bluffs, he wanted the *nChe-wana* to run in a different direction. But there was too much sage. The fish did not like the smell, so he let it go in its present channel. The trace where he wanted the river to go can still be seen. All about are the fish-traps *Speel-yi* prepared, bundles of standing rocks.

Speel-yi abandoned this incomplete fishery because of the smell of sage. He traveled on up the *nChe-wana*, leaving at various places fisheries for Indians who were to inhabit that region. He went to Wenatchee River. He made some riffles, same as he had abandoned in [other] places before completed. In these, the Indians must set scaffolding, triangular-formed posts across the river. Then poles are lashed reaching from post to post. Against these poles, willow sticks are placed up and down so the fish cannot pass. Then the fish can be speared. It is a successful fishery.

Speel-yi then went up the Wenatchee and made the Wenatchee Falls. This was the big fishery for all the tribes. The chinooks, the "blue-backs," and all the good fish are found there. *Speel-yi* ruled that spears and gaff-hooks were to be used at this fishery.[24] If a fish tore loose from spear or hook, he made a place below the fishery where the wounded fish would float out to the shore and die. The Indians could get these fish and use them while still fresh and good. None were wasted. This was *Speel-yi*'s own work, to save all the fish.

The Wenatchee tribe had the west side of the river, the tribes east of the river had that side of the stream.[25] In the middle of the river, middle of the falls, sits *Speel-yi*'s daughter, a big rock. At this place the salmon jump and she rules.[26] If any Indian caught a big salmon, if he was about to be pulled in, he was to yell loud. Then he would not be pulled into the water. *Speel-yi* ruled that Indians come there for a big time, and all must halloo when fish was caught. This was done. Salmon could be air-dried without fire.

Speel-yi planted all kinds of roots on the Wenatchee side, camas and other roots among the rocks on the side of a hill. He planted ser-vis-berry [service berries] on the steep bluffs on the Wenatchee side. These berries were for benefit of young people. The rule was that young women could go there to pick berries and any young man come and talk to them. The girl could not run away nor hide. If agreeable, they could agree to marry and go away as man and wife. This was Indian custom, Indian law. It was good to do so.[27]

Speel-yi also ruled that there is no difference how many Indians came to Wenatchee fishery to camp, all camps must be set adjoining, continuously, one opening into the other with the trail running directly through the tepees. Persons traveling on this trail, either foot, horseback or pack-train, must pass through the tepees. Fires must be on one side of trail so people could pass. The trail must always be kept clear for travelers. This trail was on the Wenatchee side of river, where bluffs are close and narrow.[28]

Speel-yi further ruled that any Indian, man or woman, coming from a distance to this fishery, if they had arranged to stay only one sun, maybe two suns, they would always stay longer. *Speel-yi*'s daughter would attract them and they would never leave under four or five suns. This was the law and ruling of *Speel-yi*. Something always occurred to detain travelers over time.

Speel-yi traveled on up the *nChe-wana*, making fisheries of various kinds. He created the "High Falls" [Kettle Falls] in the Okanogan country, and many others. But the Yakimas and Klickitats do not know about these; do not understand the mode of catching the fish and drying them there. Our tribes have not seen the fisheries of those countries.

Notes by McWhorter

These sisters are now the *Weet-weet yah*, the Cliff Swallow, "smaller than the killdeer." The Yakimas call them *tie-teah* or *tea-tic*. These active little birds travel up the river shore ahead of the fish. Salmon and even eels will not appear until after these swallows have first heralded their coming in the manner prescribed by the wise *Speel-yi*. They especially travel with the blue-backs, but they come first with the chinook salmon. The *Weet-weet yah* no longer have any control over the fish, other than where to go. The laws of *Speel-yi* stand to this day.

Why-phoht is a Klickitat name pertaining to the "mouth" of the Klickitat River. The same appellation applies to the *nChe-wana*, where it enters the *Ah-tah cheech*, the ocean. *Klah-ti-hut* is "dropping over" falls of the Big Klickitat. This name does not appear to be of the Klickitat-Yakima proper. However, Indian place names are oftimes multiform. *Y-yum* means "above." It refers to a certain locality "above" The Dalles on the *nChe-wana*. It was a noted tribal fishery opposite *Skein*, "cradle-board." The resident Indians were known as *Y-yum pums*.

This drama enacted on *Skein* Island, if not voluntary on the part of the devotee, the "charm" proved ineffective. *Al-o-tut*, whose aquatic achievements are noted elsewhere in this volume, was one who often volunteered to carry out the rules and laws laid down by *Speel-yi*, governing the fishing on the island. *Al-o-tut* died about 1900. To the Indian, there are many mystic signs to be found on *Skein*. The imprint in solid rock of the track of the blackbear, the grizzly bear, the wolf, coyote and other animals, are some of the wonders encountered. The island was a great resort of the Indians during the fishing season.

In May 1918, when camping with a band of Indians on the *nChe-wana* near Timberman's Ferry above Pasco (Washington), the tribesman called my attention to the cool dry wind which set in from the North-northwest regularly each mid-day as depicted in the legend. Eels dressed and hung on an improvised scaffolding on the beach and protected from the direct rays of the sun, were soon cured in best of condition.

The exact location of this ancient failure of *Speel-yi* was not ascertained. The interpreter pointed out from the high first river bench on the "Four Brothers Ranch" near Timberman's Ferry, a saw-like notch in the hills, far up the *nChe-wana*, as the scene of *Speel-yi's* unsuccessful experiment. He said:

"It is a considerable distance above White Bluffs. I have not been there in many years, but the channel bed is plainly traceable. The rocks placed by *Speel-yi* in building the fish traps are still in position. I do not know the location by the white man's name."

Steep bluffs of Wenatchee (west side) was place of courting. This was a romantic phase of Indian life. I was well acquainted with the daughter of *Te-yiash*, Peace Chief of the Yakimas, who was wooed and won while gathering berries on this wild bluff of the Wenatchee gorge. The aged woman was visibly perturbed when her daughter volunteered to tell me about her mother's courtship.

It will be noticed that the Yakima River is not included in the scenes of *Speel-yi's* exploits in this legend. The grandmother, *An-nee-shiat*, was raised on the *nChe-wana* proper, and was not conversant with the Yakima folklore. She said, however, that:

"*Speel-yi* created a riffle fishery somewhere in the Yakima, above its mouth and below *Top-tut*."

13

Tah-tah Kleah: A Shasta Legend
William Charley (Yakima)
1918

BEFORE THE PRESENT tribes lived peaceably in this country. Before the last creation there were certain people here who ate Indians whenever they could get them.[1] They preferred and hunted the children, as better eating. Those people, the *Tah-tah Kleah* [monsters or giants], were taller and larger than the common human. They ate every bad thing known, such as frogs, lizard, snakes, and others that the Indian do not eat. They talked the Indian language and in that way might fool the Indians. There were five of them, all sisters. But at the last creation they did not come up, only in California. Two were seen there. They were women, tall, big women, who lived in a cave.[2]

One time the Shastas were digging roots and camped. They knew that the two *Tah-tah Kleah* were about, knew that they were in that place.[3] The Indians were careful, but the *Tah-tah Kleah* caught one little boy, not to eat, but to raise him up to live with them.[4] The boy thought that he would be killed, but he was not. The *Tah-tah Kleah* had him several days. Every day the big women went out to gather stuff for food. Each had a big basket on her back and would come home with it filled with everything bad, frogs and snakes. These they would throw in the fire alive to cook, then with a stick, pitch them from the fire to the boy to eat. But he would not eat them. He went out and looked for his own food, roots and other things he liked. He did not try to escape, to get away. He was afraid of being overtaken and killed. The *Tah-tah Kleah* might roast him and eat him.

Often at night after the *Tah-tah Kleah* had eaten, there would be left in the baskets some objects the boy could not see. These he believed to be human beings. They were roasted and eaten after he had gone to bed. He was allowed to see everything brought in the basket, all but these particular beings whatever they were.[5]

Each day the boy would go farther and farther from the *Tah-tah Kleah* cave. He went in search of food and to play. At last he began searching to find his way back to his people. He kept looking out a way to reach them, but each night he would return to the cave.

One day the little boy had all plans laid. He was going to run away from the rock-den of the Monster-women, leave them and their bad, poisonous things. The *Tah-tah Kleah* left in the morning with the big baskets over their backs, and when out of sight, the boy hurried away. He ran fast, traveled over rough, wild places and at last reached his own people. They were glad, for they had supposed him dead. He was now safe. The *Tah-tah Kleah* would not venture near the village.

The boy told his parents all that he had seen at the cave of the *Tah-tah Kleah*, told of the food they had offered him and of what they kept hidden from him in the big baskets. This made the people more afraid and careful than ever.

After many years the two *Tah-tah Kleah* were destroyed. None knew how, but perhaps by a higher power.[6] Their cave-home became red hot and blew out. The Monster-women were never again seen, never more heard of. But they have always been talked of as the most dangerous beings ever on earth.

One other of the five sisters was drowned. From her eye, all owls were created.[7] The person or power who killed her said to her:

"From now on, your eye will be the only part of you to act, which shall be at night. It will go to certain birds, the owls. The sound, or the voice of this bird will scare the children only."

These stories were told [to] the little children. Masks were made to represent the *Tah-tah Kleah*, and the wearer would carry a big basket on her back. After the stories had been repeated to the children until well fixed in their heads, the *Tah-tah Kleah* [were] described so as to be known if seen. Then perhaps some evening at dusk an old person, masked and carrying the big basket, would appear to them. The parents would tell the children that if they cried or did certain wrong things, the *Tah-tah Kleah* would catch them, would carry them away in her basket to be cooked and eaten in a cave somewhere. In this way, the children grew up to be honest, to mind what was told them. They were afraid to do wrong.[8]

"It would take a half day," concluded the narrator, "to tell how the other two *Tah-tah Kleah* were destroyed."

Notes by McWhorter

Batrachia and reptiles as food-diet are held in abomination by the Northwestern tribes. Two Yakimas were made deathly sick when informed that the dish served them by an Oregon settler was "fried rattlesnake." It should be remembered, however, that this particular reptile is held in potential dread by these tribesmen, who will not harm one of them unless in actual self-defense. An occasional exception to this rule is found in some votary who has received "instructions" from his *tah* [Spirit helper] wherein the *wah^k-puch* may be sacrificed for a specific purpose. A medicine man of recent years among the Yakimas would kill the rattler, open it and extracting two cylindrical particles of fatty substance, swallow them raw, not as a food, but as a great "medicine." But with what horror these creeping creatures are regarded from a dietary standpoint once came under my own personal observation among the Yakimas.

A Catholic [Indian] and a medicine man, both clan leaders, became antagonistic over some topic during a tribal council. For well-known reasons [power to do them harm through medicine], a layman will seldom or ever oppose the wishes or contention of a medicine man, but after adjournment of the council, the Catholic approached his opponent, and startled the bystanders by the following harangue:

"Do you know what will be your lot in the hereafter? Do you know what will be my job, my business, when we both reach the next world? I will tell you! I will tell you all about it. You will be placed in an iron cage like an animal in a circus, and I will have the work of feeding you. Do you know that I will feed you, what kind of grub? This is what I will feed you. I will chop up snakes and frogs, and with an iron fork pitch them to you through the bars, raw and not yet dead, just as we feed hay to cattle. That is all you will get in the next life, and I will have charge of the job. I will do the feeding."

Without comment or reply, the older man turned away, visibly impressed by this unimaginable and terrible sentence.

In the [Plateau] Indian philosophy there were two creations of life forms. The first was the age of the Animal People, who ruled the world. The second, or last creation, marked the ushering in of the human race, the springing up of the various Indian tribes.

This legend varies among the different tribes, but it is told by the Yakimas as practically here given. I have seen disobedient Indian children frightened into subjection by the mere threat:

"*Tah-tah Kleah* will carry you off in her basket! Take you to her cave-house! Roast you and eat you!"

The owl has the eye of this sinister monster, this devourer of children. Among the Okanogans she is called *Sne-nah* "Owl Woman."

14

Coyote, His Son and Salmon
Mrs. Skouken John (Yakima)
July 1917

EAGLE LIVED EAST of the *As-soom* Trail ["Eel" Trail, south of Toppenish, Washington] where the eels went up. Coyote climbed to the top of the mountain and sat down.[1] He was thinking:

"I am going to kill my own son."

His son had a wife that Coyote wanted, a fine looking woman. Coyote sat there on the mountain. He knew where Eagle had a nest on a high tree. He would get his son to go over and kill the Eagles. He said to his son:

"I found Eagle's nest. I want you to go climb the tree and see if young Eagles in the nest have feathers. Kill them; also kill the old Eagles when they come home. Go over. Climb the tree. Kill all the Eagles and get their feathers. I will make arrows for you. You know that you have no arrows."

The son was glad. He said:

"All right! I am going now."

The son was a big chief who wore fine buckskins all covered with porcupine quill work. Coyote said to him:

"You better pull off your clothes."

When they came to the tree, Coyote placed a new tree with limbs up against Eagle's tree. This was so his son could climb. Young Coyote took off his fine clothes and began to climb. Coyote called to him:

"Do not look down till you get to the nest. See if the young Eagles have feathers suited for arrows."

The young man climbed the tree to Eagle's nest. He found where Coyote had been there, found where Coyote had befouled [defecated in] the nest. The son looked down and saw the tall tree without limbs. The new tree with limbs for easy climbing was gone. His fine buckskin clothes were also gone. Coyote had thrown the climbing tree and had gone. The young man cried:

"I am not to come down! I think that I am going to die!"

Coyote took his son's clothes to camp and took his son's wife. When he came to the son's tepee, he said to the woman:

"I am going to tell you what I was thinking. I knew you were here and I came to see you, my grandchild."

They [had] made traps from the top of the mountain to the lower ground. Coyote came where the traps were set. He took his son's wife and traveled away.

The son stayed on the top of the tree two days and two nights. Then he got down from the tree, came down to the ground. He set out to trail his father. He soon came to where Coyote had lived, but Coyote was not there. He looked for clothes and food. He got a stick used in the fire and scratched in the ashes. He found roots roasted. They had been left by his grandmother so he would live, so he would not die from hunger.[2] From this camp he trailed Coyote who had taken his wife. He trailed them five days and five nights. Then he found his wife, saw her at a distance. She was carrying a child on her back and loading another. There were three sisters, all wives of the son. Coyote had taken the youngest for his wife. He did not like the others. The little child saw its father and called to him. The mother said:

"Hush! Do not call your father. Coyote will see him and kill him. Do not call again!"

The woman had torn fringe from her dress and left it on the trail. She looked back and saw her husband stooping, looking at the fringe. The young man came up to his wife. He said to her:

"How far to where the old man told you to camp?"

She told him how far it was. He said to her:

"The other two wives are coming on the trail. Put me in your pack. I am not heavy; take me to the camp."

The woman put him in her pack, carried him to camp. Coyote was there. He [en]slaved the other two women, ordered them about. They would not do anything. The young man got out from the pack. He took a club and killed Coyote, killed his father. He threw him on the water and the body floated down to the *nChe-wana* where five sisters had a big dam at *Skein*, where Fall Bridge now stands. Coyote came back to life. He said:[3]

"I am going to stop this work. I am going to take the salmon up the *nChe-wana* to all the people."

He then thought how to do that; the sisters would take him in their tepee—in their home. He thought:

"I am going to be a little baby and lodge at the big dam. They will come after me. I will be a baby; they will hear me crying. They will think somebody is drowning and will come get me."

So Coyote became a baby and floated down against the big dam. The sisters heard him crying and brought him to their tepee. When they found that the baby was a boy, they said:

"We will keep him till he is big. He can then carry water and work for us."

The sisters had five root diggers, made of elk horn. They went out on the hills to dig roots every day. Every time they went, Coyote would get out from the cradle-board, take the root diggers and go to the dam. He dug for five days, dug till all the root diggers were broken. The oldest sister digging roots on the fifth day, broke her digger. She then knew that something was wrong.[4] She said:

"Something bad in our camp."

The sisters hurried to their camp. They look about; the baby is not there. They go to the dam to see what is happening. They find Coyote hard at work. He has the dam nearly torn out, his work nearly completed. The sisters had five horn spoons, big spoons, or ladles. These Coyote had on his head.[5] They hit him on the head with a big club and break one spoon. They hit him again, another spoon is broken. This they do till all five spoons are broken. Coyote finishes his work just as the last spoon is broken. Coyote cried:

"You did a big work, but I have torn it all down."

The dam destroyed, Coyote brought the salmon up the *nChe-wana* for the first time. He traveled till he became hungry. He wanted a salmon. When he came to a nice rocky place, he called for the salmon to come out of the water. A big salmon came out and Coyote grabbed him. But he could not hold him. The salmon went back into the water.

Coyote came on, leading the salmon up the river till he found another nice clean rocky place. He again called to the salmon to come out. The big salmon came out, but Coyote could not hold him. This he did five times as he traveled up the *nChe-wana*.[6] Then he asked his five sisters how to get the salmon, how to hold the big salmon. His sisters refused to tell him because Coyote always said, after getting the information, that he "thought so." But when he threatened the sisters with hail and rain, they became frightened and told him to call the salmon out where it was sandy and he could hold him. Coyote "knew this before," but he did as instructed. The big salmon wallowed in the sand and Coyote held him easily.[7] He baked the salmon and had a good feast.

Coyote came to the mouth of the Yakima [River] where people lived. He said to them:

"All the women are to be my wives as long as I want. I will let them have plenty of salmon."

The women said:

"All right!"

Coyote stayed there for a time. The people had lots of salmon, as long as he stayed and afterwards. When he had stayed as long as he wished, he came to the Satus. There the women treated him right and he gave them plenty of salmon. Salmon goes up that stream.

The women from Thappanish went to the Satus to get hemp for thread and other uses. Coyote said to these women:

"If you will all be my wives, I am bringing lots of salmon. The creeks will be full of salmon. You will have plenty for food."

But the Thappanish women did not want it that way. They looked at Coyote and laughed. They said to him:

"No! You are only Coyote. We do not like you! We do not want it that way."

Coyote did not like this. He said to them:

"All right! You people will have to travel to other places for salmon. There will be none come to Thappanish. Your legs will be worn out traveling for salmon."

Coyote left no salmon in the creek leading to Thappanish.[8] He went on up into the Kittitas country where the women agreed to be his wives. He left them plenty of salmon. He came to where the Teanaway pours down. He had his child, a daughter, with him. He said:

"I am going to quit right here. New people will come here for salmon. I am placing my daughter in the middle of the water so the salmon will not pass."

Coyote did this, and the daughter is still there. The salmon strike the daughter and cannot get by. Coyote made a law that all the people would come there for salmon and have big times. Coyote is there, sitting near his daughter. There is red on his face and most of his body. Most of the rock is red.

Notes by McWhorter

As-soom is "Eel" Trail which crosses the mountain south of the Thappanish Battle Field, Yakima Indian Reservation. Its steepness is proverbially "terrific," and the great number of its sinuous "cut-backs" has led many to suppose that therein lies the origin of the name Eel Trail. This, however, is in error. Eel Trail was made historic during the Yakima War. It was over this trail that Special Indian Agent, Major Andrew J. Bolon, rode to a tragic death in September 1855 to be followed a month later by Major G. O. Haller in a hurried retreat after his defeat at the hands of Chief Kamiakin's warriors. The brass howitzer abandoned by the fleeing troopers at the foot of the first "cut-back" of the trail was concealed by the pursuing Indians and has never been found.

Coyote's son had seven wives, five of them were *Cilk-cilk*, or "Mice," and they were sisters, while the other two were *Luk-ki-yi*, black crickets inhabiting the rocks. This black beetle is usually known as *luc-kus*, so named from its chirping notes. The *Cilk-cilk* were fine-looking women, while the *Luk-ki-yi* were unattractive. Coyote was attracted to the former when staying overnight with his son. He observed them from his couch while they were building a fire. His repugnance for the *Luk-ki-yi* was obtained from the same source. In some of the legendary lore of the Yakimas, Coyote's son had an eighth wife, *Me-meme*, the turtle-dove.

15

Coyote and the Two Sisters of the *nChe-wana*
I-Keep Swah (Wasco)
July 1918

SALMON AND ALL fish were held from the people. Two Sisters had a big dam at mouth of the *nChe-wana*.[1] Coyote made his body into a nice piece of *op-cod-id* [alder-wood], which is fine wood for fire. Burns good, makes no sparks. This *op-cod-id* was all carved, looking good. The youngest of the two sisters found the *op-cod-id* floating on the *nChe-wana*, when they were out in a canoe catching wood. She said:

"Look! See the nice wood! We will take it to burn."

But the older Sister said:

"No! Let it alone! It is bad wood! Do not take it!"[2]

The sisters let the wood go. Coyote then went back up the river. He changed his body into a small baby, laced on the *skein* [cradleboard]. He floated down the *nChe-wana*, crying. The two sisters heard him. The youngest sister said:

"Look! There is a nice baby. Maybe its people all drowned. Maybe it is left alone. We will take it, raise it for ourselves."

The older sister said nothing. They took the baby, took it to their lodge. They cooked a big salmon for it. The baby ate it, grew fast.

The sisters went out to dig roots. Coyote took five arrow-wood sticks. For five days he worked hard to tear out the dam to let fish go up the river. Every night he was a baby, a growing baby on cradleboard. But in daytime, he was a strong, big man digging fast with his five arrow-wood sticks at the dam.[3] On the fifth day he finished the big dam going down. All the fish came up the *nChe-wana*, Coyote driving them. He changed the two sisters into *chi-col-lah* [Cliff Swallow], a small bird. That bird comes up the river ahead of the salmon. Coyote made that rule, that law.[4]

Driving his salmon before him, Coyote came up the *nChe-wana*, building fish traps as he came. He also did many other things. At [present-day] Vancouver, he found a people without mouths. They took food by smell only. Cooked salmon, deer, bear or anything. They smelled it, then threw it away. Then they took another piece, do it same way.

Coyote watched these people for a time, watched them eat by smell. Then he took a sharp flint arrowhead from his pack. He stepped up to one of the men sitting smelling food. He said to him:

"What you doing? What is wrong with you?"

Then Coyote jerked back the man's head. He slashed him across the face with the sharp flint. Made a mouth for him. The man went:

"*Wa-a-au-au-u-a!*"

Then he found he had a mouth. He jumped! He called:

"*I got mouth! I got mouth!*"

Then that man ate salmon, did not throw it away. Other people wanted mouths. Coyote cut mouths for them. After that the people knew how to cut mouths, knew how to make them good. They did it for each other until all had mouths.[5]

The chief of these Vancouver people [Chinooks] asked Coyote:

"What your name?"

Coyote told him:

"I got no name."

The chief offered Coyote his daughter for wife. Coyote said:

"No. I do not want any wife. I get woman when I want. I go on now. I want to be free."

16

Sho-pow-tan and the *Tah-tah Kleah Tamwash* (Yakima)
1919

THIS HAPPENED AFTER the days of *Speel-yi*, and in the days of the present Indians.¹ *Sho-pow-tan* [Small Owl] was the man.² He was a big chief, who lived at *Po-ye-koosen* [near the junction of Tieton and Naches rivers]. He went up the Naches [River] to hunt deer. Many men went with him. They hunted all one sun, and when evening came, *Sho-pow-tan* did not return to camp. The hunters called to each other:

"*Sho-pow-tan* is not here! *Sho-pow-tan* is away! *Sho-pow-tan* is lost!"

Tah-tah Kleah, the evil old woman with her basket, heard that call in the twilight: '*Sho-pow-tan* is lost!' and she said to her four sisters:

"We must go hunt *Sho-pow-tan* who is lost from his people. We will get him for ourselves."

Sho-pow-tan knew that *Tah-tah Kleah* was coming for him, so he went up to a hollow place in the *Tic-teah* [Eagle Rock on the Naches River]. You can see the trail where he traveled up the face of the rock, to the cave high up in the wall of *Tic-teah*. Grass is growing along that narrow trail. You can see it when you are out from the rock, where it winds up the cliff.

Sho-pow-tan had killed a deer. He had filled the tripe with the blood of the deer. He heard *Tah-tah Kleah* coming, and he knew that she would kill him. He knew, and he placed the blood-filled tripe in front of him. She came to the hollow place. *Sho-pow-tan* had a stick in his hand. He sat back of the tripe, under the hanging rock. *Tah-tah Kleah* entered the mouth of the cave. She looked! It was a little dark, but she saw it, the strange thing lying there. She does not know! She is afraid! She called to *Sho-pow-tan*:

"Take it away! I do not like it!"

Sho-pow-tan said:

"No! That is something powerful. Step over it!"

Tah-tah Kleah did as told, stepped her foot over the tripe. *Sho-pow-tan* was ready. He did not get up. He sat there, and when *Tah-tah Kleah* stepped, he punched the tripe with his stick. He punched it often and it went:

"*Kloup! kloup! kloup!*"

Tah-tah Kleah was scared! She screamed! Threw up her hands and fell from the cliff. The *wana* [river] ran by the base of the cliff, deep and swift. *Tah-tah Kleah* fell into the water and was killed. Had she caught *Sho-pow-tan*, she would have carried him away in her basket, cooked him and ate him. But *Sho-pow-tan* was brave, was wise. He was too much for *Tah-tah Kleah*.

Notes by McWhorter

Sho-pow-tan is a species of owl smaller than the great horned owl, noted for its "wisdom."

The definition of *Po-ye-koosen* is undetermined, but it is the name of the country immediately up the Tieton River and adjacent to the confluence of that stream with the Naches.

Tic-teah is "Eagle Rock" on the Naches River. It is an imposing pile by the side of the highway on the south side of the river. Its appearances would indicate that the river; at no remote time, swept the base of this rock as narrated. The channel is now several rods to the north. *Tic-teah* would indicate that the scene of *Sho-pow-tan*'s feat was named for the "pilot" bird of the salmon. The natural habitats of this bird are the river bluffs and cliffs. In places, the perpendicular banks of the *nChe-wana* are frequently festooned with their nests.

17

How *Speel-yi* Tricked *Tah-tah Kleah*
Anonymous (Yakima)
No date

COYOTE WAS TRAVELING along the mountain slope on the north side
of the *nChe-wana*, above [present-day] Fall Bridge.[1] He looked ahead
on the trail. Something coming! Something meeting him on the trail. It
is big! Something bad. It looks frightful! Coyote stops and looks again,
takes a good look. Yes! He knows what it is, knows what he is going to
meet. It is *Tah-tah Kleah*! The monster who devours people, devours
everybody she meets. It is too late to run. He cannot escape by running.
Coyote must act quickly or he is gone.[2] He knows what he will do. The
great leaning wall-rock in the mountain side! It hangs over as if it would
fall down. Coyote hurries! He places his hands against the face of the
ancient cliff! He braces! He pushes hard! *Tah-tah Kleah* comes up to him.
She looks at him and says:

"What you doing? Why do you do that?"

Coyote answered:

"Do you not see that the rock is falling from its place? Come hold it
while I go bring a pole-brace and prop it. Push hard! Do not let it fall!"

Tah-tah Kleah put her hands against the cliff and bore with all her
mighty strength. Coyote ran away looking for a timber-brace, a big pole
of some kind. He went fast, looking everywhere along the trail. There
was no *ilquis* [timber] growing there. Coyote knew this. He went faster.
He wanted to get away from the *Tah-tah Kleah*. When Coyote stayed
long, when he did not come back, *Tah-tah Kleah* grew tired. She slacked

pushing. The rock does not fall! It stood there firm and fast; nothing could pull it down. Then *Tah-tah Kleah* knew. She said to herself:

"That was *Speel-yi*! He tricked me and got away."

18

Battle between Eagle and Chinook:
Origin of the Horn Spoon
Sitting Rock (Wasco)
October 1921

IT WAS AT *Win-quat* [The Dalles].[1] One old man, a big chief, had good children, had a nice daughter. This chief was rich. He had a great *Too-noon* [mountain sheep] horn. He wanted somebody to split that horn, but nobody could do it. He wanted to make spoon, make ladle or any thing from that horn.[2] But nobody could split it for him. The chief said:

"I will put up [marry] my daughter. The man who can split the horn can have my daughter as his wife."

The chief called all the people, all the young men to try strength for his daughter. None could burst the big horn. One big chief, Chinook Salmon, at the salt-water, at the mouth of the *nChe-wana*, heard about this trial for the *Win-quat* woman. He said:

"I must go see about this business. I will see what is being done."

So Chief Salmon went, and on that same day, Eagle, a big strong man, also came to the *Win-quat* chief's lodge. Eagle had heard about the trial of strength, so he came on same day as Chief Chinook. They both go in that lodge, a great mountain, a cave in the big mountain. I can show you that lodge, a cold place. We call it Eagle's Cellar. Eagles build nests in the rocks about that cave, live there. When in that lodge, Chinook said to Eagle:

"You try first! Try your strength on the horn of *Too-noon*."

Eagle did so. He squeezed that horn in his hand and split it. Eagle threw the horn on the ground all split. Chief Chinook made that horn whole, made it sound as at first. Five times Eagle crushes that horn. Five times Chinook makes it sound and good. Chinook said:

"No use trying to split the horn. We cannot split the horn."

Then Chinook takes up that horn. He crushes it, throws it on the ground. Eagle cannot make that horn sound again. It lay there all split, busted open. The old chief said to his daughter:

"You must go with this man. You must marry him."

Chief Chinook took the girl, married her.

Eagle was mad. He called all his people together. He said:

"We have got war! I was first man to split the horn of *Too-noon*! Chinook became jealous. He spoiled my work, he took the girl. We will fight Chinook; we will fight his people."

The Eagle people said:

"All right! We will make a war! We will fight!"

Chinook's people were all fishes, all in the water. It was below *Win-quat* where the big fight took place. *E-tal-i-pus* [Coyote] put up rocks, all level on top. He made long grooves in that rock where he shot arrows straight. He shot Chief Chinook in the eye, killed him. Eagle said:

"We have killed the big Chief Chinook! Come! We will eat!"

All the birds, all the animals eat the big Chief of Salmon. They eat all but one little egg. That egg dropped down in a crevice of the big rock. It lay there several suns. No bird, no animal can get that egg. Then rain falls; water is in the rock where the egg lay. A little salmon comes out of that egg. It gets into the water of the creek; it goes into the *nChe-wana*. The little salmon grew to a big man. He found [Meadow] Lark. He thinks that Lark killed his father. He tore open the leg of Lark. Lark cried! He said:

"You fix my leg and I will tell you all about it. I will tell you who killed your father."

Chinook fixed Lark's leg, made it sound and strong. Lark said:

"At *Win-quat* a big Chief had a fine looking daughter. Your father won this daughter from Eagle. He crushed the big horn of *Too-noon*. *E-tal-i-pus* shot your father in the eye and killed him. Five *Lalawish* [Wolf Brothers] got your father's wife, the handsome daughter.[3] The youngest of the wolf brothers married her. They put up a lodge at *Schumn*, below *Win-quat*. They live there. Every morning five wolves go hunt the deer. They leave the woman alone. You go see her in the morning."

Lark told all this to Chinook. Chinook now hunts for a strong spirit in the mountains. He piles up rocks, tears rocks out from the cliffs. He grows strong, more strong all the time. He comes after the *Lalawish* comes to their lodge.

Next day wolves all go to the mountains to hunt. Chinook makes it warm, makes it hot. All water dries up, all in creeks, all in rivers dry up. Wolves cannot find water; they are dying for water. They come home staggering like drunk men, almost drunk with thirst. Chinook [had] made one spring, a big spring at *Schumn*. Water is cold, nice. Wolves come there, put heads in water and drink just like crazy men. Chinook takes bow and arrow, shoots oldest wolf, kills him. He shot four oldest of the brothers, the youngest running off to the mountains. He escaped with his life.

Chinook took his father's wife home in a canoe. They went just below mouth of the Klickitat River. There Chinook grows sleepy. He sleeps with head on woman's lap. Worms come out from his mouth, his nose, his eyes and ears like he is dead. Woman is afraid, is scared. She drops Chinook off her lap. When he drops, he comes to life. There are no worms.[4] Chinook takes up canoe paddle, takes the woman on it, throws her to a cave in the cliff along the river [Washington side]. I can show you that cave up in the rocks, up in the side of the wall-rock. It is there today.

Young Chief Chinook now went home to the salt water at the mouth of the *nChe-wana*. He has two grandmothers. They are the *Esh-kolloh* [Raven] man and wife, always two. They look something like the crow. They find dead people. They eat nasty things [crows and ravens eat the dead]. One of them went east every day. This grandmother said to Chinook:

"Our grandchild! I find a woman in the rock cave. She is nearly bones now, nearly dead. Some day we will eat her."

Chinook said:

"No! You must not eat her. Bring her here."

The grandmother replied:

"All right!"

The next day the two grandmothers go to that cave. They bring the woman, all starved and poor, bring her to Chinook at the salt water. They fly side and side, carry her on their backs. Chinook puts lots of grease, lots of fat on her body. He made her well and young again. Young Chief Chinook took that woman for his wife.

Notes by McWhorter

Win-quat means "moving" or "washing sands" and is located today at The Dalles, Oregon.

The raven is truly a bird of ill omen with the *nChe-wana* tribes. It appears ahead of coming epidemics, such as smallpox and other scourges. Traveling alone or in pairs, it is ever on the watch to pick out the eyes of the exposed dead. The raven winters on the *nChe-wana*.

19

Coyote's Adventures
Anonymous
No date

ONE DAY FOX and his half brother Coyote were traveling together. Fox had a little bell on the end of his tail which Coyote admired very much, and he asked Fox for it. Fox gave the little bell to Coyote as they turned the curve of the river and told him that they will then part, but he must remember and bear in mind always that he must never take a short cut of [at] the river, but must always follow the river or else he would have trouble with his little bell, because it will never follow him, and he will die.[1] But Coyote thought he would never tire of the bell, so he took it after the warning and tied it on his tail and ran by the riverbank, as he left Fox behind.

He ran on the ice very proud of his new bell. He was proud by nature, and he glanced from side to side to see how nice he looked, and he would give little bounching [bounding] jumps to hear the sounds of his bell, which pleased him very much. As he disappeared in the distance of the curve of the river, Fox turned and left in a different direction with a smile on his face; he knew how fickle Coyote was, and that the bell he would gladly give back to the owner.

Coyote turned all the long curves of the river for a few days, and grew tired of the bell, as a child does with a toy, and its tinkling sound didn't appeal to his ear anymore. As he came to a great long curve of the river, he thought how easy it would be for him to make a quick short cut.

He thought:

"I could give a long jump then run across; I would be there in a moment, and the bell can't catch me, to kill me anyway."

He thought, how could a bell kill him, Fox must be fooling him. It must be one of Fox's jokes, he will never know, he thought.

So he made a dash across the curve. As he reached the river again, he fell over dead, for his interals [internal parts] were strung across the curve, leaving his tail with the bell on by the river as Fox warned him.

It was some days afterward when Fox came across Coyote half-decayed. Fox gathered his remains and stepped over it. Coyote jumped up, rubbing his eyes and yawning.

"Oh, how long I have slept."

Fox answered him:

"Yes, you have slept. I told you never to make a short cut of the river or else you die. I will now take my bell back, because you have disobeyed me. You can go, but if you see a woman on the ice do not pay attention to her. She is Salmon Trout and will kill you."

Coyote promised that he wouldn't mind the woman; he ran along the ice, and singing his war songs gaily he went for a long ways. When he turned a long curve of the river, he noticed that a woman was standing on the ice. As he drew near he saw that she was fishing, and a beautiful woman, which won his heart at once. Her face was painted with many hues of colors. She laughingly called to him:

"Come here, Coyote, let us wrestle. I am cold and want to get warm."

Coyote asked her what she wrestled for.

"For myself," she answered. "If you throw me, I will take you as a husband, and follow you and obey you."

This flattered Coyote and he forgot his promise to Fox. He threw off his wrap and wrestled with the woman, and before he knew it, she threw him so hard on the ice that his stomach burst open and he laid there dead, while the woman dove back into the hole in the ice, turned back into a salmon trout, as she really was.

It was some days before Fox came across Coyote's dead body, which he restored back to life. Coyote said:

"Oh how long I have slept here. I got sleepy and laid down here," he lied broadly. Fox scolded:

"Yes, you have slept. You have disobeyed me again. If I didn't find you, you would have rotted away here."

Fox took Coyote along with him, and they traveled for some days, and without having food, they grew very hungry. So Coyote suggested to Fox that he pretend that he is a hunting dog, that Fox would sell him for food, and he would run away and that they divide the food.[2] To this Fox agreed, tying Coyote by the neck with a string he led him to an encampment of people and sold Coyote for food and then he ran away with it and ate it all. It was sometime before Coyote got away from the hunters, and catching up with Fox he saw that he was fooled, which made him very angry and that much more hungry. Coyote ran after Fox with the intention of killing his brother. Fox ran away with a laugh, and they went a long ways, and at last Fox grew tired, so he thought of fooling Coyote.

As Fox got out of sight over the top of a steep hill, Coyote ran behind him, almost catching him. When he came in sight of Fox, he saw Fox was trying to hold a large rock that laid on the side hill. Coyote cursed Fox, and told him that he was going to kill him, but Fox made a motion for him to be quiet. To this Coyote wondered, and he kept quiet and whispered to Fox, asking why he was holding up that big rock. Fox told him that it took all his strength to keep that rock in place, and couldn't tell him right away, but would he hold up that rock, while he went and found something to hold the rock in place, because the enemy people were close by. This Coyote readily believed, and he held up the rock in place, while Fox made a pretense of sneaking away slowly out of sight. Then he ran off at will.

Coyote waited a long time, but Fox didn't return. He grew tired and hungry, so at last he thought he would let the rock roll, even though it made the enemy people hear. He yelled at Fox, but an answer failed to return, so he grew impatient, and he made a great jump away from the rock, expecting it to roll down the steep slope, but the rock was in its usual place and it would never roll. Then he found that he had been fooled again by Fox. He then decided that his eldest brother was the wisest of them all, and he returned back to his country to live.

20

How Coyote Trapped Wind
Anonymous (Klickitat)
September 1921

WIND WAS BLOWING all the time, never ceased blowing. Nothing could stop him, nothing could stand before him. Everything was being killed by Wind.[1] Coyote saw this, saw how all the people were being killed by strong, cruel Wind.[2] He studied what to do, how to stop Wind from his bad work. He went to the mountains. He found a *sim-coye* [low gap or a pass] in a mountain ridge. Coyote said:

"This is the place I am looking for. This is a good place to trap Wind. He shall not be killing people all the time."[3]

Coyote then fixed his trap. He stretched a grass-rope across the *sim-coye*, from one ridge-point to the other. With other ropes he completed his trap. Everything fixed, Coyote went off for the night.

Next morning Coyote came and found Wind in the trap, caught around the neck. Wind had big ears, great ears, with which he made the gales. These ears he fanned, stirring a strong, bad wind. Wind had no hands, no feet. He was very much like a person, yet he was Wind. There he was in the trap, his mighty ears swinging back and forth! back and forth! creating a coming storm. Coyote looked at Wind. He said to him:

"Eeh! So you are here! I have you fast! I am going to kill you."

Wind begged for his life. He promised to do better, not to do as he had been doing. Coyote agreed to let him live, but he should quit blowing all the time.

Coyote freed Wind from the trap. Wind rushed away in a great gale, sweeping Coyote off his feet, knocking him down as he passed. Coyote was killed, but he came back to life again. Since then, Wind blows hard only at times, doing damage at certain periods. At most he breaks down trees in the forest, drags sand from the *nChe-wana* and the sea, piling it along the shore or drifting it across the desert. Occasionally he kills people, but not all the time as he did before Coyote trapped him in the mountain *sim-coye*.

21

How Coyote and Wood-Tick Took the Sweat
Yakima Male Elder, told in an Indian Hunting Camp
April 1921

"HE BIT ME, this man," exclaimed the Indian, displaying a lively *ub-sch^{ch}* [wood-tick] which he had amputated from his shoulder.[1] Carefully avoiding injury to the insect, as he permitted it to crawl from hand to hand, the young hunter continued:

"You know how Coyote and this man take the sweat? No? I tell you. Coyote goes somewhere and sees this man. Coyote always gets in trouble. When he leaves to go see this man, his wife tells him:

'Now you do no mischief today. Be good! You always get left; get the worst of it.'"

Coyote promises to be good, to do no wrong, do no bad things. He takes bow, takes arrows, goes to see this man. When he gets there to this man's lodge, this man takes the sweat. *Whe-acht* [sweat house] made of *yahmas* [deer] ribs.[2] No poles like the sweat house yesterday. Coyote sees *yahmas* ribs. He likes to eat ribs. Coyote is always hungry. He thinks: "I go in there to sweat. I like to eat *yahmas* rib fat." Coyote says to this man:

"I sweat with you!"

This man tells Coyote:

"All right! You make the sweat with me."

So Coyote goes in the *whe-acht* with this man. Soon pretty hot! Grease drops down from *yahmas* ribs. Coyote catches grease in his mouth like this [imitating].[3] This man says to Coyote:

"Aw, that's no good! Do not eat that! Wait till get in lodge-house. Then you eat all you want."

Coyote hears him say that. Coyote thinks: "I will kill him. Take all *yahmas* meat home. Have plenty! I get everything this man has."[4]

So Coyote kills this man. Cuts off his neck! When Coyote does this, when he cuts off this man's neck, the man calls out:

"Everybody go! Everything go hurry!"

When this man says those words, when he calls those words, everything goes quickly.[5] *Whe-acht, yahmas* meat, lodge-house, all goes. Coyote's *yahmas* skin shirt goes. Coyote's *yahmas* skin leggings goes. *Yahmas* sinew-string on Coyote's stick-gun [bow] goes. Everything goes, leaves that place. Coyote has only his stringless stick-gun and arrows left. Arrows no good. *Yahmas* sinew that holds feathers goes. *Yahmas* sinews holding stone points goes. No shirt, no leggings. All naked Coyote. His wife gives him hell when she sees him come like that. She know he was doing bad work somewhere.[6]

His story ended, my companion got up from his blanket, and going a short distance from camp, deposited the wood-tick well within the protection of a great boulder which sheltered the windward side of our camp, explaining:

"I will not kill him, this man. If I kill him, I won't find deer."

That same evening I handed him the weathered fragment of deer antler which I had found in a short hollow stub showing the suture-like surface where it had joined the head, with some idle question concerning the relic, but more for the purpose of noting what he would do with it. For a moment he handled it in a careful, and musing manner, and then carried it a short distance and dropped [it] in a thick growth of wild rose bushes; from which it was subsequently secured to be converted into a rustic match-box, which now adorns a shelf near my desk.

22

How Coyote Was Cheated by *Cusho*
Anonymous, told in an Indian Hunter Camp
April 1921

COYOTE WAS CHEATED. He had big book; in [it were] all names of any-one to be made chief, to be made head man anywhere. When Coyote want to make a chief for any place, he look in the book. There he find name of man to be made chief. One time *Cusho* [pig or hog] say to Coyote:[1]

"We try who can stay up five nights, five days without sleep. Who can do this will be first man, will be biggest chief."

Coyote say:

"All right! We will do this. We then see who is to be first man, who will be biggest chief."

Cusho had four brothers; five, all. They look just alike. You cannot tell them apart; Coyote know only one. So Coyote and *Cusho* sit all night, no sleep. All day they sit, no sleep. Then *Cusho* go away, his brother come. He sit all night, all day with Coyote, no sleep. Then he go away, another brother come. He sit all night, all day with Coyote, no sleep. Then he go away, another brother. He sit with Coyote all night, all day, no sleep. This is four nights, four days, Coyote no sleep. Awful sleepy, Coyote. Then last brother come. He sit with Coyote, no sleep. Coyote sit half night, no sleep. He cannot stand it longer, must sleep. So Coyote fall over, sleeping. He know nothing, sleeping tight. Then the four *Cusho* brothers come steal Coyote's big book, run away with it. When Coyote wake up he miss his book. He say to *Cusho*:

"Where my book?"

Cusho answer:

"I do not know! I not see your book."

This is way Coyote lost out, cheated by *Cusho*. Before that time, *Cusho* was wild, poor. Not much to eat, *Cusho*. But when he get the big book, when he get the big laws for himself, then he have plenty, everything. *Cusho* eat all; eat everything he see.[2] Coyote then get poor himself, broke. Always broke, Coyote. I guess *Cusho* was white man.[3] Both alike, *Cusho* and white man. Take everything, eat up everything. Always rooting for more. Indian like Coyote, lose out, all. Everything white man takes from Indian.

23

How *Speel-yi* Was Tricked by *Too-noon-yi*
Anonymous
No date

SPEEL-YI WENT TO visit *Too-noon-yi* [mountain sheep].[1] He was hungry as usual. *Too-noon-yi* said:

"I will cook some meat for you."

This please *Speel-yi*. He said:

"Yes! That is what I came for, for something to eat."

Too-noon-yi made hot water in the cooking basket, then cut a piece of meat from his wife's breast and put it in the water. *Speel-yi* thought:

"*Aw-w!* I do not think that I want to eat that! I cannot eat that."

But when the meat was cooking, it smelled good. *Speel-yi* was very hungry. He thought:

"I guess I will eat that meat. It smells fine. It must be good."

Too-noon-yi now made two sticks and stuck them in his wife's nostrils. He held her head over the cooking basket, while the blood came and ran in the basket. *Speel-yi* was surprised. He thought:

"*Aw-a!* I cannot eat that! I do not want to eat that stuff."

Too-noon-yi stirred the blood all up with the meat, made soup which smelled very good. *Speel-yi* was growing more hungry. He thought:

"I think I will eat that! Yes! I will eat that."

Speel-yi ate all that he wanted, ate all that he could hold. Then he said to *Too-noon-yi*:

"You must come see my wife and I. We live just as you do; we eat just as you do. After five days you must come."

In five days *Too-noon-yi* went. *Speel-yi* built a fire, heated the rocks. He put them in the cooking basket, made the water hot. Then he began to cut away his wife's robe in front. She screamed and said:

"What you doing? Are you bad in your head?"

Speel-yi said to her:

"*Hus-s-sh!* keep still! Do not let *Too-noon-yi* hear you!"

Speel-yi tried to cut some meat from her breast. She screamed louder and said:

"I do not want you to do that! I will not let you cut meat from my breast."

Speel-yi again said:

"*Pc-s-h-hh!* Keep still! Do not let *Too-noon-yi* hear what you say."

Speel-yi now sharpened two sticks to put in his wife's nose. She drew away, screamed again. She said to *Speel-yi*:

"I will not let you do that! I will not let you put the ilquis [wood] in my nose."

Speel-yi spoke in low voice:

"*Pc-s-h-hh!* Do not let *Too-noon-yi* hear you say that! Keep still!"

But his wife would not let him cut the meat, would not let him put the sticks in her nose. *Too-noon-yi* feeling sorry for them, cut meat from his own breast and with the sticks made blood run from his own nose. Then he went away. The lying *Speel-yi* said to his wife:

"There! That is what I thought he would do. You see we now have something to eat."

24

How *Speel-yi* Was Tricked by *Ots-sp^l-yi*
Anonymous
No date

SPEEL-YI WAS A hunter, but he killed nothing but young *yahmas* [deer].[1] One time he killed two young *yahmas*, and coming to where *Ots-sp^l-yi* [deer-teats] and wife lived, he threw the *yahmas* down and went into the lodge to visit the old people. The lodge was dug in the ground, and poles set up over the sunken place. These poles were covered with *yahmas* skins and over them was earth. Every thing about the lodge was of the *yahmas*. Skins and plenty of meat was everywhere. *Speel-yi* liked this house. He went with *Ots-sp^{l}yi* to sweat in the *whe-acht* [sweat house]. *Yahmas* meat was hung up in this sweat house. *Speel-yi*, always hungry, smelled at the meat. He wanted to eat it. When the sweat house got hot from the water on the fire-rocks, the fat from the meat dripped down on *Speel-yi*. He licked the fat; he was eager for a chance to eat the meat. When through sweating, *Ots-sp^l-ti* called:

"*Who-o-oah!*"

A young *yahmas* came and lifted the door-covering of *yahmas*-skin, and *Ots-sp^l-yi* and *Speel-yi* came out. *Speel-yi* now thought:

"I will kill *Ots-sp^l-yi* ! I will get all the meat, all the skins, everything that *Ots-sp^l-yi* has. I will then own his lodge, all that is in it. I will have this fine *whe-acht*, all this good meat. I will no longer be hungry."

Now *Ots-sp^l-yi* was wise. He knew that *Speel-yi* was wanting to kill him, knew everything. When *Speel-yi* grabbed him, he hallooed:

"*Too-o-o-tah-ni-tic!*" [all run away quick].

136

Speel-yi laughed. He said to *Ots-sp^l^-yi*:

"It will do you lots of good to call your *Too-tah!* [papa]. It will do you lots of good to call your *Nah-too-tus!* [father]. You will now see what I am going to do with you."

Speel-yi threw *Ots-sp^l^-yi* on a rock which had small holes in it, like worm-holes. He commenced beating him with another stone, hitting him all over. *Ots-sp^l^-yi* went into the holes and *Speel-yi* thought that he had killed him. *Ots-sp^l^-yi* was gone. *Speel-yi* looked for him, looked good. He saw one of the little *yahmas* he had killed, standing over the other one. He thought:

"Well! You have come to life and now going to eat your dead brother."

Speel-yi looked around again. The lodge and the sweat house were gone. The deer-sinew on his bow and arrows had also disappeared. His weapons lay useless on the ground. *Speel-yi* thought:

"Well! This is very strange! I killed *Ots-sp^l^-yi*, and now everything of *yahmas* that was here is gone. I do not understand this business."

Now *Speel-yi*'s wife was at home in their lodge. All at once her clothes made of *yahmas* skin left her. She had on no clothes, was stripped naked. She said:

"Now what has my man done? He had done something that he had no business to do. He is always getting into trouble."

Speel-yi came home and his wife went after him. She said:

"What have you done? You have done something bad, something you had no business to bother with. See! My clothes have left me. You have brought home no *yahmas*."

Speel-yi felt a little shamed. He answered:

"I thought to kill *Ots-sp^l^-yi*! His lodge was good. I thought we would go live in his lodge. Everything he had would be ours. We would have plenty of meat, plenty of skins. His *whe-acht* was good. All would be fine for us there."

Speel-yi's wife scolded him:

"You were foolish! You could not do that to *Ots-sp^l^-yi*. He owns all the *yahmas*, is part of them. You cannot do that way to him. Now you have lost all. Your bow and arrows are useless."

Speel-yi said:

"That is what I thought."

Notes by McWhorter

Because of this signal called by *Ots-sp^l-yi* from the *whe-acht*, the Indians to this day sacredly observe the rule and never leave the door-covering from within until after uttering aloud this peculiar call. Anyone on the outside may perform this duty [opening the door flap] for them. If alone, or if all parties are inside the *whe-acht*, then the door-flap may be drawn by the votary, but not until the signal has been given.

The *whe-acht*, if not personified, is the sanctuary of a magnanimous, yet exacting spirit essence. While "sweating" with some Indian friends in the fastness of *Tahoma*, I inadvertently pulled aside the door-covering and emerged from the steaming interior without observing the accustomed signal. The older of my companions, who was on the outside, was displeased. He said:

"Why did you do that without calling? I was here and could have opened the door for you! If you treat him right, he will treat you right."

It is needless to say that the offense was not repeated. After five successive "sweats" alternated with "dips" in the icy pool near by, I remarked:

"Five sweats! The five rules of Coyote! I quit now!"

The Indian, with a degree of reverence in his tone, replied:

"Your work is done!"

25

How *Speel-yi* Tricked *Twee-tash* (Klickitat-Yakima)
July 1920

SPEEL-YI WAS ON the trail.[1] He looked ahead and saw Grizzly Bear [*Twee-tash*] coming. *Speel-yi* stopped quick. He said to himself:

"The *Twee-tash* is coming! He will make me trouble. I do not like the *Twee-tash*. I must do something quick."

Speel-yi then called two of his sisters from his body, made them into fierce dogs, big dogs not afraid of anything.[2] *Twee-tash* came on, came up to *Speel-yi* who was sitting on the ground. The two dogs, *Te-lil ki* and *Mo-mah* stood up, tails in air. They walked slowly around *Twee-tash*, watching closely. *Twee-tash* stood still, head raised. Dogs growled loud, growled fierce. They made a big roar with their growls. *Twee-tash* was afraid of *Speel-yi*. He said to himself:

"This is *Speel-yi*! He had dogs! I do not want any thing to do with them. I want no trouble with *Speel-yi* and his dogs."

Speel-yi wanted no trouble. He was afraid of *Twee-tash*. He said to his dogs, spoke sharp and quick:

"Here! *Te-lil ki!* Here *Mo-mah!* What you doing? That is your Master! Do not bother him! Come here! Keep still!"

The dogs quit growling. They quit stalking *Twee-tash* and came back to *Speel-yi*. *Twee-tash* then went on, leaving them on the trail. There was no fight, no trouble between them. This is the way that *Speel-yi* outwitted *Twee-tash*, how he scared him out from fight.

26

How *Speel-yi* Was Tricked by *Schah-sha-yah*
Anonymous
No Date

SCHAH-SHA-YAH [FISH HAWK] and his wife lived by the side of a river. He had a hole cut in the ice where he caught fish.[1] A tall tree stood over this fishing place, and Fish-Hawk had cut all the limbs from its trunk, leaving it bare and slender. Taking five willow switches, he would twist them separately, and sticking them under his belt, ascend the tall tree. Looking down into the small opening in the ice, he would call:

"*Te-y-y-e-te-e-e-w-h-ee!*"

Then from the height Fish Hawk would plunge into the water and come up with all five of the willows strung full of fish. *Speel-yi* went to visit Fish Hawk. Fish Hawk asked him:

"Would you like some fish to eat? I will catch fish for you."

Speel-yi, always hungry, answered:

"Yes! That is why I came, to get fish to eat."

Fish Hawk said:

"All right! I will get you some fish."

Fish Hawk, with five twisted willows in his belt, went to perch on top of the tall tree. He watched in the water, watched very closely. Soon he called:

"*Te-y-y-e-te-e-e-w-h-ee!*"

Shooting down through the ice opening, Fish Hawk came up with his five willows strung with nice fish. He took them to his lodge and his wife began cooking them. *Speel-yi* ate as long as he could swallow. He had a good fill of fish, for Fish Hawk's wife kept cooking them till *Speel-yi* was hungry no more. *Speel-yi* wished to be friendly with Fish Hawk, and he said to him:

"In five days you come to see me."

Fish Hawk said:

"All right! In five days I will come."

Speel-yi went home and prepared for the coming of Fish Hawk. He made a hole in the ice under a tall tree standing on the river bank. He cut all the branches off the tree, leaving the trunk stripped and bare. His wife saw him and thought:

"What is he doing now? He has seen some one working in their way. He wants to do like them. He is always getting into trouble."

In five days Fish Hawk came. *Speel-yi* said to him:

"Now I will get some fish for you to eat."

He took five willows, twisted them, put them under his belt and started up the tree. His wife was scared. She said:

"Do not go up the tree! Do not try the tricks of others. It is not your way. You cannot do it."

Speel-yi answered in a whisper:

"*P-ch-ch-h-t*! Do not say that! Fish Hawk will hear you. Do not let him know."

Speel-yi went to the top of the tree, looked down and whistled. Then he jumped for the hole in the ice. He missed it, struck the ice and was knocked dead. Fish Hawk saw him lying there on the ice, unmoving and still. He felt sorry for him. He took the twisted willows and went to the top of the tree. He watched in the water. When he saw fish he called:

"*Te-y-y-e-te-e-e-w-h-ee!*"

Down he went through the ice! Up he came with the willows strung full of fine fish. He laid them by the side of poor *Speel-yi*, then went away. Soon *Speel-yi* came to life. He found the fish. He believed that he had caught them. He felt himself a great man, was proud. He said to his wife:

"I thought that I could do this thing. You now see we have fish to eat."

27

How *Iques* Stole the Favorite Wife of *Enum-klah*
Anonymous, told in a Yakima Hunting Camp
April 1921

ENUM-KLAH [THUNDER] had five wives, always digging roots every day.[1] One was favorite wife of *Enum-klah*. *Iques* [Rabbit], after he killed *Tah-tah Kleah*, went to these women digging roots. He grabbed the favorite wife and said:

"Come! Go with me!"

The woman laughed. The other four women said to her:

"Yes! Go with the man."

They wanted her to go. She was the youngest, best looking. *Iques* held on to her, held to the favorite wife of *Enum-klah*. She laughed, went away with him. She went from that place with *Iques*. When *Enum-klah* came home and found his favorite wife gone, he asked where she was. The other four women said:

"*Iques* stole her from you. You have lost her."

Enum-klah was mad. He went after *Iques* and the woman. He found their trail, their tracks where they had traveled. He followed and found them. *Iques* and the woman heard *Enum-klah* coming, heard his voice as he came overhead. *Iques* hovered over the woman as she lay on the ground, sheltering her from the bolts [of lightning] shot by mad *Enum-klah*. Three times *Enum-klah* struck at *Iques*. The fourth time he hit *Iques* a little on the neck. You can see the red spot made by the blood of *Iques* where *Enum-klah* struck him on the back of the neck. *Iques* had the flat shoulder bone of *Tah-tah Kleah*, which he had dried. He held the bone up, held it towards *Enum-klah*. *Enum-klah* saw this bone, this strong "medicine." He was afraid! He could not strike *Iques* again. He went back home, leaving *Iques* and the woman alone. *Iques* tricked *Enum-klah* out of his favorite wife. *Iques* was bad man.

28

How Coyote Was Changed into an Eagle
Anonymous, told in a Yakima Hunting Camp
April 1921

COYOTE WALKS ALONG a river when he sees Eagle flying. Coyote thinks he like to be like Eagle, to fly high through air.[1] He talk to Eagle:

"I want to be like you, to fly. Make me like yourself."

Eagle tells Coyote:

"All right! Sit on the high rock. I will fly by you four times. Fifth time I come, you will go with me."

Coyote climbs on the high rock, sits down near edge. Eagle goes up in air, comes down passing near Coyote. Four times Eagle does this, passing near Coyote. Fifth time he comes Coyote gets scared! He say:

"I do not want to jump! I am afraid to jump!"

Eagle tells Coyote:

"Do not jump! Sit down on rock."

Coyote sits down where Eagle tells him. Eagle comes down, passes close to Coyote. Four times he does this. Fifth time he comes Coyote is scared! He gets back from edge of rock. He is afraid to jump. Eagle again tells him:

"Do not jump! Sit here on edge of rock. I will try again. Fifth time I come you will go with me."

Coyote sits on edge of high rock, on top. Eagle comes four times close to him. Fifth time Coyote jumps out of way, scared! He is afraid to jump. Eagle tell him that he does not have to make jump. Only sit still on rock. Then Eagle try again, passing close to Coyote four times. When he comes fifth time, Coyote again jumps back from edge of rock, jumps out of Eagle's way. Coyote says:

"I am afraid to jump!"

Eagle again tells Coyote:

"You do not have to jump. I will make you to fly. Only sit still. This is last time I can try changing you to an Eagle. If you do not sit still I cannot change you to an Eagle. This is last time I can try."

Coyote for last time sits at edge of high rock. Eagle passes him four times. Fifth time he strikes Coyote. Coyote flies away an Eagle. He likes it, to fly through the air. It is nice. He flies over the trees, catching squirrels as he wishes. The other Eagle eats only twice a day. Coyote eats all the time, is always hungry. The first Eagle is glad. He watches Coyote, who looks fine as he flies.

Another coyote sees the two Eagles, one flying high, the other flying low, catching squirrels. He thinks that he would like to be an Eagle. Coyote comes down, sits on same high rock. The new coyote said:

"I will go talk to him."

So this coyote goes up the rock and talks to the Eagle. Coyote tells him how he had been changed to be an Eagle. The coyote wants to be made an Eagle. He asks Coyote Eagle to make him an Eagle. Coyote Eagle tells him that he will do so. He instructs the coyote how to do, where to sit on edge of the high rock. He said to the coyote:

"I will come four times, fly by you four times. The fifth time I come I will strike you, when you will become an Eagle and fly away with me."

This second coyote sits on edge of highest rock as instructed. Coyote Eagle flies four times close past him. When he comes fifth time, the coyote is scared, gets out of the way. Four times this is done. Coyote Eagle then tells the coyote that only one time more is left. If he does not sit still this time, he cannot be changed to an Eagle. This time the coyote sits still. Coyote Eagle strikes him on fifth pass, but he is not changed to an Eagle. Instead, Coyote Eagle is changed back to Coyote again. Two coyotes now on the rock.

Eagle is sorry to lose Coyote Eagle. He chases this second coyote for making trouble. Poor Coyote wants Eagle to change him once more to an Eagle. But this cannot be done. Eagle says to him:

"No! I cannot do this. One time is all. I cannot do it anymore."

That was the way Coyote became an Eagle, and how he lost his feathers. Coyote now had to remain on the ground all the time.

29

Isti-plah
Chief Stwire G. Waters (Klickitat-Yakima)
No Date

ISTI-PLAH LIVED IN the *nChe-wana*, about three miles above Fall Bridge [lower Colorado River], north side of the river.[1] He would swallow everything that passed by, no living thing could escape. *Isti-plah* would draw them in with his breath and swallow them. Coyote heard of this and decided to kill him.[2] He said to himself:

"I will go see about this. I will know more about it."

Isti-plah knew of Coyote and was afraid of him. He did not want to swallow Coyote, was afraid to swallow him. Coyote said:

"I will go! Too many are being swallowed by *Isti-plah*. He must stop this work. There will be a different people coming to the *nChe-wana*, a higher people.[3] *Isti-plah* must not be swallowing them. I will go kill him."

When Coyote made his mind to kill *Isti-plah*, he started on some trail leading by where *Isti-plah* lived. He walked slow, going very slow. *Isti-plah* saw Coyote, saw him going slow on the trail. He knew him and said:

"I will not swallow Coyote. He knows me. He is too smart. I will let him go."

Coyote talked to himself, talked so *Isti-plah* could hear him. He said:

"I am afraid he will swallow me. I am afraid of this big fellow. He will swallow me and kill me."

But *Isti-plah* would not come out, would not swallow him. Three times Coyote passed, but *Isti-plah* would not swallow him. Four times he passed, and four times *Isti-plah* would not rise out of the water, would not swallow him. Coyote then said to himself:

"Well, *Isti-plah* knows me. I will go back on another trail. I know what I will do, I know how I will fix it."

Coyote went back and the next day he said:

"I will make a pack of mud and carry pack like an old woman to make mud house. I will cry like an old woman who has lost her man, like an old widow woman who has lost her husband and is sorry."

Coyote now went on another trail and when he came close where *Isti-plah* lived, he bent over, walked slow, crooked over with a stick, just like an old woman. He cried:

"*Oh-ho! 0-h-o-o-ho! Oh-o-o-ho! o-h-o-o-ho!*"

Coyote was crying, sad. *Isti-plah* thinks:

"This is different! This is not Coyote! It is a crying old woman."

He then swallowed Coyote deep in his belly.

Coyote had a pack where he carried bow and arrows, stone knives and other things. He had pitch and dry wood. He made it all himself, he knew how. Coyote looked around where he found himself, where he was. It is just like a lodge inside of *Isti-plah*, but it is cold. There are lots of people in there. Some are poor, not much meat on their bones. Others are dead, bones scattered around. There are all kinds of people, birds and animal people. Coyote said:

"I will build a fire so the people can [be] warm. I will stop this cold."

Coyote took out his pitch and fire-sticks and kindled a fire. He looked above him. There is something big hanging over him. He looked at it and said:

"Well! This is the heart of *Isti-plah*. I will cut it down."

Coyote had five stone knives. He used one until it was dull, then took another knife. He cut away for a while and that knife grew dull. He took a third knife. This knife grew dull and he came to the fourth knife. *Isti-plah* now knew that something was wrong inside of him. He feels pain, a bad pain. It grows deeper, grows worse. *Isti-plah* grows sick. He said to himself:

"Oh my heart! It pains me awfully bad! Awful pain! I make mistake, make bad mistake! I swallow Coyote and he will kill me! Coyote will kill me!"

The last knife Coyote took and cut the heart down. It fell on the floor. *Isti-plah* shook with pain. He shook and said:

"Now he kills me! Coyote kills me!"

Isti-plah then vomited Coyote and all the people up. Coyote made all the dead people alive and called:

"Come out!"

Coyote wanted all the people out from there, did not want any left in the belly of *Isti-plah*. He now looked back at the water. He looked at the *nChe-wana*, where *Isti-plah* [had] lived and said:

"I now command you never to swallow any more people. When people come in canoes, you can swim, but let the canoes go by. Soon another people will come, another generation of people. They will be different kind, a good people. You cannot swallow them. You can only swallow us. We are *Wah-tee-tash* [ancient people or Animal People]. We are only animal people, birds, insects, everything. We are not real people. You cannot swallow the good people when they come."[4]

After this talk Coyote looked around and said:

"I am all right now. I killed *Isti-plah*, the bad [monster] of the *nChe-wana*. I will now go."

Coyote then left and the animal people went home.

At this day, sometimes a steamboat will come to the place where *Isti-plah* lived, where he was, and it cannot go. The boat stops and goes:

"*Chug! ch-ch-u-gu-ch-ch-chu-chug! chug! chug!*"

The boat goes back and comes up again and maybe gets past. The old Indians, when they see this, say that it is where *Isti-plah* lives and maybe is still there, but cannot swallow things as he once did. Coyote killed him. The water there is awfully deep, deep and dark looking.

30

Ne-siwa-nu-way-pah-cin
Hemene Moxmox, Yellow Wolf
September 1914

THERE WAS SOME kind of Animal [monster] which could swallow all the people.[1] There was one Man [Coyote] from any [every] place who could kill anybody. He knew that the big Animal had swallowed his brother, *Te-lep-pah*. He thought about going to see this Animal, but he did not know the way. The Man knew of another man who could show him where the Animal was, so he went to him. This man's name was *Qats-qats* [Meadow Lark]. *Qats-qats* would guide the Man.

They went up *Com-mune-nu* [Snake River] to the mountains, but on the way *Qats-qats* broke his leg. He cried because he broke his leg. He cried and said:

"You cannot find the Animal which swallowed your brother."

The Man said:

"My grandmother, can you not tell me the place where my brother died?"

Qats-qats replied:

"I cannot tell you. My leg is sore. I cannot talk loud."

The Man then said:

"I will make your leg good as it was before you broke it."

Qats-qats was glad. He said:

"Thank you! I will then tell you all about the Animal."

The Man had some kind of a bone the length of your hand. He split the broken leg, put in the bone and made the leg as good as ever. *Qats-qats* stood up. He did not feel pain. *Qats-qats* danced, so glad he was that his leg was well. He said:

"I will tell you all about it. The Animal is down at *Kam-yah* [Kamiah]. It was there he swallowed your brother."

McWHORTER: *"What kind of an animal was it?"*

YELLOW WOLF, LAUGHING: *"Oh! I will give you the story."*[2]

The Man said:

"Thank you, grandmother. I will now know where the Animal is."

Qats-qats replied:

"It was at *Peo-peo-Hi-hi* [White Bird] and the Animal was there. I knew that Animal when I climbed on the hill."

All kinds of Indian fruits and paints the Man had tied on his back. He took them out of his pack. He prepared. That Indian painted himself white. One mountain was high, so that the Man could not look over it. From his pack he took a bone implement [a gouge]. With this he chiseled a gap, like a saddle in that mountain: *Wee-i-cops* near Kamiah. He looked through this saddle and saw the Animal. He then passed through it, over the mountain.

The Man crossed four mountains and had one more to climb. At this last hill, the last to go over before reaching the Animal, he tied bunch-grass on his head.

The Man reached the top of this mountain, got on top of it and saw the Animal. The Man laughed when the Animal did not see him. He stepped back down the hill. He could see a day's travel away, the Animal who swallowed people. The Man laid down, his legs back down the hill, with bunch-grass on his head. He peeped over the ridge. He hallooed to the Animal:

"Come swallow me now."

The Animal was afraid of the voice, afraid of the Man. He could not see him and was afraid. The Animal looked around, but could not see what made the voice. Looked on the ground, looked in the air. Looked in the sky, but could see the Man nowhere. He would like for him to come close so he could swallow him.

The Man stood up on that hill, on top of that hill. He pointed his crooked finger at the Animal. The Man laughed. He called to the Animal:

"You cannot see me. Your father was blind and could see nothing, just like you. My father could see any [every] thing. You are young. I am old. I am older than you. That is what you are, young and blind. You cannot see anything. I am the oldest. I can see any [every] thing plain. I could see you from five big mountains. You were close, but you could not see me. You are my brother."

The Animal thought:

"I am the oldest. I was from the beginning of the earth."

The Man said:

"Go ahead and swallow me. I am getting in a hurry. Go ahead and swallow me first."

The Animal said:

"*Wet!* [No]."

The Man now thought:

"He cannot swallow me, he will not swallow me at all. How can I make him mad?"

He studied and then called:

"Your father was a poor man. My father was smart and could swallow you. He could swallow you easy."

The Animal thought:

"I do not know when he was like me, to swallow people."

Then he said to the Man:

"If your father was like me, could swallow people, you go ahead and swallow me. Swallow me first, if your father was such."

The Man was one sun's travel from the Animal, was thirty-five miles away as the white man would measure, when talking. The Animal again called:

"Go ahead! Swallow me first."

The Man laughed. He made fun of the Animal, who was big as any mountain. The Man sniffed his nose at the Animal. He sniffed, and the Animal was moved a few steps. The Animal was scared. He cried:

"*Ah-ah!* [surprised] *Ta-loch! Ta-loch!* [hold on, hold on]."

The Man said:

"I was smelling something that stinks around here. I was not trying to move you. I never said: '*Ta-loch! Ta-loch!* when you were going to swallow me.'"

The Man laughed and went towards the Animal. The Animal got mad. He swallowed the Man, drew him in with his breath when he came close. The Animal opened its mouth as big as this room and swallowed him.

The Man now found himself inside the Animal. He looked around to see what was there. He began to walk. He did not go far until he met

Ha-ha-hots [Grizzly Bear]. *Ha-ha-hots* tried to kill the Man. The Man said to him:

"Why do you take this means to kill me? Why did you not kill the Animal? Why do you not kill him now?"

The Man drove *Ha-ha-hots* off to one side, made him stay there. *Ha-ha-hots* has always been mean.

The Man was now close to the Animal's heart. He meet the *Wah^k-puch* [Rattlesnake]. The *Wah^k-puch* tried to bite him. He stepped on his head, and the head of the *Wah^k-puch* has been flat ever since. He drove the *Wah^k-puch* back to one side, away from everybody.

The Man went but a short ways when he met *Yah-kar* [Black Bear]. He talked to *Yah-kar*, who was nearly dead. *Yah-kar* said to him:

"You are *Me-o-ket* [Chief] come in here. Your brothers and relations, half of them have died. Half are dead, but half are still alive."

The Man heard this and called:

"All you [still] alive come around this way!"

They came. The Man found his brother, *Te-lep-pah* [Fox]. He laughed when he saw his brother, laughed at *Te-lep-pah*. He said:

"What makes you so poor?"

Te-lep-pah answered:

"Well, brother, a little more and I would be dead. Can you not see trees and all things on the inside on which the Animal fattens?"

The Man pulled out his flint knife and cut fat from the Animal and gave it to his brother to eat. He kindled a fire with *is-ka* [pitch]. This was a long time ago, and Indian match was rubbing two sticks together. Fire was in the sticks. The Man burned the pitch and made a good fire for the people to warm by. They were cold. The smoke came out of the Animal's mouth and nose. The Animal said:

"*Ta-loch! Ta-loch!* I will let you out alone."

The Man said:

"You cannot let me out. I will stay in here. These are my brothers and relations. I do not want to come out.[3]

The Animal again said:

"I will just let you out. You are *Me-o-ket*. I will let you out now."

The Man answered:

"Yes, I am *Me-o-ket*. I cannot go alone and leave my friends, my people here."

The Man thought:

"I would like to kill the Animal."

He talked to his brother, *Te-lep-pah*, and family and told them:

"Right there is the Animal's *tet-soon* [anus]."

The Man piled the bones of those who had died, right at the Animal's *tet-soon*. The Animal's heart was as big as this house. The Man said to the living people:

"I am going to cut his heart out. I am going to kill the Animal."

He drew his knife, a flint knife. He took that knife and cut at the heart. He cut for a long time. He broke his knife. The Man could wish for a knife, from any place, and it would be there. He took another knife and cut and broke it. He had left three more knives. He took another knife and cut at the heart, and that knife broke. He took another knife and cut, and it broke. That left one more knife. He had a little more to cut. Now the Man picks up his last knife to cut. The Animal is going to die. He is shaking with pain, shaking all over. The Man said to the people:

"You run down to the Animal's mouth, and before he is dead, as he is dying, you must all run out."

The Man still had the length of your hand to cut around when he broke his fifth knife, the last knife he could use. The Man hung to the heart and broke it down. When he broke the heart down, the Animal opened its mouth wide. It was dying. The people all ran out, ran to the outside. The Man took all the bones of the dead people and everything with him when he went out. He got out about this time of year [September]. Then the Man, the Chief, said to the people:

"You can go to your own house, anywhere and I will tell you about it afterwards."

Then the people said:

"You are *Me-o-ket*. You are the Big Chief."

The Man was *Et-si-yi-yi* [Nez Perce for Coyote], the bravest and wisest of all the people. He had killed the monster: *Ne-siwa-nu-way-pah-cin*, the *Ilts-wyochi*, the *Il-swou-iske* [Swallowing or Swallower] who had been swallowing all the people.

The people went home. *Et-si-yi-yi* got his brother and they thought [counseled] what to do with *Ne-siwa-nu-way-pah-cin*. They knew what they would do. *Et-si-yi-yi* had power to get from anywhere whatever he wanted. After awhile he got a new knife and skinned the *Ne-siwa-nu-way-pah-cin*. He cut the legs off at the joints. He cut the body in pieces and scattered them about.

The *Si-coult* [Sioux] are back East. The breast of *Ne-siwa-nu-way-pah-cin* thrown there, *Et-si-yi-yi* called the *Si-coult*. They are brave and not afraid. The Blackfeet are from the hind legs, all tall and slim fellows. The front legs are the Omahas. This was the way all Indians were made, from different parts of the body of *Ne-siwa-nu-way-pah-cin*. While *Et-si-yi-yi* was doing this work, his brother, *Te-lep-pah*, was standing a little ways off. The brother said:

"The people here! There is nothing to give them, nothing to make them from."

Et-si-yi-yi replied:

"Why did you not tell me this before?"

Te-lep-pah could say nothing. He had been sleeping.

Et-si-yi-yi rubbed blood in his hands and sprinkled it on the ground, all around. The Chief said:

"There will not be many people in Kamiah. BUT THEY WILL BE GREAT FIGHTERS."

From this blood sprang the Nez Perce. They are good warriors and have whipped the tribes all around. This is all.

McWHORTER, GREATLY AMUSED: *"I think they were made from the belly; from the insides of the belly."*

"Are there any traces of the body of the *Ne-siwa-nu-way-pah-cin* to be seen in the Kamiah country at this day?"

"The heart is still to be seen near the Presbyterian Church at Kamiah. It is a mound back of the church."

"*Et-si-yi-yi*, the coyote, is the most cunning of all animals."

"Coyote is slick. His kids kill chickens."

Notes by McWhorter

This monster could draw down its throat flying birds, buffaloes, deer, elk, and every living thing for two or three sleeps around. Coyote anchored himself with grass ropes to the three big mountains, widely distributed. They were: *Wah-wamax*, near the Wallowa Valley, *Ce-cak-ka-mas* (called "Seven Devils"), and *E-pat-took-mox*. Thus secured by his ropes, with bunchgrass tied about his head, he lay close on his mountain outlook and drew in a long breath from the direction of the unsuspecting monster. The monster was moved from his place a few steps. In alarm, he ejaculated:

"*Yi-yi in, Its-i-yi-yi*" (That is you, Coyote).

When finally the monster was incensed to the extent that he drew on Coyote with his mighty breath, Coyote found himself almost cut in twain by the restraining ropes. Struggling, he severed first one and then the other with his flint knife, and was then speedily swallowed up in the yawning mouth. In his descent, the grizzly attacked him. He struck the grizzly on the nose. He drove the grizzly back from him. The heart of the Monster is below the Presbyterian Church at Kamiah, instead of in back of it. Perhaps the difference lay with the interpreters. This correction comes from Many Wounds. One version of the legend is that Coyote tied himself with a grass rope to the "Seven Devils" mountain, lest the monster drag him into its maw with its breath prematurely.

31

Nihs-lah: A Legend of Multnomah Falls
Ana-whoah, Black Bear (Wasco)
September 1911

I WILL TELL the whole story. A chief's son from the ocean [coast] came up the *nChe-wana*, looking for a girl [wife].[1] He found a young woman at Multnomah Falls. He had come without letting his parents know. The girl went with him without letting her parents know. The boy took her to his people at the big water [Pacific Ocean], unknown to her people. Coyote claimed the girl as his granddaughter, so he went with her. She took all kinds of berries found in the country about the Falls, as gifts to the boy's people. Coyote came along, following behind. When they arrived at the home of the boy, his parents told him:

"You cannot keep her. She must go back home."

They would not keep her, so Coyote and the grandchild sat down for five nights, waiting for the boy to come out of the lodge. He did not come, did not return to the girl. Coyote then went alone to consult his five sisters.[2] When he asked his sisters, they answered:

"We will not tell you. You always say: 'That is what I thought.'"

Coyote must know, so he said:

"If you do not tell, I will make the rain and hail come down and kill you."

The sisters were scared. They said:

"We will tell you. For five days the boy has come not. It is no use. His parents will not have the girl. She must go back home."

Coyote was great, was brave. He could change anything as he chose.[3]
He said to the granddaughter:

"Never mind! We will go back."

Coyote and his granddaughter then came back to Multnomah Falls
and said:

"Here we will stay."

The girl brought with her all the roots and berries that she had taken
to the big water, and today they are found about the Falls. Coyote said:

"From the ocean the boy came out. We will never be friends, but
enemies always. He had no respect for you, my granddaughter."[4]

Coyote then called the boy from his distant home and made him half
fish and half human. The tail part was salmon, the upper portion was
man, with long flowing hair. This being was as large as the largest sturgeon. Coyote placed the transformed boy in the *nChe-wana*, near the
Falls. He named him *Nihs-lah*.[5] Coyote announced to the boy:

"When the people pass by the Falls, you will come out and be seen
about every two moons. You will become mad. The wind will blow hard,
the waters rising high will kill the people. This will be well, for we are
enemies."

Coyote placed the girl on the opposite side of the *nChe-wana*, and
called her *Sko-lus*. She is there to this day, the tall cliff, the rim-rock above
the river. This story my parents told me when I was a little girl, nearly
one hundred snows ago.

When the fish and man-image would rear itself from the water near
the Falls, immediately would the wind sweep up the *nChe-wana*, a mad
gale. The water would rise high up the rocky cliffs, and all the people in
boats in mid-stream would be killed. When a girl, I saw the *Nihs-lah* rise
from the river and several people killed out in the middle of the stream.
The monster appeared to stand half as high as the mountains. It was vis-
ible only for a moment.

It was learned that by keeping the canoes near the girl's side of the
river, the people in them would be saved. In an earlier day, some white
people were drowned when *Nihs-lah* suddenly stood high above the
water. It was bad.

When Coyote transformed the boy into *Nihs-lah*, he became mad
and caused the Bridge of The Gods to fall.

32

Coyote's Attempt to Circumnavigate the Land: Origin of the Southern Tribes
Blazing Bush (Klickitat)
January 1911

COYOTE LIVED AROUND here some place and he said to himself:[1]
    "I am going all around the land, at the edge of the big water [Pacific Ocean], to see if there are other people and where they live. I will find out all about this business."

Coyote then went west to the ocean, there he saw *Wah-yah-mah*, the big eagle, chief of all birds, flying down from the clouds to meet him.[2] Coyote told the chief what he wanted to do. *Wah-yah-mah* said:

"This is good! You do as I tell you and I will make you a big chief. Go all around the land, along the water's edge. If you see a strip of land extending into the sea, you must not walk across it, you must walk around it, along the edge of the big water. Go around all the land. When you come back here, I will make you a big chief."

Coyote started on his journey along the edge of the big water. He found that there was a small rattle tied to the end of his tail, and one around his neck. They made nice music as he ran. In these rattles lay his big power, given him by *Wah-yah-mah*. This made his heart strong, his traveling light. Coyote traveled many days, cheered by the rattles and the prospect of becoming a big chief. He was now going eastward. He came to a long narrow strip of land, extending far into the sea. Coyote stopped. He could see across the land to the water beyond. He looked all around, back over the trail he had come, up into the sky, but he could not see Chief Eagle anywhere. He said to himself:

"*Wah-yah-mah* cannot see me. I am very tired. I am weary with this walking. I will cross this strip of land. *Wah-yah-mah* will not know."

Coyote crossed the land. When he reached the other side, the little rattles were gone from his tail and his neck. His power was lost. He could not continue his journey; neither could he retrace his steps to his old home. The land he crossed was far in the south. He married some women he found there. From them grew the Choctaws, Osages, Creeks, Seminoles, and all the far Southern tribes.

33

How *Its-i-yi-i* Was Thwarted in Attempt to Change the Course of the *In-che-lim* River
Hemene Moxmox, Yellow Wolf (Nez Perce)
24 October 1924

ITS-I-YI-I [COYOTE] WAS going up the *In-che-lim* [Columbia River], speculating, looking around.[1] He got tired, was always tired. Got tired and went up the mountain called *Swa-we-lah* ["rolling or swaying around" Moses Coulee, Washington]. Then *Its-i-yi-i* went back down the mountain, went across. He studied which way the river could run. He decided that it would run a certain way. He thought:

"Too far round by Wenatchee [Washington]. I will make it to run through this way."

Its-i-yi-i had a bone as long as a man's hand. It was from *ha-pots-cots*, a sharp bone. He cut the channel, now "Moses Coulee," with the bone. This will be a short cut for the river. Too far to go round by Wenatchee, *Its-i-yi-i* now said:

"I think that I will go back below and try the river, when I turn it through this new way. There is no Indian fruits, no Indian roots below here. I am going to take a raft load of all kinds of roots and plant them all along the river."

Another Coyote saw *Its-i-yi-i*, what he was doing. He said:

"What is he doing? River is all right where it is. What is that man doing, cutting a new way for the water? How will the people pass across the cliffs? They will have to travel clear round, as far as to Wenatchee."

If it was not for the high cliffs on either side of the new way, it would be all right. This other Coyote told Frog:

"You better go now to head of the ditch. Go there and sit down."

Its-i-yi-i had his raft done. He had it loaded with all kinds of Indian roots, good for food. He went up towards the head of the new way, the ditch. He walked fast. *Its-i-yi-i* got tired, was always tired. Frog was sitting there, most covered with grass. Only a little of Frog was exposed, a little of her top-side. *Its-i-yi-i* stepped on her. She suffered, she cried. *Its-i-yi-i* fell over her. He looked back [around] and said:

"I hurt you?"

Frog was the aunt of this other Coyote. She answered *Its-i-yi-i*:

"You broke my leg."

Its-i-yi-i replied:

"This is my work, my business. Why did you come over here in the way? I am going turn the water through here right away!"[2]

Frog said:

"It is not my fault. The other man told me to come, told me to tell you not to turn the water on."

Its-i-yi-i inquired:

"Who is the chief here?"

Frog pointed and said:

"You see that man sitting away over there? He owns all the land! You are only a traveler, going up and down the river. He told me to stop you."

Its-i-yi-i made reply:

"Yes, if he feels that way. I am going make cliffs on both sides of it and let it go at that."

Its-i-yi-i then traveled on and left it that way. The raft, ready loaded with all kinds of roots, he left where it is seen today, the Indians' fruit [roots] *camas, cowse, cheo-weet,* carrot, *cah-cate, lah-kopt-tut, ye-kum, chach-um, tom-tok-le-kot, chop-che-le, lo-lus, posch, eches, ki-o-pus,* and many other roots, numbering twenty or thirty, *Its-i-yi-i* left growing on *Swa-we-lah*; where he had built it to float down the new channel of the *In-che-lim* [Columbia River], for the new people who were to come.[3]

The other Coyote saw the aunt with broken leg and called to her:

"Come over here!"

Its-i-yi-i placed big rocks across the *In-che-lim* and, jumping from one to the other, crossed the river. These rocks can be seen there to this day.

The other Coyote came to his aunt. Her leg was broken above the knee, close to the knee-cap joint. He said to his aunt:

"I will doctor you up. I will fix you! Do not worry about your leg."

This Coyote grabbed her leg, and rubbed the broken bones together. He said to her:

"Stand up!"

The aunt at first was afraid. But she tried and found that she could stand good. She walks just as if she is well. *Its-i-yi-i* asked:

"How you feel? Does it hurt you? Does it pain you?"

The Frog aunt replied:

"No! I am well now."

This Coyote told his aunt:

"I am saving your life. The water, half way up the cliffs, would wash you to the ocean. Every animal, deer, elk, and all others who try to swim across could not climb the cliffs. The water would carry you to the ocean."

That was Coyote's rule. Fish, anything in the water, could not go any place. All would have to stay there between the cliffs.

34

Coyote and Crow
Anonymous
No date

COYOTE CAME FROM towards the sunrise, traveling through the country.[1] He was destroying monsters, preparing the land for the new people, the Indians who were to follow. Coyote crossed the Cascade
Mountains and reached the Sound country. He was hungry, very hungry.
He saw Crow sitting on the peak of a high cliff, with a ball of deer-fat in
his mouth. Coyote looked at Crow with this fat and thought how good
it would be. His belly grew more hungry, and he wondered how he could
get the fat for himself. He studied hard, thinking what to do. Then
Coyote laughed. He said:

"I know now what to do, how I can get the fat from Crow."

Then Coyote came close to the base of the cliff and called up:

"Oh Chief! I hear that you can make a good noise, make a nice noise
with your voice. You are a Chief, a big Chief and wise! Let me hear you
make your voice sound. Chief! I want to hear you, my Chief!"

Crow heard Coyote and felt proud to be called Chief. He said:

"*Cou!*"

Coyote called again:

"Oh Chief! That was not much sound. Chief! Make a good noise!
Sing a good song for me Chief! I want to hear you. You are a big Chief!
Chief! Make your voice loud for me. I want to hear you loud, oh big
Chief!"

Crow was flattered. He was glad to be called Chief. He called loud
from the high rock:

"*C-a-a-w!*"

Down fell the ball of deer fat from Crow's opened mouth. Coyote grabbed it up quick. Coyote laughed at Crow. He said:

"You are no Chief! You are not smart! You are not great. I called you Chief only to fool you! To trick you and get your deer fat. You are not wise! Not a Chief. Go hungry for your foolishness! I will eat your deer fat. I will not then be hungry."

35

Battle between Eagle and Owl
Simon Goudy (Yakima-Klickitat)
April 1920

THERE ONCE LIVED an aged woman and her grandchild, a girl. Another party lived at a great distance, a long ways from them.[1] This was *Why-am-mah* [Eagle] and his four brothers. They had a slave, a medicine man. This was *Amish* [Owl], who cared for the tepee, managed everything in the tepee. Eagle was a great hunter and every day went hunting with his four brothers. Most of the time he killed deer. Owl was the tepee-keeper, stayed home all the time. It was known all around among the people that Eagle was the best hunter of all. He had no wife, neither had Owl a wife.

One day the old woman took notice of the grandchild. She saw that she was a nice looking girl, that she was old enough to get married. She thought of the girl's parents, of all her people who were dead. She thought of the two of them being alone. She said to her grandchild:

"Would you like to have a man?"

The girl thought for a time and then answered:

"Yes! If you think that I should have a man. I want one to take care of us, to take care of both of us."

The grandmother knew of Eagle, knew him to kill more game than anyone around. They lived a long distance from Eagle. The grandmother said:

"I will give you good instructions. If you take my counsel, if you listen to my words and do as I tell you, you will have a nice man."

The girl was industrious, an early riser all the time. She said to her grandmother:

"I will do it! I will do as you tell me."

Then the grandmother waited five days, let five days pass before giving the instructions. When the five days had gone, she said:

"Now I will give you good advice. You want a man. I wish first thing you do, make yourself clean."[2]

The girl answered her grandmother:

"I will do that."

Then the grandmother said:

"I will now show you. There are five brothers living together. They are *Yeet-yeet*, the smallest brother. *Kaka-lo Kaka-lo* [Always Flying], is second smallest brother. *Ka-ka-no*, the next brother. *Kle-yah* [Wings Pointed Over Head] is the fifth, and largest brother. This is Eagle, the best hunter of them all."

After the girl had sweat in the *whe-acht*, after she had bathed in the river, after she had combed her hair and painted, the grandmother said:

"Go to a certain tepee. Go the way I am pointing, the way I am showing you to reach that tepee. When you get there, when you enter that tepee, the first thing look to your right. The first bed is that of *Why-am-mah*. There will be other beds, a feather hanging over each bed. Sit down by the first bed. Do not pay attention to other beds. Do not pay attention to anyone who may be in the tepee, who may laugh at you. You sit by the bed, say nothing. It is the bed of *Why-am-mah*, the Eagle, the greatest hunter of them all. He is the one I want you to marry. The other four beds will have smaller feathers hanging over them. The big feather, the big *skein* [center tail feather of Eagle] hangs over the bed of Eagle, where you must sit. If any people in the tepee make fun of you, laugh at you, pay no attention till this man Eagle comes home from hunting. If any other people, pay no attention to them or other beds. Sit by Eagle's bed only."

The old woman knew that *Amish*, the Owl, was there. He was the slave-manager of the tepee, to keep everything in order, to have all food cooked when the five brothers return from hunting, cooked for their eating after a short rest on their beds.

When the girl arrived at the tepee, she went in. She saw the bed to the right and sat down on it. She looked up and saw the big fine feather all white on edges, hanging over the bed. There were four other beds, four beds with feathers hanging over them. All smaller feathers, tapering

down to *Yeet-yeet*, the smallest of the brothers. *Yeet-yeet*'s bed was opposite that of Eagle's. She saw Owl looking at her, smiling from the head
of the tepee. The girl got scared, was afraid of him. He was a big medicine man, the big doctor. Soon he spoke to the girl:

"What you looking around for?"

The girl is half scared! She remembered what her grandmother had
told her, remembered her advice. The girl never answered Owl. Owl said
to her:

"Why did you come here?"

The girl never answered. Owl said:

"You better get off that bed!"

The girl did not look up, smiled but made no answer. Owl laughed.
He spoke the fourth time, made the fourth question:

"Would you talk?"

The girl did not answer, sat there without speaking. Owl stood up.
He walked close to the girl. He asked the fifth question:

"Who sent you here?"

The girl is scared! She looked at Owl! She answered:

"My grandmother sent me here."

Owl laughed, laughed loud. He said:

"O! Your grandmother sent you here! If your grandmother sent you
here, you are making mistake. Your grandmother sent you to me. That
is my bed over there."

The girl stood up, scared! Stood up from Eagle's bed, went over to
Owl's bed. That was where she made big mistake.[3]

In the meantime, when the girl stood up from Eagle's bed, when she
went over to Owl's bed, Eagle's bow broke, broke while he was hunting
far away. Eagle knew that something had happened at home, knew at
once that something was wrong.[4] He said to his brothers:

"Let us go home! We better go home right now."

All five brothers started home. They had some game, had killed a little game. This they packed and then went. They came close to the tepee
and stopped. They sat around till almost sundown, nearly supper time.
They did this to give Owl a chance to cook. He must always have supper
ready, have it all fixed when the hunters return. Supper must be ready for
eating after the hunters have rested.

When rested good, the five brothers went to the tepee. *Yeet-yeet*, the
youngest, entered first. Then the next youngest, on up, Eagle going in
last. All took certain places on their own beds. They saw Owl sitting,

nothing cooked. He had played with the girl till he heard the brothers coming, then became busy. He had been tickling the girl among the skin robes. Eagle said:

"What is it? What is wrong? Why not supper ready for us?"

Owl answered:

"I have been sick all day, not feeling well. I have been sleeping. I heard you and then got up."

Eagle said:

"Well, it is getting late. Better hurry and cook supper."

Owl laughed. He replied:

"If anybody was here they would think me a slave, to cook for you."

Next morning, after breakfast, all five brothers go hunting again. Owl was hiding the girl. That girl should have been Eagle's wife. The grandmother had sent her to him, but Owl got the best of him. Eagle knew it, knew everything. On that day when out hunting, when his bow broke, it came to his mind. But he was going to test Owl, if Owl would come out and say:

"Here is the girl. I have been hiding her for you."

Eagle and his brothers hunted all day. Each had a deer. Eagle said to his brothers:

"I think that I have a girl. Owl is hiding her. I am going to lay a plan for him. I am going to pack this whole deer, take it not too close to the tepee. I will leave my deer in the canyon, go home without it. You will go home with your deer, the rest of you, each taking his pack. I will sit down and rest. Let *Yeet-yeet* go now to the tepee. Let him leave his pack near, and look through the crevices of tepee. Let him see what Owl is doing."

Yeet-yeet did so. He went. He heard laughing inside the tepee. He peeped, and saw the girl, a nice looking girl. None of the other brothers knew of this. None of them had thought of what might be wrong. Eagle had said to *Yeet-yeet*:

"If you find a girl there, come and tell me."

Yeet-yeet came back to Eagle and said:

"Yes! I saw the girl. She is there, a nice-looking girl."

Eagle then told them:

"That is supposed to be my girl. Your packs, take them home. When you get there, tell Owl to come meet me. Tell him I cannot travel more. If Owl asks: 'What is wrong? Why does not Eagle come home, tell him: 'Eagle has heavy pack. Go meet him. He is over there near the ridge. Go help him.'"

Then the four brothers went home, leaving Eagle behind. When *Yeet-yeet* entered the tepee and told Owl to go help Eagle, Owl said:

"No! I must cook. Let Eagle leave his pack. He can get it another day."

The next brother came and laid his deer outside the door. He said to Owl:

"Come! Carry the deer inside."

Owl laughed. He said these words:

"If lots of people in this tepee, if anybody was here, they would make fun of me. They would think me a slave. No! You people must not take me so. I am a hunter myself."

Soon Owl stood up. He went and carried the game inside. It was his duty, his business to carry game into the tepee. That was his own ruling, his own law.[5] But he wanted to break away. He did not want the girl to think:

"No! I made mistake. It was the other man."

Soon the next brother, the third brother came. He said to Owl:

"Go ahead! Finish your job! Carry in the game."

Owl laughed. He said:

"If any people in this tepee, they would make fun of me. They would think me a slave to work for you. No! You people must not take me so. I am a hunter myself. No! You never used to act this way."

Owl went out. He carried the deer in quickly. He looks toward the bed where the girl is sleeping [hid]. All the brothers know it now. Yes! It is Eagle's "lay out." It was for Eagle to make Owl get out of that place. Soon the fourth brother, next to Eagle comes in. He drops his deer outside the door. He enters the tepee and says to Owl:

"I am tired! (puff puff) Heavy pack! (puff puff) Go ahead! (puff puff) Get the meat in! (puff puff)."

Owl laughed, laughed long and loud. He said:

"If lots of people in this tepee, they would make fun of me. They would think me a slave. No! You people must not take me so. You never used to act this way. No! I am a hunter myself."

The girl had a peep-hole where she looked from the robes and saw the hunters. She saw Owl go bring in this last pack of the larger brother. When he had brought it in, this older brother said to him:

"Eagle is far back on the ridge, across the canyon. He wants you to come help him in with his pack. It is heavy, Eagle is very tired. Go! Go help him! It is the orders of Eagle!"

But Eagle, resting out in the woods, knew that Owl would pass away the time, a long time before leaving the tepee. This was true. Owl said:

"Do you people think that I am *Tah-mi-lah kah-lat* [one who cares for the camp]?"

Kle-yah made answer:

"Hurry up! Go right away! It is Eagle who gave the order."

In the meantime Eagle had started home. He walked slowly, to meet Owl near the tepee. Owl went outside the tepee. He started to go, but stopped and said:

"I forgot something."

Owl went back into the tepee, went up close to his bed. He did this often, going a little ways and then coming back. It was Eagle's work. Owl was a medicine man. He would fight! All the four hunters lay on their beds resting. They paid no attention to Owl. Soon one of them said:

"There comes Eagle!"

Owl gets scared! He better start out right away! Eagle comes through the doorway. He said to Owl:

"What is wrong? I waited a long time for you. I left the pack there."

Owl replied:

"I was a little sick. I am going right away. Where you leave the pack?"

Eagle replied:

"Right over the ridge, across the canyon. Packing rope is there, I left mine. Take no rope. Use mine. I am tired; I can travel no more."

Owl starts out. He runs, stops and looks back at Eagle. Owl starts again, goes on the run. Eagle stands outside the tepee for a time. Then he goes back inside, lays down on his bed to rest. Soon they hear a noise! What is it? Owl is coming back! He had seen Eagle enter the tepee, saw him go inside and he came back. Owl enters the tepee. He goes up to his bed. Nothing has been disturbed. Eagle said:

"What is wrong? Why do you come back?"

Owl replied:

"Oh! I forgot— [so-and-so]."

Owl sits on his bed resting. He sees nothing disturbed. Nobody knows about the girl. Owl now gets up and goes for good, goes to bring in the pack left by Eagle. When Eagle laid down his pack, he left with it a small string, the dried guts of deer. When touched, they break. This was to keep Owl away a long time, bothering him tying the pack rope of dried guts. There was no other pack rope. Owl takes up the pack; he places it on his back and starts on return to the tepee. The rope keeps breaking all along the trail. Owl is detained splicing the brittle rope of guts.[6]

In the meantime, Eagle is busy. He goes to Owl's bed. He takes the girl out from among the robes. He looks at her! Nice looking girl. Eagle asks her:

"Who sent you here?"

The girl answers him:

"My grandmother sent me here. I was scared at Owl."

Eagle said to her:

"Then come to my bed. Owl is *Tah-mi-lah kah-lat!* He is no good. Pay no attention to him. You are my girl, my wife."

Eagle took the girl. All five brothers hurried from the tepee. Owl was having bad luck back on the trail. Eagle said to his brothers:

"We must go fast! Go fast and far as we can. Owl is a medicine man, bad. He is liable to kill us all. We must go fast, must carry the girl with us."[7]

The brothers hurried! They took the girl up in the air! This was to hide their trail. They started away, going as fast as they could. They traveled a long ways before Owl reached home. When Owl reached home, he looked inside the tepee. All were gone. He looked in his bed for the girl. The girl was gone. Owl cried for the girl. Owl made *muk* [mark or medicine against Eagle]. He said:

"I am going to kill them all, kill every one of them."

Owl was a strong medicine man. He prepared himself. First he made medicine. Owl counseled with the spirits, how to find the brothers and the girl, which way they had gone, where they were going to. Outside he starts from the tepee, looking for their tracks. Only where they had stood, did he find. Only their tracks where they had stood outside the tepee. Then Owl circled. Circled, circled, circled farther and farther about the tepee. At last he found their trail. Found where they had started traveling. Owl trailed them, following their tracks. He found that they were getting away from him, traveling too fast for him. He cannot overtake them. That was the first night. Owl traveled all night. Eagle and his brothers traveled all night, hurrying for their lives. Eagle knew that if caught, Owl would kill them. That was Owl's intention, to kill them all.

Owl traveled until daylight, traveled all that day. He could not catch up with the brothers, could not overtake Eagle and the girl. He called for hail and rain, called that the feathers of the brothers might get wet. This would hold them back. It rained and hailed, rained long and cold. When Eagle and his party reached the other side of The Dalles on the *nChe-wana*, *Yeet-yeet* was wet, soaked and chilled. He said to Eagle:

"I am now done! I can go no further."

Eagle took his little brother, *Yeet-yeet*, up into a high cliff and hid him there. He said to *Yeet-yeet*:

"Good bye! my little brother. I will never see you again. Owl is coming close. Take care of yourself. Hide close."

Eagle then came back to his other brothers. He said to them:

"Owl is close now. We better go fast, better travel hard."

Eagle and his three remaining brothers started again with the girl. They did not go far until the next youngest brother was wet, soaked and cold. He said to his brothers:

"I am done! I cannot travel further. I guess we are all going to die."

Eagle hid this brother in the cliff. He spoke to him:

"Good bye! my brother, I will not see you again. Owl is coming close, is not far away. Take care of yourself. Hide in the rocks."

Eagle with his two remaining brothers hurried on with the girl. Soon the youngest of the two brothers gave up the struggle. Wet and numbed, he said:

"I can go no further! I must stay here, must leave you."

Eagle hid him in the cliff. He said to him:

"Good bye! my brother. I will see you no more. Owl is coming very near. Hide close. Take care of yourself."

Then Eagle and his last remaining brother, the biggest one next to himself, hurried with the girl. They hurried on their way, going fast to escape Owl. But soon this last brother of Eagle's gave up. It was near the [present] Idaho state line, when this, the largest and strongest of Eagle's brothers was done. He said to Eagle:

"My brother! I am finished! I must leave you now, must leave you alone. Do the best that you can."

Eagle hid his last brother in the cliff. He said to him:

"Good bye! my brother. I will see you no more. Owl is nearly here. Take care of yourself. Hide deep among the rocks."

Eagle now took the girl and started on alone. It was still raining and hailing, cold and chilly. They hurried fast as they could.

During this time, Owl made travel through hills and canyons, coming fast to overtake Eagle. A bad medicine man! He was strong to do evil things, to do mean things. Owl was mad! So mad that he would kill Eagle and all of his brothers. He hurried. He came to poor little *Yeet-yeet*, cold and shivering where Eagle had hidden him in the cliff. Owl found him. *Yeet-yeet* said nothing when Owl came up. He could not fight Owl, too small and weak. He knew that he must die. Owl said nothing. He caught *Yeet-yeet*, twisted off his head and threw him away.

Owl kept going, following on after Eagle and his party. He came to the next youngest brother, *Kaka-lo Kaka-lo*. He did him as he had *Yeet-yeet*. Tore him up and threw him away.

Owl was mad. He kept going. He came to the third brother, to *Ka-ka-no*. *Ka-ka-no* was not so weak. He was brave, and they had a fight. *Ka-ka-no* held Owl back for a while, fighting for his life. But he was killed. Owl tore him to pieces, scattered him about.

Owl hurried on again. He came to the last of Eagle's brothers, *Kle-yah*, hiding in the cliff. There was a hard fight. *Kle-yah* was brave, was strong and made a big fight for his life. They battled long, but Owl killed him, killed the last of Eagle's brothers. Only Eagle now was left. Owl, the bad medicine man was mad. He hurried on the trail of Eagle, hurried to finish his work.

While Owl was doing this, killing the four brothers, Eagle knew it all. He knew when the last of his brothers had been killed. He said to himself:

"My brothers are all killed! I will be next."

Eagle repeated this to the girl:

"My brothers are all dead! Killed by Owl. I will be the next one. I must look for a level place, a good place where I can stand up. I will fight for my life! I will fight for you."

Eagle now took the girl to a level place in a canyon where there were no big boulders. Where there were no trees, no brush to interfere with the coming battle. Eagle knew that there must be a fight, knew that a hard fight was coming. Eagle made the girl sit down. He takes a long rest, he is preparing himself for the fight.[8] Eagle is not scared, is not afraid. Now he sees Owl coming! He will not run! He will meet Owl. They will have a fight. He says to the girl:

"Owl is coming!"

The girl is scared! Eagle says to her:

"We will fight on the ground first. We will commence the fight on the ground, then raise in the air. We will go up fighting, up! up! up higher and higher. You will see feathers falling. You will see feathers from my body, see many of them. Do not care from what part of my body they are from. You will know that I am still living, still fighting. But when you find my *skein*, when you see the middle tail feather fall to the ground, you will know that I am dead, killed by Owl. Then save yourself if you can. I will not be alive to help you."

At that moment Owl came up. He came close to Eagle. He was mad. He looked at Eagle and said:

"Ah-hah! I have caught you at last. It is what I thought, that I would catch you some time. I have chased you far. I am good tired. I will take a little rest."

Eagle replied:

"All right! Take your rest. Take your time."

Owl sits down. He questions Eagle:

"How did you come to find my wife? Who told you to take my wife?"

Eagle spoke:

"No! The girl was not sent to you. She was sent to me. I am trying to get her back, to take her to myself. She was mine from the first. It should be as I am trying to make it now. She was for me first."

Owl laughed. He laughed long and harsh. He said:

"You are mistaken! I got her first. Her grandmother sent her to me, sent her to be my wife."

The girl heard the words of Owl, heard the words of Eagle. She said:

"No! Grandmother sent me to this man. You beat me out of it. You scared me. You told me lies, told me many lies. I do not want you for my husband. I was sent to this man. I will stay with him."

Owl laughed. He told her:

"No! You are my wife. We will have to fight for it."

It was then that Eagle and Owl began the battle, fighting for the girl. Both stood up. Owl took hold; Eagle took hold. They start on the ground, tearing each other. They keep on, whirling, leaping in air and then settling down again. They leave the ground! Rising! Rising! Rising higher and higher. Up they still go! Fighting hard. Feathers are dropping through the air, dropping to the earth. The girl looks up, looks at the fighters overhead. A big feather drops. She picks it up. No! It is not *skein*. Eagle is still alive.

Higher go the fighters. The girl watches them growing smaller and smaller. They are going nearer to the sky. Feathers still fall about her. She picks them up. She finds that Eagle is still alive. He is battling hard for his life, fighting for her. Now they have disappeared in the blue. She cannot see them. The girl waits a long time. Feathers still come down, Owl's feathers. Only the big feathers she picks up, looking to see if it is Eagle's center feather, the one that holds up, bears up. She knows which feather will tell the death of Eagle, the one that will drop when he is killed. The girl waits long before another big feather falls. They fall now, keep falling. Then *skein*, the center feather, the main feather of Eagle comes down. The girl picks it up. Yes! This is the feather. He is dead! Eagle has been killed.

The girl's home, where the grandmother lived, was not far away, not far from where the fight took place. Soon as the girl picked up the feather, she started for her grandmother's tepee. She reached there. She told all, told her grandmother everything. Told how Owl had deceived her, what she had done. The old woman said:

"You have done wrong! We will both be killed! Owl is bad. He never stops killing when he is mad. We may as well give our lives right now. When Owl comes, he will kill you. He will kill me. It is best for us to manage together how to save ourselves, to put our ideas together, what is best to do before he comes. Owl will trail you here. He will never give up."[9]

The grandmother and her child now thought many ways how to kill Owl. They planned how best to kill him, but no! None of them would do. Then the old woman thought of one thing, the sweat house. She said to the grandchild:

"We will make a *whe-acht*, a good sweat house. We will have plenty of pitch-wood. You bring pitch from the woods. When Owl comes and takes a rest, when he sits down, we will be ready for him."

The girl said:

"All right!"

They got ready. The grandmother built the sweat house, the girl bringing pitch from the woods. She brought lots of pitch. The girl brought rocks, brought many rocks. She laid wood and on this placed rocks. She laid wood on these rocks, then placed more rocks. Built up wood and rocks, all in order. Then she set fire to the wood. The rocks get hot, good and hot. The old woman finished the sweat house, everything done. Soon the grandmother sees Owl coming close. He arrives, comes where the women are. When he comes up, he sits down. Owl says:

"*A-e-h!* I am tired. I am traveling a long ways for this woman. At last I have got her."

The grandmother had instructed her grandchild what to do when Owl should arrive. She must sit by him, put her arm about his neck, must say to him:

"All right! You are my man. You are a good man. Make him think that you like him."

Soon as Owl had spoken so, the girl did as her grandmother had told her. She sat down by Owl, placed her arms about his neck. She said:

"You are a good man, my man."

The grandmother came where Owl and the girl were sitting. She said to Owl:

"You been traveling somewhere? You going somewhere?"

She spoke as if she knew nothing about the trouble. Owl answered:

"Yes! I have been traveling for this woman. I have got her now, have found her at last."

The old woman was surprised. She said:

"Oh! That your wife."

Owl made answer:

"Yes! She is mine!"

The grandmother acted as if she knew nothing, knew nothing about Owl's case. Owl said to her:

"I been traveling, fighting. Killing people for this woman."

Owl had no feathers on him. No flesh on his bones and head. He was bloody, only bones and sinew. When he walked his body went:

"*Skloph-skloph-skloph!*"

The grandmother looked at him, looked at his condition. She said to him!

"Too bad! Your sinews and bones are dirty. You wash and clean up."

Owl said to her:

"No! I am all right!"

The grandmother spoke again:

"Too bad! You are a young man. You are all blood. Clean up! I was going to sweat, but you must sweat first. Everything is ready. Rocks all hot, everything fixed ready."

The old woman out-talked Owl. Owl said:

"All right! I will go. Where is sweat house?"

This was what the old grandmother wanted. She answered:

"*Whe-acht* is ready. I saw you coming. You might be a stranger! I waited for you first. This is your wife. Only two of us live in this place."

Owl took the old woman's advice. He went as directed to the sweat house to sweat, to clean up. The grandmother followed behind to show him. All was ready. Hot fire, big fire. Rocks in the fire, all hot. Nice creek running by the *whe-acht*, clear, cold water. Owl told the old woman to put the rocks in place, to fix everything up. Sweat house was made solid, small door to go through. They had pitch-wood covered up outside the sweat house. Girl had brought lots of pitch, had carried plenty. Owl did not see it. Owl crawls inside, crawls through the door. He draws a long breath: "*A-h-h-h!* [sighs]." The old woman closes the door-flap. Owl throws water on the hot rocks. Soon he sweats, sweats good. After sweating for a time, he calls:

"*Who-o-oah!*"

The old grandmother lifts the door-cover.[10] Owl crawls out, goes to the creek and bathes. He takes a good wash. The girl carries pitch, piling it outside, away from the sweat house. Owl comes again to sweat. He crawls inside, the old grandmother closing the door. This he does twice, sweats twice, going to the creek each time. He sweats a third time. He sweats good, longer each time. Then he comes out, goes to the creek for the cold bath. A fourth time he sweats, sweats longer. The girl has pitch piled all around the sweat house, piled near the door. Owl stayed in longer this time. He came out, the old woman lifting the door-flap at his signal call. He bathed in the cold water, bathed a good while. Now Owl comes back for the fifth sweat, which would finish his work. This must be the longest sweat of any. He crawls in, the grandmother closes the door. She said to the girl:

"Hurry with the pitch!"

They cover the *whe-acht* with pitch-wood. All about the doorway they pile the pitch, closing it strong. Owl is singing of his work, what he has done, what he will do. To kill the girl when he comes from the sweat house. He will be greatest in all the country, none so strong as he. No one will be able to stand before him, none fight or kill him.

The women heard the song, the *tahmahnawis* [power] song of Owl. They hurried. When the pitch-wood was all ready, they started the fire. Pitch was on every side of the sweat house, was on top of it. A big fire was soon over it all. The door was closed tight, fire was over the door.

Owl still sang of his work, what he had done, what he would yet do. He sang in the *whe-acht*; sang, not knowing of the pitch fire. The women keep piling on wood, heaping the pitch. Every time pitch is placed, the fire leaps bigger, blazes hotter. It grows hot inside. Soon Owl sees light where the door has burned away. He tries to jump through the door! He cannot do it. He tries to get out the other way. He cannot get out. Not long till the *whe-acht* burns down, burns up. Owl, the bad medicine man, is dead.[11]

The grandmother and the girl stood looking at Owl, watching his head, when it would burst. They did not wait long. The head burst, exploding. One side of it, one eye flew across the creek to a cliff. There was a split, a crevice in the rock. The eye flew there, hit in the crevice of the cliff. It stuck there, hung up. That eye is still there. It can be seen as on that day when Owl was killed, killed by fire in the sweat house. When Owl's head came apart, when the grandmother saw the eye shoot to the cliff, she said to Owl:

"*Ah-hah!* I got you now! From this time on you will be nothing but an owl! Once in a great while people will talk about you, when you make a noise: '*Whoo! whoo! whoo! whoo-ah!*' You will be nothing but a scare for children, only scare little children. That is all, only a child-scare. You will be harmless. There are lots of people coming, a different people. You cannot hurt them. You are now nothing but an owl, a harmless *whoo!* owl."

Notes by McWhorter

That the eagle occasionally slays young deer cannot be gainsaid. Indian hunters have told me of witnessing such scenes. The eagle, plunging like a bolt from a great height, strikes the deer, tumbling it on the ground. If not disabled by this first crash, the deer may regain its feet, but outside of thick woods there is no escape. It cannot long stand the repeated onslaughts of the tyrant of the air. Finally disabled, the deer fails to arise when it is soon dispatched by talons at its throat. Mr. A.M.V. Arbogast, an old nimrod of the Trans-Alleghny, once killed an eagle which had swallowed the fragment of a deer's rib six inches in length. The broken end, sharp and pointed, protruded from the eagle's back two and a half inches, while the jointed, or round end rested in its craw. From all appearances the bird had carried the rib in that position for many years. See *Border Settlers of Northwestern Virginia* (Hamilton, Ohio: n.p., 1915), 353-54.

Tah-mi-lah kah-lat means "the one [to] stay in camp." *Muk* is "marking." Owl made "marks" or secret medicine against his enemy. The machinations of the "medicine man" has ever been a source of dread to the primitive minded tribesman. [McWhorter used the term "primitive," a word that is not appreciated by Native Americans because of its perjorative connotation. Many Indians from many different parts of the country believe that owls can speak of death.]

Skein means "bearing up" or "holding up." It is the center tail feather of the eagle. It is because of its resemblance to this feather, and the use to which it is put, that the Indian cradle-board is called "*skein*." It was this center, or main feather of the eagle, that was usually set up over the vacant bed-space of the warrior, or any one going on a venturesome journey. So long as the feather remained in place, the absent one was known to be free from serious harm. But there was mourning in that lodge if the feather fell, for it was a precursor of misfortune if not death to the wanderer. This feather has always been prized for its talismanic properties.

Who-o-oah: a signal call for the door-flap of the sweat house to be lifted.

36

Eagle and *Tis-kai*: How Porcupine Came by His Quills
Blazing Bush (Klickitat)
1918

IT WAS MANY ages of snows ago when *Why-am-may* [Eagle] was an older brother of the Four Hawks.[1] They had *Tis-kai* [Skunk] for a tepee-keeper and cook.[2] He cooked during the day, for Eagle and his four brothers were all hunters. Eagle was the leader of his brothers in hunting, while *Tis-kai* was only a servant who cooked for them.

Not far away there lived an old woman and her granddaughter, a good-looking maiden. The grandmother told her grandchild that she should marry Eagle, the great Chief and bold hunter. The girl, obeying the wish of her grandmother, journeyed one morning to the home of Eagle. But the old woman had neglected to tell her of *Tis-kai*, the servant. When she arrived at the lodge of Eagle, she found a man there in full possession. When *Tis-kai* saw the young woman, he said to her:

"Come inside the tepee. Be yourself in a home."

The girl went inside the lodge and *Tis-kai* married her. She became the wife of *Tis-kai* by mistake. This was before mid-sun, and when the sun was going down the sky, *Tis-kai* said to his wife:

"I have five cousins who are out all the sun hunting *yahmas* [deer]. Very near this time they will return from their hunting up in the mountains."

Tis-kai hid his young wife between two mats, where none could see her. It was coming sun-down when the smallest Hawk brother returned. He had no game. The next-sized brother returned. He had game. He called *Tis-kai* to come out and take the game inside the lodge. *Tis-kai* laughed, but he went out and brought it in. The third-sized Hawk-brother arrived with game. He called:

"*Tis-kai*! Come take the food inside."

Tis-kai laughed and said to himself:

"She will think that I am a servant."

But he went out and brought the game inside the lodge. The young woman was there, but the hunters could not see her. She was standing between the mats, could see all who entered, but none could see her.

The fourth Hawk-brother came. He was loaded with game. He called *Tis-kai* to come out and carry it inside the lodge. *Tis-kai* gave a big laugh. He said:

"The cousins must think that I am a servant."

But he went out and brought in the game. As the Hawk-brothers came through the door-way, the hidden girl could see them. She saw that their looks were good, that they were handsome men. She had been fooled by *Tis-kai*.

The fifth hunter arrived, the great Chief Eagle. He called:

"*Tis-kai*! Come carry the food inside."

Tis-kai laughed. He spoke loud:

"They must all think that I am only a servant, a slave."

But he went out and brought the deer inside. It was near eating time, and he must wait on the hunters when they eat. Now when the young woman came, she began to cook, to fix up the mat-lodge in the way that a woman does when she is the good wife that a man wants. *Tis-kai* used to grind sunflower seed in the mortar, and he had given the seed to the girl to grind. She ground it nice and fine, all before the hunters had returned. She had the food all prepared when *Tis-kai* hid her, made her stand between the two mats till they would go to bed. She was there but none could locate her. She saw the four Hawks, She saw Eagle. She viewed them all and said to herself:

"I made mistake! I married the wrong man. I married *Tis-kai*."

Tis-kai spread the food then called his cousins. Everything looks good. The hunters think:

"This cooking is all right. It is better than usual."

Eagle ate some of the sunflower seed. He found it well ground, fine for eating. He said to *Tis-kai*:

"My cousin, you have done well! You have ground good this time in your life."

Tis-kai laughed. Eagle continued eating the sunflower seed. He found a long hair. He said to *Tis-kai*:

"This is a long hair."

Tis-kai answered:

"That is my hair, out of my head. My cousin, give it to me."

Eagle handed the hair to him, and *Tis-kai* slyly doubling it, measured it with his own hair and said:

"Yes! This is my hair, out of my own head. See! It is the same length."

Eagle told *Tis-kai*:

"It does not look the same as your hair."

Eagle was suspicious of *Tis-kai*. The hair bothered his mind.

After all were filled, they went to bed. *Tis-kai* got his little wife from hiding and lay down with her. He whispered and laughed, kept his cousin Eagle awake. Eagle called to *Tis-kai* to sleep. *Tis-kai* said:

"My cousin! The mouse tickles my back. That is the reason I feel funny and laugh."

Eagle replied:

"Sleep! Do not laugh. You keep me awake with your laughing."

Morning came. *Tis-kai* hid his wife in the same place, between the two mats. Eagle went early, killed a deer up in the mountains and left it there. It was a plan to get *Tis-kai* to go after it the next morning. So when Eagle returned from hunting in the evening, he brought no game. While they were eating, he said to *Tis-kai*:

"In the morning you will have to go after the deer. I left it there, too tired to bring it home. I left a rope with the deer. You need not take a rope when you go."[3]

Tis-kai replied:

"All right, my cousin."

Eagle found another long hair in the sunflower seed. He said to *Tis-kai*:

"More of your hair!"

Tis-kai laughed. He said:

"Yes! Give over my hair, my cousin."

Chief Eagle now knew that *Tis-kai* had someone in his possession, hidden about the lodge. They all went to bed, *Tis-kai* whispering and laughing as before. Eagle said to him:

"Keep quiet! You disturb my sleep."

Tis-kai said:

"All right, my cousin. I will be quiet."

They then went to sleep.

Next morning everyone got up early. *Tis-kai* hurried, cooking food and they all ate. *Tis-kai* said:

"I must hurry!"

He started to bring in the deer. He went but a short distance, when he came back and said to his cousin:

"I forgot the flint knife."

Eagle told him:

"Knife and rope are there. Everything is there."

Tis-kai started a second time, but soon came back. A third, a fourth, a fifth time he came back, and then he went running. Chief Eagle caused it to rain hard, so as to delay the return of *Tis-kai*. He did not want him to return that sun.

Soon as *Tis-kai* was out of sight, Eagle made search of the lodge. He found the young woman in the hiding place between the two matting. He took her out and saw that she had been fooled by *Tis-kai*. He pressed an arrow over her and she became as when with her grandmother.[4] Chief Eagle then took the woman to the top of a high cliff of rocks where they stayed.

In the meantime, *Tis-kai* hurried to return with the deer. But the rope broke often, causing him trouble. Eagle had made the rope of twisted deer-guts. After many trials to carry the pack, *Tis-kai* left the bundle and ran home with all speed. He arrived there late in the night and found his wife gone. In her stead, were five little *Tis-kai* mah [skunk children]. When morning came, *Tis-kai* made search for the tracks of Eagle, to find which way he had gone with his stolen wife. He went to the river. There he saw them both far down under the water. *Tis-kai* said to himself:

"I have found them at last! They will now both die."

He then shot [at] them with his poison. He had lots of poison, like small bullets.[5] He saw Eagle and the young woman laughing down in the water. Five times he shot [at] them, and still he saw them laughing at him.

Then he heard them above him, up on the high cliff. He looked. *Eh!* They are on the tall rock over the water. He had only been poison-shooting their picture. *Tis-kai* called to Eagle:

"How did you get up there?"

Eagle replied:

"I tied myself about the waist. My cousins pulled me up. You must do the same way."

Tis-kai agreed, and asked Eagle to let down the rope. Eagle did this, and *Tis-kai* tied it around his body. Hawk-brothers were all there, and they began pulling *Tis-kai* up. As they were doing this, Eagle ordered a small round rock heated hot. They were bringing *Tis-kai* up very slow. He called to Eagle to know how far they had brought him. Eagle called down that he was far from the top. Every time *Tis-kai* called to know how far he had come, how far they had pulled him, Eagle would fool him in the distance by saying:

"You are far down."

Tis-kai had his poison ready, plenty of poison. Again he called:

"How far to reach where you are? How far to where you are now?"

Eagle still fooled him:

"You are yet way down!"

Tis-kai was planning to shoot them all with the poison he carried, and when near the top of the rock, he again asked how far they had to draw him. Eagle blinded the distance by speaking low:

"You are still far down from the top!"

Eagle now saw that *Tis-kai* was getting ready to shoot his poison. He took his buckthorn pincers from his pack and squeezed hold of the little hot rock. He shoved it into *Tis-kai* and at the same time cut the rope. *Tis-kai* fell from top of the high cliff, landing in the water. The bullets of poison, forced by the hot rock, came out of his mouth as he was falling. They struck the water far ahead of him, and floated down the river.

Tis-kai was now helpless. He followed down the river to see if he could find his Power again. He came to people living along the river. He asked them if they had seen his Power floating down on the water. They answered him:

"Yes! We saw your Stink float down the river."

This answer *Tis-kai* received different times. He would cry and say:

"If I ever recover my Power, I will fix you people."

Tis-kai kept on down the river and came to a different village. He asked if any of the people had seen his Power floating down on the water. They answered:

"Yes! We saw your Power and Wealth floating down the river."

Tis-kai laughed. He said:

"Good, my people! I will remember you when I come back."

Tis-kai continued down the river, looking for his Power which he had lost by the hot rock. It was night when he came to another village-settlement. He heard a big time, heard the enjoyment, the people singing in the long mat-lodge. He looked through a hole in the door. He saw that it was his Power the people had. It had been caught by canoe-fishermen as it floated on the water. They had brought it to the village, having a big enjoyment rolling it across the building. Rolling it like a hoop-ball.

Tis-kai now began studying how he could recover his Power from the people. He studied and then went to work. He dug a hole not far from the long-lodge. He knew how far he must go under to come up in the lodge where they were playing. He then opened a small hole where the Power stopped in its rolling. When he had finished this work, day had come again. He stayed under ground and the people did not know he was there. He waited to be ready to recover his Power-bullets when the time came.

It was evening when the people again commenced their sport in the long-lodge. They did not know that *Tis-kai* was there underground waiting to recover his Power. The players rolled it several times, but it missed the hole made by *Tis-kai*. But *Tis-kai* wished for it, and it rolled to its former old place.

Tis-kai now stood up in that long-lodge. He laughed at the people. He walked to the door, and as he passed out, he sent a shot to the whole gathering. No one there escaped the poison-bullets of *Tis-kai*. All were killed, none lived.

Tis-kai gathered all the costly shells, all the ornaments those people were wearing. He made them into a pack and returned up the river. He wanted to get back to his old home. When he came to those people who had made fun of him, he killed them all with his posion-bullets. He took their best shells and beads to wear on his neck. He had a big bundle to carry, packed on his back. He had killed all who had laughed at him. He was now all alone, traveling up the river. The friendly village he did not bother. Those people he had passed far down the river.

Chi-kash [Porcupine] saw *Tis-kai* coming on the trail and was scared. He lay down and made himself dead, with worms on his body. *Tis-kai* came up and looked at dead *Chi-kash*. He said to himself:

"I have found something to eat for myself. It will carry it along and when awfully hungry, I will eat it."

So *Tis-kai* put dead *Chi-kash* on his pack and journeyed on. As he went, he said to himself:

"I am afraid of nothing but *Qui-klah* ["Whistler" or marmot]. I am afraid of him only. He may meet me and I will leave all that I am carrying. I will get scared of *Qui-klah*."

Chi-kash was not dead. He was alive. He knew all. He knew that he was being carried by *Tis-kai* to be eaten by him when hungry. When he heard *Tis-kai* say that he was afraid of *Qui-klah*, he thought:

"Now I will try! I will see what I can do."

Chi-kash then made a very low whistle. *Tis-kai* stopped. He said:

"*Eh!* I heard a whistle."

Then he made a run, and *Chi-kash* whistled a little louder. *Tis-kai* ran the harder, while *Chi-kash* continued whistling, getting louder all the time. *Tis-kai*, running his best, said to himself:

"I am being overtaken by *Qui-klah!*"

He dropped his pack, his whole bundle and ran fast away. *Chi-kash* was on the pack, and he whistled louder than ever. *Tis-kai* fled for good, did not come back again. *Chi-kash* earned *Tis-kai's* costly pack of shells and neckwear. He untied that bundle of shells and beads, put them all on himself. It is what *Chi-kash* wears to this day.

Notes by McWhorter

Qui-klah is the Klickitat name for the hoary marmot of the Northwest. *Wow-she-thon* is the Yakima appellation for the same animal. Both names appear to pertain to the peculiar whistling call of this interesting rodent. In the Okanogon legend, "How Skunk Came By His Tail," Whistler is a ghost or spook.

The hoary marmot is locally known as "whistling jenny." It is interesting to note that a Mohammedan legend has it that *jin-nee* was a pre-Adamite order of beings, both good and bad. They were endowed with power to assume the forms of animals and of giants. The *jin-nee* were the followers of Chief of the Jinns.

37

How Young Eagle Killed *Pah-he-nux^t-twy*
Che-pos To-cos, Owl Child (Wishom)
October 1923

PAH-HE-NUX^T-TWY, A CHIEF, was cutting off the heads of the people.[1] A bad man, he killed people when playing the bone game. He was not satisfied without killing some people.

Eagle heard about this. Eagle had two wives. One was Cricket, [and] the other was Dove. These wives had two children, two boys. Eagle said to his wives:

"I am going over there to find out who is killing all the people. I am putting up this feather. Watch it! If blood appears on it, then I am dead. You will know that I have been killed."

Eagle hung the feather and said again to his wives:

"Watch the feather all the time."

Eagle had fine hair, long hair, lots of shell wampum and buckskin, leggings and shirt. He looked fine! All dressed in best of everything.

Eagle went! Traveled one sun and camped. The next sun, he did the same thing, traveled and camped. The third sun, he traveled and camped. The fourth sun, he traveled and camped. The fifth sun, Eagle traveled all the time that it was light. It was about sundown when he came to where Indians were camping. He sat down on the ground close to camp. He saw a lodge off to one side and thought to go to it. Eagle found two old women there. One of them said:

"Oh! My sister! A man comes into our lodge. I think he is a chief."

Eagle is a tall man good looking and clean. One old woman said to him:
"I never see you anywhere before. This is the first time that I see you."

Eagle made no reply, did not talk. The old women told him:
"There is the chief at the bone game. He destroys men! Young man," the two old women said, "you have come only to get killed. He has destroyed many chiefs."

The bad chief was on his knees at the bone game. He said:
"Eh! Somebody has come."

This bad chief knew! He said to Bluejay:
"Go over to the old women's lodge and see who is there."

Bluejay comes to the doorway of the lodge and said to Eagle:
"The chief wants you to come and gamble the bone game with him."

Bluejay looks at Eagle and was nearly blinded. He went back to the chief and said:
"You sent me! I am nearly blind. My eyes are put out."

The chief told White Fish to go see who was over at this outside lodge of the old women. White Fish went and said to Eagle:
"The chief wants you to come and gamble."

Eagle looks at White Fish. White Fish's mouth is cut way back. White Fish ran home, his mouth big. The next fish, a fish with a small mouth said:
"I will go! I will put finger in my mouth."

Small-mouthed fish went and told Eagle to come and gamble with the chief. He then put his finger in his mouth. Eagle looks at him, burns his mouth red.

The chief told Crab to go see who was at the old women's lodge. Crab went and said to Eagle:
"The chief wants you to gamble with him."

Eagle looks at Crab, burning him red. Crab ran home, scared! He said to the bad chief:
"You asked me to tell the chief to come and gamble with you. I am all burned up!"

Then the bad chief sent Cotton-Tail. The chief said:
"Go tell him, who is chief, that I want to gamble with him."

When Cotton-Tail delivered this message, Eagle went to gamble with the bad chief. Took all the people who were in the old women's lodge to go gamble with him. That was the way, the rule. They got to the bad chief's lodge. They go in and all sat down. The chief said to Eagle:

"If I beat you, I will cut your throat. If you beat me, you will cut my throat."

They commence to gamble. The best are *Cas-te lah* and Cotton-Tail. They are against Eagle, and Eagle loses. The bad chief said:

"I will have to cut your throat."

Eagle was not afraid. He answered the bad chief:

"All right!"

Then the bad chief cuts Eagle's throat. Cut off his head and hung it up like a flag, left the body lying on the ground. Eagle had told his wives:

"Watch the feather! Watch it all the time! If blood appears on it, then I am dead. You will know that I have been killed."

When Eagle was killed, blood dropped from the feather. The wives said:

"Eagle is dead!"

When the blood came, the two wives with the children moved camp. Coyote was not far away. He knew that Eagle was dead, and he took the two children. He was a chief! He played Eagle to get the two women and children.

Now Cricket thought that it was Eagle, her husband, but Dove knew better. Dove cried all the time. They go traveling for one sun, then camp. Next morning they travel, then camp at night. Dove follows behind, crying. The third sun they travel till growing night, then camp. Fourth sun they travel, then camp. The fifth sun they travel, then camp and travel no farther. They will stay in this fifth camp a long time.

The two boys go out and do the same as Indians. They grow up like Indians. The youngest boy is strong, powerful, strong! He practices every day how to make his strength grow. He pulls up small trees, twists them like ropes. He casts heavy rocks from him, practicing all the time. Then he pulls up big trees, throwing them like spears. Big rocks are hurled out into the river. Bigger rocks, still bigger! Pitched across the *nChe-wana*.[2]

Finally Young Eagle is a grown man, and he sets out, going on the trail of his father. He follows his father's tracks, resting where his father had rested, where his father had sat down, camping where his father had camped.[3] Four times, four suns, he traveled and camped. Then the fifth sun, he came to the lodge of the two old women. Young Eagle sits down and looks. The lodge is far from the village. That was why his father had gone there. For a long time Young Eagle sat and looked at the old women. Looked and looked at them! He was better looking than his father: buckskin moccasins, leggings and shirt, and many shell wampum strings. His hair is long and fine looking. One old woman said to him:

"Oh! young man, you have come to the wrong place! There is a bad man, a bad chief near here. I do not want to see you killed!"

Then the two old women told him all about how his father was killed. A fine big man, all fixed up nice, Young Eagle went to gamble with the bad chief. He won the points, won the sticks fast. Only one more stick, one more point to win. The bad chief is scared! He said:

"We better quit right now."

Young Eagle will not quit. He made reply:

"No! When you gambled with my father, he did not say quit."

Young Eagle won the game. When the last stick went across to his side, the bad chief said:

"Let me go safe! Do not kill me! Save me!"

Young Eagle would not let him live. He answered the bad chief:

"No! I will not do that. I must cut your throat off!"

Three times the bad chief asked to be let go alive. Three times Young Eagle refused. Four times the bad chief wanted not to be killed. Four times Young Eagle would not let him remain alive. He said:

"No! When you won the game from my father, you killed him."

The fifth time the bad chief asked to live, he offered Young Eagle everything he had for his life. But Young Eagle refused. He cut the throat of the bad chief and told him:

"After this there will be no more killing at the bone game. Only play in gambling. That will be all the bone game will be used for."[4]

The bad chief had lots of people on his side. They wanted to get away, wanted to escape when their Chief was killed. Young Eagle had five *ᵉQue-quy mah* [Grizzly Bears] on his side. Two fires were burning not far apart. Young Eagle had his *ᵉQua-quys* on either side from these fires. The people who escaped the flames were killed by the fierce *ᵉQua-quys*.

This was the end of *Pah-he-nuxᵗ-twy*, the bad chief. Since that time there has been only betting in the bone game and no killing.

Young Eagle took his father's head down from the pole. He took it to where the body still lay on the ground and put it back in place again. He had some paint and he rubbed it all over his father's dead body. He did this a second time. Three times, four times he painted the body. The fifth time he rubbed the paint, Eagle came back to life. He got up and went home to his two wives. Coyote was there, and when he saw Eagle, he cried:

"Oh! my grandchild! I took care of all while you were dead. All are here now!"

Eagle replied:

"All right! I know what you have been doing. You go up on top this tree. A nest of birds is there."

Coyote went up the tree. When he got to the nest, no birds were there. Young Eagle commanded him:

"You stay there forever!"

That tree, and Coyote, is a great cliff along the *nChe-wana* [between Wishom and Hood River]. It was Coyote's punishment for what he had done. He can be seen there to this day.

Notes by McWhorter

^eQue-quy mah is the plural in Wishom for grizzly-bear. The scene of this legend is along the *nChe-wana*, between Wishom and Hood River, Oregon, the closer proximity being in favor of the first named place.

38

How a Water Ball Was Made
Che-pos To-cos, Owl Child (Wishom)
March 1932

YOU KNOW THE sweat house, how it is made.[1] How the rocks are first heated and then put into the small hole in the ground just inside the door-way. How water must be brought and sprinkled on these hot stones to make a fog for the sweat.

Three men had the rocks hot all ready for the sweat. Then they found they had no water basket to bring water from the lake. They must try their power. See who could bring the water.

One man took an open woven basket, all full of holes, and dipped it into the lake. He brought the basket full of water, and set it down at the sweat house. He had a strong power.

Another man took a dip-net—used to catch fish—and going to the lake, dipped into the water and brought it filled and sat it by the basket that had been filled. The water did not leak out.

The last man must now try his power. He waded into the lake until the water came above his knees. Then he began making a water-ball, piling it up and shaping it with his hands. He made a round ball of water, large as a good-sized cooking basket. He lifted it to his shoulder and carried it to the sweat house, and sat it down by the basket and the dip net of the other men. The water ball held its shape, did not melt down. Then the man stuck his finger into it, and the water ran out. It was great work.

You do not know what power this man possessed? I will tell you. When a small boy, he was sent out somewhere in a lonely place to try find power from something. The Seal came and talked to him.[2] It told him to do as it was telling him, and when he should be grown up he would have this power to handle the water. Inside the fish, inside the seal, is the sack which you can take out. It was given the fish and the seal to help them handle themselves in the water. Blow it up with air [the air-bladder]. Land animals do not have this, and it was this power given by the seal to the boy when alone in the night-darkness. No other man had such power as did this man.

39

Girl Rock
Billie White Thunder (Nez Perce)
14 September 1924

IN THE *IN-CHE-LIM* below Newport [Washington] are falls of considerable height [Kettle Falls], at the base of which is a peculiar stone, resembling in formation, somewhat that of a woman with lower limbs extended.[1] Salmon in attempting to scale the falls, and in such attempt striking, or landing at the juncture of these limbs with the body, are invariably killed on the instant. The legend is that in the days of the beginning, *Its-i-yi-i* [Imitator or Coyote] chased a girl, who, in a desperate effort to escape his attentions, leaped over the cliff, where she has remained to this day, changed to the stony formation spoken of. The stone is light in color.[2]

Often the fishduck, in attempting to fly upwards over the falls, is killed by coming in contact with the pouring cascade. Too high for the bird to scale.[3]

40

How the Mountain Broke
Anonymous
July 1922

A TIME WAS when no slide showed in the desert mountain below Toppenish, on the Yakima Indian Reservation.[1] All was sound and unbroken to the top of the ridge. That *knute* [land slide] came this way.

The *Pom-pom* [or] drum with singing voices in worship was first heard [here]. There were also tones of a bell, such as the Dreamer [*Washat*] priests now use.[2] The people heard this in the night darkness, they heard it in the light of the sun. The worship continued for a time, then there was a change.

Another kind of drum was heard, a war drum and the war song broke on the night. It was as if warriors were making ready for war, dancing the war dance. The drum and song sounded in the night, sounded in the sun light. No one could tell where it was, only that it came from the mountain somewhere.

For one moon this continued, when suddenly as the sun was on the evening trail, a great rushing noise burst where the drum was going. The people saw a cloud, dense and black come surging up over the mountain, wrapping its summit in folding shrouds of darkness. Immediately the thunder broke in such booming volume as to rock the ground. The swirling mass, aflame with ripping tongues of lightning, poured a deluge of water down the mountainside, flooding all the adjacent low lands. Then came a jarring, grating rumble, ending in a crash that rattled the lodge-poles of the village. The side of the mountain had crumbled and fell.[3]

Immediately, the sun hanging low, flashed forth, melting away the storm-rack. The people beheld a terrible form writhing and twisting in the hollow of the broken mountain. A body longer than the tallest tree and thicker than the girth of a horse, wet and glistening flashed in the slanting sunbeams. A great antlered elk-like head was reared on high, while a tail bearing rattles of prodigious size, vibrated filling the air with a thousand clanging notes. This was the mighty Head Chief of all the *Wah^k-puch* [Rattlesnake].[4]

The people now knew that the mountain had been shivered by the quivering contortions of the huge reptile in its struggles to emerge from its underground home. The self-liberated chief set off towards the sunrise. He traveled till he reached the Rocky Mountains, where he has remained ever since. The ruins of his fallen lodge attests to his ponderous size and strength.

Two other big *Wah^k-puch* chiefs were seen at the *knute*, just after the slide. They had horns like the buffalo. The coiled body of the one forms a small pond or lake at the sunset end of the ruins. Another pond some distance away on the sunrise side marks in like manner the finale of its mate. The trail of this chief is seen in a well defined slough leading the entire distance from the *knute* to the pond in question. These two great serpents preyed on the beavers inhabiting the creek and water-ways.

41

Bridge of the Gods
Ana-whoa, Black Bear (Wasco)
September 1914

WHEN THIS EARTH was first made, the Animal and Bird People were living all over the land.[1] They were the only tribes at that time and that day. Some animals were great and could kill people, could do mighty wonders. I will tell you of one and how the Bridge was made.

From [at] sundown in the west was a great bird. It lived there, and all the people were afraid of it. This animal was *Noh-we-nah klah* [Thunder-bird]. A law was made by this bird, made in five high mountains. The bird made five high mountains and said:

"I make this law, the law that if people pass over the five high mountains, I will kill them. They must not come where I live."[2]

Hal-ish [Wolf] was one of the greatest of animals. He did not believe the law.[3] He said:

"I will go! I will be the first to see what *Noh-we-nah klah* will do to me."

Hal-ish were five brothers. They said:

"I will go."

Hal-ish went to the first mountain. The brothers stood in a row, all stepped the right foot at the same time. Nothing hurt *Hal-ish*. Then the left foot was stepped, all at the same time. The five brothers were dead.[4] When the people learned that the five brothers were dead, *Twee-ti-yah* [Grizzly Bear] said:

"I will go! I will take a chance! I do not think that I will die like the five *Hal-ish*."

There were five brothers of *Twee-ti-yah*. They went to the first mountain. They stood in a row, stepped the right foot, all at the same time. But when the left foot was stepped, *Twee-ti-yah* fell dead, as did *Hal-ish*.

Wy-you-wee [Cougar], five brothers said:

"I will go try! I will take a long step. I will leap over the mountains."

Wy-you-wee went; and at the first leap, all were dead.

Then *Yeh-kah* [Beaver], five brothers said:

"I will try! I will go under the mountains. I will not get killed like *Hal-ish*, *Twee-ti-yah* and *Wy-you-wee*. I will go see about this law."

Yeh-kah tried, and all five brothers were killed.

Coyote's oldest son was a great man, greater than all others. He said:

"I will go talk to the mountains. I will go talk to this great law, the mountains. I will break the law down, or see if it will not break down, that the people may live and pass to the sunset."[5]

Coyote's son was five brothers. They went and two of the sons talked to the five mountains, the law. The mountains were made to move up and down, dance and shake, but nothing more.[6] The five brothers were killed the same as had the others. The five laws in the five mountains still stood. None could pass them to the sunset.

Coyote's son, the five brothers, had not told their father what they were going to do. Coyote had instructed them never to go away from home to stay overnight, and when they did not return, he knew that they were dead, killed by *Noh-we-nah klah*. The old man knew all. He was wiser than his sons, wiser than all others.[7] He had been told from *Wha-me-pom-mete* [Land Above]. The Great Man Above had instructed him in wisdom.[8] After his son, the five brothers had been gone five nights, Coyote said:

"I know that my sons are all dead. The Animal has killed them. *Noh-we-nah klah* has killed them with his five laws, the five mountains."

After five days and five nights had passed, Coyote cried. He cried long, wailing among the mountains and caverned rocks.[9] He went to a lonely place and cried. He rolled on the ground lamenting, for he was sad and miserable. His heart was poor, heavy and lonely. He prayed to the Great Man for strength to save his five sons, strength to bring them back to life. Coyote cried and prayed. After he had cried and prayed for a time, the answer came:

"You cannot break this great law of the Animal. You cannot go over the five mountains, the five laws. The law stands there as made by the Animal, by *Noh-we-nah klah*."

But Coyote continued praying, rolling on the ground in a lonely place in the mountains. He was far away from everyone. Then he was told:

"The only way you can do is to go up to *Wha-me-pom-mete*. It will take you five days and five nights to go. There you will be instructed how you may get your five sons back to life."

Coyote heard and went up. Went up for five days and five nights, into *Wha-me-pom-mete*. There he told about his troubles. He said to the Great Man:

"You are wise. You know of the great Animal who has made the five mountains, the five laws. None can pass over them, none can go to the sunset. My five sons are killed. I wish you could give me a law, the strongest kind of law, so I can whip the Animal, that the people may live."[10]

The Great Man answered Coyote:

"Yes! I know the five mountains. I know the mountains, the five laws. I know that people coming from the sunrise are not to pass over the five mountains. They must not see the Animal, *Noh-we-nah klah* who lives at the sunset. He must not be seen by anybody."

This was told Coyote by the Great Man who lives in the land above. The Great Man said:

"Yes! You know yourself. You are a strong man. You are most as strong as I am. You ask how to kill *Noh-we-nah klah*. I will tell you. We will kill him. I will help you. I made the earth. I made all the animals. Some I made greater than others. *Noh-we-nah klah* is the strongest, was made the strongest. I will help you. I will blind the eyes of *Noh-we-nah klah*. Then you can go over the five mountains, the five laws and kill him."

Coyote answered:

"*Ay-ow!* [All right] I wish you would help me."

The Great Man said to Coyote:

"Do you know on earth a great bird called *Why-am-mah* [Eagle]? Do you know his sons and daughters, his children? When you go back to earth, find *Why-am-mah*? He has law, has powerful strength. Find his son, his youngest son. Pull a feather from under his wing, a small feather and downy. This feather has strength, has power running out from the heart. It is strong of the heart, because it grows near the heart."

Coyote heard and he turned back towards the earth. For five days and five nights he came and landed on earth. He knew where *Why-am-mah* lived, where his five children lived. The Great Man had said:

"You go to *Why-am-mah*. Tell him about me. How I have given you strength to come to him. Ask for his youngest son's feather. Ask for the feather light and down, the feather growing next to his youngest son's heart."

Coyote went to *Why-am-mah*, told him all that the Great Man had said. Then he asked:

"Can you give me the feather from your youngest son? Can you give me the feather growing next his heart? All the people are being killed by *Noh-we-nah klah*."

So *Why-am-mah* picked this feather from his youngest son, where it grew under the wing next to his heart. Coyote was to be turned to a feather, small and so fine that it could not be seen going through the air. Such feather goes too fast. The Great Man [had] said:

"Ask *Why-am-mah* for his strength, for great power to help you. I will help you. If you go ten days and ten nights without a drink, without food, you will be changed to a feather. You can then go anywhere."

So Coyote went hungry for ten days and ten nights, no food, no water. He was then turned to a feather, like the one given him by *Why-am-mah*. He flew through the air towards the five mountains, but he remained a great distance away. Coyote was instructed to create a noise like *Enum-klah* [Thunder], rolling far away, as he passed through the air. This he did for the first time, rumbling and low, off towards the sunrise. The second and third time, he made a slow, deep noise in the distance. *Noh-we-nah klah* heard and said:

"How is this? I alone was given power to make that noise from sun to sun. This noise I now hear must be given from *Wha-me-pom-mete*. I am dead! I am dead! I am dead!"[11]

The fourth time, Coyote made the noise louder and closer to *Noh-we-nah klah*. *Noh-we-nah klah* became angry. He said:

"I will kill whatever this is that is coming close to me."

Noh-we-nah klah then made a mighty noise, a greater thunder in answer to Coyote. Coyote went into the air, higher and higher, darting and whirling so rapidly as not to be seen. Then *Noh-we-nah klah* was afraid! Scared! He felt sure of death. He sought the deep water to hide there. He heard Coyote far above him. He knew that if one more noise, the fifth thunder, came, he would be dead. Coyote prayed again to the powers of *Wha-me-pom-mete* to help him one more time.[12] Help him kill *Noh-we-nah klah*, that the people might live, that his five sons might come back to life. The Great Man of *Wha-me-pom-mete* heard Coyote and helped him.

Noh-we-nah klah shrank deeper in the water. Scared! Coyote, above him and invisible, now brought a greater noise than ever, a crash like the bursting of this world. The five laws, the five mountains, crumbled and fell. The fragments, floating down the *nChe-wana*, created the many islands along its course. The giant body of *Noh-we-nah klah* formed the great Bridge across the *wana* at the Cascades. This Bridge was of the first mountain and was mostly stone. It stood for many hundreds of snows, no one knows how long, and then it fell. The Indians said that in time it would fall and it did. Some of my ancestors, old people, saw and passed under that Bridge. I do not know the number of snows since that time, but they are many. It was the law, the rule, that when the canoes journeyed through the waterway, no Indian was to look up. None must see the Bridge, must not look up at the rocks of the Bridge.[13] After killing the law made by *Noh-we-nah klah*, after breaking down the five mountains, Coyote said to *Noh-we-nah klah*:

"The people are coming, lots of people. A second people, the Indians, are coming. You shall not kill them as you have killed the present people. Once in a while you may produce a great noise, make the earth tremble and the people will be afraid. You can strike the trees and high places, but you can never be as great as you were."[14]

The five sons of Coyote and all the people killed by *Noh-we-nah klah*, came back to life.

When I was a little girl, this story was told me by my father [early nineteenth century] who heard it from his father [mid eighteenth century], who heard it from his father, and perhaps still farther back. I do not know, but some of them saw the Bridge, passed under it in canoes. I was not to tell all the story, not even to my own children. But I have told it to you and it is true. There is no more to tell.[15]

This last statement by the narrator, who must then have numbered closely to her century milestone, was confirmed by her daughter, *Yes-to-la-lemah*, who was acting as interpreter. She said:

"I had never heard all of this story as given you by my mother. She never told it to her children in full as she told it today. One way that I have heard it—not from my mother—is, that when the five mountains were destroyed, the Bridge, which was in the first mountain, was also broken down. Most Indian stories are rehearsed in various ways, by different tribesmen. It is the same as with white people, the preachers. But my mother, who is the oldest living member of her tribe, must have it correct, as the Wascos knew it. She has always had a good memory, and her mind today seems as clear and strong as when I was a child."

At this point *Yes-to-la-lemah* conversed with her mother for a few moments, when the aged woman again spoke for interpretation:

"Do not go to the young Indians for these old stories. Do not depend on the young people to tell them in the true way. They do not know. They do not listen to the stories as did the old Indians when they were young. The wisdom of my people will soon be forgotten."

Notes by McWhorter

During the narrative, *Ana-whoa* handed me a small plume of downy eagle feathers, plucked from under the wing, as typical of the one presented Coyote by *Why-am-mah*. Of course the down of the young eagle is more pronounced than that of the matured bird. The Klickitats tell me that when passing up or down the *nChe-wana* by canoe, the occupants, excepting those necessary to man the oars, would land when the Bridge was approached, and walk around to the opposite side where they would again reembark. Those who took the canoes through the tunnel, or bridge, always bid their friends goodbye; for it was believed that the great natural structure would sometime fall, as prophesied by the ancient seers. The catastrophe might take place during transit of the boats. The final destruction of the Bridge formed the Cascades, the first real salmon trap to be met with on the *nChe-wana*.

42

Spalding Memorial Rock
Heyoomyummi, Woman Grizzly Bear (Nez Perce)
No date

ONE TIME THERE was an old man, *Pe-li-yi-yi* [pestle], who lived where this rock stood on the bluff overlooking the land of the *Lap-lap* [Lapwai, Idaho, the Place of the Butterflies].[1] Very wise, he knew everything. He was supposed to be a Chief or Governor.[2] Any people camping from down the river, going towards the sunrise, he knew it. Coming from anywhere, going any direction, he knew. Any information asked, he could give it. Anything important for the people, different people, *Pe-li-yi-yi* could be consulted with success.

But one time *Its-i-yi-yi* [Coyote] disagreed with *Pe-li-yi-yi*. Coyote said:

"If we do not get rid of him, some way he will kill the people."

He said to the old man:

"We do not want you to be controller of anything. I am going to call you, and you will become a rock."

The old man answered Coyote:

"You will turn to be rock too!"

Then both became rock. The old man [had] said:

"I will become rock, and so will you! Because, real human beings are approaching. They will be here instead of us alone."

The old man was on the hill above the highway-arch over the railway at Spalding [Idaho]. Coyote is against the bluff across the Clear Water, opposite side of the valley.[3] Coyote is still seen there, as a rock crag standing out prominently from the hillside.

On the same side, above where the sand accumulates, where the people from Lewiston come to swim, you can see *Al-lah-who-ee-yi-yi*. He helped Coyote, and the old man made him to rock. He is there.

There is also a woman and a child to be seen nearer to Coyote. She came from down the Clear Water, going up the river. The old man had sharp eyes, seeing everyone passing. He would stop them or else turn them to rocks. You can see the woman and her child there as part of the group forming the bluff or cliff.

This is our story. The white people moved *Pe-li-yi-yi*, using him for the Spalding Monument. It was not right to do this. This rock belonged to the Nez Perce, a "heathen" tribe.[4] Spalding came against our religion, and this hidden man has been taken for his monument. This was not right.

Interpreter's comment: "Spalding declared in his sermon that our religion was heathenish, that 'All heathen people will be punished at the last day. Their punishment will be hell-fire without end.' He said that the medicine man 'works through the power of the Devil, doing the work of the Devil.'

"We take this rock, look upon it, as an image *of something. Spalding was against images [symbol]. This rock was taken against the command: 'Worship no images.' The whites worship Spalding by placing this image as his monument.*

"The rock was fallen, lying on the ground. It was an old landmark. In the white man's Book of religion [Holy Bible] it is written:

'Thou shalt not remove thy neighbor's landmark, which they of time have set . . . [Deuteronomy 19, 14],' and, 'Remove not the ancient landmark which thy fathers have set [Proverbs 22, 28].'

"The Christians do not regard, or follow their own declared teachings. This is why I have let my hair grow long again."

Notes by McWhorter

Woman Grizzly Bear (Mrs. Susie White) is the daughter of the late Short In The Head, Nez Perce warrior, 1877. Mrs. White's mother, *Pe-nah-we-non-mi*, was present when the legend was told, and aided her daughter in correctly portraying it. True to the patriotic principles of the Indian race, the narrators deplored the sacrilegious usage to which the old man, *Pe-li-yi-yi*, has been subjected. He should have been allowed to remain at his ancient rest, placed there by a superior power. The rock referred to in the story is located near Spalding's mission site on the Clear Water River in Idaho.

When interrogated as to his familiarity with certain phrases of the Bible, this "Long Hair" replied with a wan smile: "I was once teacher of a Methodist Sunday School class. *I think being honest is the best religion.*"

43

Big Skukum Inlet
(Nisquallish)
1921

BIG SKUKUM IS a long narrow arm of Puget Sound, reaching to the town of Shelton [Washington].[1] Its name is derived from the swiftness of its current, both at the setting in and ebbing of the tide. At such time the inlet may well be compared to a very rapid river.

A "line of boulders paralleling the shore" are, at half tide, a menace to small craft and always fatal to the Indian. Woe betide the unlucky tribesman whose canoe ran afoul the lurking danger. If he escaped drowning at the time, he would not live long afterwards. A prescribed song was always sung by the unfortunate one, which might well be termed his death song.

An aged and blind Indian ran his canoe on the rocks. He was heard chanting the wailing refrain and was rescued. True to tradition, he died within three weeks time.

At night or in foggy weather, the experienced canoe man gauged his proximity to the danger line by repeatedly striking the water with his oar. If there was a shore echo, he immediately sheered in the opposite direction, holding to the center channel. In this way the deadly rocks were avoided.

44

Origin of the Name *Lapwai*
Many Wounds (Nez Perce)
November 1926

WE WERE PASSING alone through the old Indian Celebration Camp Grounds in Spalding [Idaho], when I asked Many Wounds the meaning of the name *Lapwai*.[1] He turned towards the river, east side of the mouth of Lapwai Creek, and going to a spot near the largest cottonwoods still standing a few yards from the mouth of the creek, and only a few rows from the Banks of the Clear Water, he replied:

"I will show you something that not many white men have heard about. You see these two biggest cottonwood trees. It is here, a damp place, sometimes a muddy spot. Butterflies come here thick in the spring and summer. Many colored butterflies. Settling on this damp place, they wave their wings like this: (Imitating with hands the well-known movement of this insect when settled as described). That motion of the butterfly wings we call '*Lap-lap.*' The whites not knowing what I have shown you and told you, changed the word to *Lapwai* [place of the Butterfly], giving it to the entire stream, and naming the fort some miles from here, the same. *Lap-lap* is only this one spot I am showing you."[2]

45

Coyote and Flint
Anonymous
No date

RICH AND POWERFUL was Flint. His lodge was towards the sunrise. It was guarded by Crane, who watched and spied for him.[1] When anybody approached Flint's tepee, Crane called to warn him, and Flint would come out and meet the visitor on an open flat that lay before the lodge. Warriors came and paid Flint big prices for the privilege of chipping off arrow points and spear heads. Some hunters who needed stones for their weapons were too poor to buy, and Flint turned them away.

Coyote heard about Flint, and he wanted some arrowheads. He asked his *Squ-stenk* [medicine] power to help him.[2] At first, *Squ-stenk* refused, and Coyote warned:

"Hurry, or I will throw you away and let the rain wash you to pieces, wash you cold."

Squ-stenk then gave Coyote three rocks that were harder than flint-rock. Also, it have him a little dog with only one ear. This ear was a knife-ear. To his wife, Mole, Coyote said:

"Go and make your underground trenches in the flat where Flint lives. When you have finished and see me talking to Flint, show yourself so Flint and I can see you."

Coyote set out for Flint's lodge, and, as he drew near, he called on his power to make fog cover the land. Thick fog came, and Crane, the watcher, did not see Coyote until too late. Coyote took Crane from his high perch on a lone tree and broke his neck before he could utter a warning call to Flint.

Coyote went on to Flint's tepee. As he approached, Grizzly Bear, who was Flint's dog, started for him, showing great, white teeth. Coyote was not scared.

"Stop your dog, Flint!" he advised. "My dog will kill him."

That amused Flint, who saw that Coyote's one-eared dog was very small. It didn't even have a tail. Flint laughed and said:

"You'd better take your dog away. Grizzly Bear dog will eat him up."

"No, stop your dog," Coyote said. "One-Ear will eat Grizzly Bear dog."

"No dog is big enough to kill my Grizzly Bear dog," laughed Flint.

The words were hardly out before Coyote sent One-Ear at Grizzly Bear dog, who growled terribly and opened wide his jaws to grab One-Ear. One-Ear jumped right into the other's big mouth and went right on through Grizzly Bear. The knife-ear cut Grizzly Bear wide open.

"See," gloated Coyote. "I told you One-Ear was bad! He can kill anything."

Flint had not recovered from his suprise when Mole appeared at the edge of the flat. She was dressed in red-painted skins.

"My friend," said Coyote, "see that woman there. Let us run to her. Who reaches her first will marry her."

They ran towards Mole, who was pretending to be digging *spitlum* [bitterroot]. The underground trenches Mole had dug were a bother to Flint. Each time he put his feet on them, he fell. Coyote, jumping over Flint, shouted:

"Eh! Ha-yea! My friend, what is wrong?"

Flint was heavy and he fell often. In fun, Coyote would jump over him twice each time before he could get up. Just as they reached Mole, she changed into a real mole and skipped into an underground trench. Flint looked very tired. Coyote began striking him with his three *Squ-stenk* rocks, scaling off chips of Flint at every blow. Flint fought as hard as he could, but he was tired, and he fell at almost every step because of the trenches Mole had made. At last Coyote killed Flint, but only after he had chipped away his entire body from about his heart. The heart Coyote threw across the flat, where it stands to this day as a hill. It is there that the most flint is found. The body of Flint, which lay scattered in flakes and fragments, Coyote gathered and threw all over the earth for warriors to use as spear and arrowheads. That done, Coyote said to Flint:

"You will be a man no more. From this day you will be only dead stone."

That is why the flint rock is senseless and cannot fight back when chipped for arrowheads. Coyote made it so before the New People, the Indians came.

46

Octopus and Mink
(Puyallup)
1921

THE PEOPLE HAD a great gathering, an assemblage of all the nation in the Long House.[1] Mink came as usual. As he entered, he kicked Octopus, who was near the door-way, and said to him:

"What you doing all flobbed out on the floor?"

Octopus raised up on his many feet, looked at Mink, but said nothing. Mink soon passed again with a kick and the same remark. Octopus raised up, but said nothing. But when Mink kicked him the third time, using the same words, Octopus caught him and started off to the Sound-shore with him. Mink became scared! He said:

"Let me go! I was only playing. I meant no harm!"

Octopus did not stop. He replied:

"I am not playing!"

He took mink to the water's edge. He carried him under the water, placed him on the bottom and laid a rock on him. Octopus then went back to the council, forgetting all about poor Mink. Not until the council was through, did Octopus think:

"My prisoner! I better go see my man under the rock."

He went down to the shore, went under the water where he had placed Mink. All that Octopus could see of him was a "batting" at the edge of the rock. This was all that was left of the mischievous Mink. The "batting" is kept up to this day when the tide is in.[2]

47

How Deer Stole Rabbit's Coat
Anonymous, told in an Indian Hunting Camp
April 1921

DEER AND RABBIT are sweating in the *whe-acht* [sweat lodge].[1] Deer comes out from *whe-acht* and steals Rabbit's clothes. Deer runs off to the mountains and leaves his own clothes for Rabbit.[2] He says to Rabbit: "You stay in sage-brush country. I will be in the mountains."

This is why Rabbit is found in desert country, in sage brush country. This is why Deer is found in mountains where there is timber. Before that time Deer had a fur coat and Rabbit had a hairy coat, the coat Deer now has. Deer cheated Rabbit out of his coat.

48

How Ant Came by His Small Waist
Anonymous
No Date

THE PEOPLE WERE given the dried meat, sinew and skins of *Yahmas* [deer], all [that they] needed.[1] But they were to follow certain rules for a time of five suns. All obeyed; all were quiet, doing none of the forbidden things; all but Coyote.[2] Always getting into mischief, he had to break [the rules] over on the very last sun.[3] Following this act, the meat, sinew, buckskin, and everything, *Yahmas* came to life, became living and fled away.[4] *Su-le-sah*, ["turning around" or Ant], thought to retain this buckskin, so [ant] tied it about his waist. But nothing could hold the new-lived deer. He fled fast and far, dragging Ant with him. The buckskin was drawn tighter and tighter, cutting deep into his body. *Yahmas* continued running, and finally broke loose. Poor *Su-le-sah* was left squeezed small at the middle, which shape has been with him to this day.[5]

49

How Blue Jay Outwitted Dog Seal
(Tulalip)
1921

A DISPUTE AROSE among the people as to who was the best diver.[1] The contest grew between the Animal-kind and the Bird-kind. Dog Seal was selected by the Animal side, but the Birds could not agree. Finally Loon was chosen, when Hell-Diver rose up and contended for the honor. The council had to continue. It was then that Blue Jay challenged:

"I can dive farther than both of you men. I will dive against you both! One after the other."

It was then settled that Blue Jay was to dive against Seal.[2] The people all went out in their canoes to be ready to help their man when he should come up from diving. Blue Jay asked his people to throw everything out of the canoes, matting and all articles. They did not want to do this; they refused to do this. Blue Jay explained that he wanted the canoes light, to be ready to come to him quickly when he came up from the dive. This satisfied the people and they did as requested.

It was the middle of the sun's traveling down the sky when Dog Seal and Blue Jay dove. Both stayed under a long time. Dog Seal was gone a long time, then he came up, floating on his back. Dog Seal was drowned.

Blue Jay continued under the water, out of sight long after Dog Seal came up. He stayed till nearly sundown, then came up. He was flopping his wings, puffing hard, almost dead. The canoes hurrying to help him, his head was caught between them and crushed to its present flattened appearance. The people asked him:

"How did you stay under the water so long? How did you manage it?"

Blue Jay replied:

"I will tell you, but the other side must not know. I went under the mat. I stuck my bill just through the mat. I could breathe; I did not drown. I could hear all, knew when Dog Seal came up drowned. Do not tell how I tricked Dog Seal.[3]

50

Raccoon and Grizzly Bear
(Yakima-Klickitat)
1916

KAH-LAS [RACCOON] AND his grandmother lived together.[1] *Kah-las* cried all day long. The grandmother asked the boy why he cried. He answered:

"I want acorns!"

The grandmother said:

"Go get some from the basket-bucket."

They had a basket-bucket made of cedar roots. So the little *Kah-las* went to where the acorns were under water in the mud-cellar. The grandmother had told the boy not to go out on the trail, but little *Kah-las* forgot all about it. He went out on the trail and left an obstruction there. When coming back he hit his leg against this obstruction and fell down spilling the acorns. When they spread out on the ground, *Kah-las* sat down and ate them all. He had none to take home. He went back for more acorns, but fell and spilled them again. He ate these and returned for more. Every time he fell, spilled them and then ate them up. This he did five times. He ate all the acorns stored in the basket in the mud.

Now there were five holes filled with acorns which belonged to *Kah-las* uncle. By this time the boy had become bad. He ate the acorns in four of the holes. His grandmother went to look for him, to see what was wrong that he did not return. She took in her hand a stick from the fire. This stick had a live coal on the end of it. When she came to where the acorns had been stored in the holes, she saw that all had been eaten from four of them. *Kah-las* was in the fifth hole. She caught him by the tail, pulled him out, and began to whip him with the stick. She struck him on the tail first, then on his body. The last lick she struck him on the nose and killed him. She laid the *Kah-las* boy there and went to her tepee, crying on the way. Arriving at her tepee, she continued crying for little *Kah-las* whom she had killed. She cried all the time for her grandchild.

In the meantime, *Kah-las* recovered his life. Getting up, he went to the river. When he came to the water he looked down under [into] the water and saw a funny looking shadow. Finally he discovered that it was his own shadow under [on] the water.

Kah-las grew hungry. He began to look for something to eat. He looked under [in] the water for crabs and found them. He ate the crabs. He made a belt out of the hazel-nut bushes.[2] He twisted the brush together, used them as a belt. He found flint rocks and used them for his knife. He found five good flint knives. He put them all in his belt.

There came to the other side of the river, *Twee-tash*, the Grizzly Bear. He called to *Kah-las*:

"Where did you get across?"

Kah-las said:

"Where the *Twee-tash* sternum is at the riffle."

Five times *Twee-tash* asked this question, five times *Kah-las* made him the same fun answer. This made *Twee-tash* mad. He jumped in the river to swim for *Kah-las*. When he was in the water, *Kah-las* called:

"Big sturgeon swallow *Twee-tash!* Big sturgeon swallow *Twee-tash!*"

But when *Twee-tash* came near to this shore, he called:

"Swim hard! Big sturgeon will swallow you! My grandfather!"

Kah-las was smart. He wanted *Twee-tash* to hear what he said, so he would take pity on him and do him no harm. But *Twee-tash* had no pity for *Kah-las*. He was very mad. He asked *Kah-las* what he had said to him while he was in the water. The boy replied:

"I said swim hard my grandfather! Big sturgeon will swallow you!"

Twee-tash rejoined:

"You never said such words. I will swallow you alive."

Then he swallowed the *Kah-las* boy.

When *Kah-las* came to the stomach of *Twee-tash*, he thought to do some work.[3] He had his five flint knives in his belt. He took one of his knives and began to cut the heart of *Twee-tash*. Grizzly Bear felt pain at his heart. He said to himself:

"This *Kah-las* is a painful food! I had better throw him out."

So *Twee-tash* threw *Kah-las* boy out in the rear.[4] When the boy fell to the ground, he jumped up and laughed. *Twee-tash* said:

"I will swallow you again!"

Kah-las boy replied:

"All right! Go ahead and swallow me!"

Twee-tash was mad! He swallowed the boy a second time. When *Kah-las* landed in the stomach of *Twee-tash*, he took another flint knife and began cutting the heart again. *Twee-tash* began to feel the heart-pain as before. He said:

"This *chil-wit* [bad] boy is painful food!"

Twee-tash threw the boy out a third time. *Kah-las* jumped to the ground. He laughed! A big loud laugh! This made *Twee-tash* mad! Worse mad! He swallowed *Kah-las* the fourth time. *Kah-las* began work on the big heart with his fourth knife. He worked hard. *Twee-tash* felt the awful pain! He could not stand that killing hurt. He said:

"I do not like this *Kah-las* food! I will throw him out."

Twee-tash threw *Kah-las* out the fourth time. The boy made a big laugh! He laughed loud! A fun-laugh at *Twee-tash*. This made *Twee-tash* madder than at any time. He said:

"I will swallow you for good this time!"

Kah-las boy answered:

"All right! I am not afraid!"

Twee-tash swallowed *Kah-las* the fifth time. The boy began cutting at the heart for the last time, cutting hard with his fifth knife. It was his last knife with which he finished the job. Finished cutting off the heart of the great *Twee-tash*. When the heart fell down, *Kah-las* jumped out. Poor *Twee-tash* staggered around. Soon he died. *Kah-las* boy felt proud! Felt brave! He had slain the mighty! The powerful *Twee-tash*, the cruel *Twee-tash*, who had killed so many people.[5]

Kah-las now began skinning *Twee-tash*, dressing the meat for food. He piled it up. Remembering his grandmother, he said:

"I will go tell my grandmother. We will pack the meat home. We will have food for a long time."

Kah-las set out for his grandmother's tepee. As he went he sang:

> I have slain the mighty *Twee-tash!*
> I have killed the big *Twee-tash!*
> I have killed the Chief *Twee-tash!*
> *Kah-las* has killed the great *Twee-tash!*
> Who is so brave as *Kah-las?*

Those were the words sung by *Kah-las*. The grandmother was crying in her tepee. Crying because she had killed her little grandchild, *Kah-las*. When she heard the song, she stopped crying, stopped her lamentation. She listened! Yes, it was the voice of *Kah-las*. She heard the words of his song. *Kah-las* came into the tepee. He said to his grandmother:

"I have come after you, my grandmother. I have killed the big *Twee-tash*. Get ready! We will go bring in the meat."

But the grandmother did not believe him. Scared! Lest the *Twee-tash* hear him, she said:

"Hush! my grandchild! Do not talk that way! That is a very dangerous thing you are talking about my child."

Kah-las repeated his song:

> I have slain the mighty *Twee-tash!*
> I have slain the big *Twee-tash!*
> I have killed the Chief *Twee-tash!*
> I have killed the great *Twee-tash!*
> *Kah-las* has slain the cruel *Twee-tash!*[6]

Five times *Kah-las* told this to his grandmother, and then she believed him.

The grandmother got ready to go. She took her pack-rope, and they started. When they came to the place, *Kah-las* told his grandmother to pack and carry the neck part. But she refused. She said to *Kah-las*:

"Your grandfather, now dead, forbid me to carry such parts."

Then the boy told her to carry the hind-quarters. The grandmother said:

"All right! My good child."

In a happy spirit the grandmother tied the hind-quarters with her rope. She placed the pack on her back, went away hurrying. Leaving *Kah-las* behind, she made haste-steps, made fast steps on the trail. She arrived at the *whe-acht*.[7] There she made herself a home, took the meat inside for herself alone. She laughed in the *whe-acht*. When *Kah-las* found his grandmother doing this, hiding with the best of the food from him, he took her out and clubbed her to death.

Comment by the narrator: "Here ends the story; the story told to me by my grandmother when I was a little boy. I give it for the foreign nationality which has come, that the whites may know the learning of the Indian, may know the wisdom of the race that they have destroyed."[8]

Notes by McWhorter

The Yakamas prepare the acorn for food in various ways, but the favorite method is to bury them in a certain kind of mud under running water, or at least pure water, letting them "pickle." At the Soda Springs, Yakama Indian Reservation, the mud is of excellent quality, imparting to the nut a peculiar and pleasing flavor. Owing to the intrusion of the white man during the outing season, the springs have been practically abandoned of late years by the tribesmen. Because of their medicinal properties both for bathing and drinking, these waters have always been held in high repute by the Yakamas.

51

The Small Mouthed People
(Klickitat)
March 1918

THREE MEN SAW a large cedar tree floating down the *nChe-wana*,
below The Dalles.[1] They looked! It is a fine tree, fine for canoe. They
said:

"We will go get that tree. Make it a canoe. It is big! Bigger than any
tree we have seen.[2] It will be a fine, big canoe. Finer than any on the
nChe-wana."

The men went out to the tree, tied it fast to their canoe. When the
tree was good and fast to the canoe, it started down the river at a more
rapid rate. It went still faster, faster than any *yak-akes* [drift wood] driven
by wind and water. The men became scared! They paddled hard, but
could not stop. They found themselves going with the tree. They worked
hard with their paddles, but they could not fight the strength of the *nChe-
wana*.[3] It was pulling the big cedar tree, pulling it with their canoe. The
men were afraid! They tried to get loose their canoe, but could not. They
could not turn back. They said to each other:

"Now we will die! We will be killed on the *nChe-wana*! Nothing can
save us!"

The tree never rested, never grew slower.[4] That night it reached the
Ah-tah cheech [ocean], the big water. The men now said:

"We are going to die! We will be killed! Killed out on the big water!"

Faster went the tree, never stopping for the night. It was far from
sight of land. Finally the tree went into a bay among some islands. It

entered a river, went up that river considerable distance. It took the men ashore, dragging the canoe from the water. Then that tree stood up straight. That tree grew fast in the ground. It was a growing tree, finest in all the forest.⁵ The men said to each other:

"We are lost! We will die! We cannot get away from this place."

The three men stayed there that night. Next morning they look out over the water. Eh! They see something coming down the river! They look! Take a good look! That canoe comes opposite where they are hiding! It stops! The man anchors the canoe with stone and line! Then that man stands up in the canoe! He pauses over its side! Looking into the water! He looks! Then quickly dives overboard! Disappearing under the water!

The man stayed below for some time, stayed longer than any Indian could stay under water. Then he came to the surface, a big salmon in each hand, holding them by the gills. He put them in the canoe, then dived again. He did not come up soon. Finally he appeared. They saw him holding two more salmon in his hands. He placed them in the canoe with the other two salmon, then dived out of sight. Again he came up with two salmon, big fish. He made several dives, each time bringing two salmon, placing them in his canoe.

The three men watching, saw what the strange man was doing. They were hungry. They had no way of getting fish. They saw that the diver stayed under water a long time. They said:

"We will go steal a fish while he is under the water!"

So while the man was diving again, they pushed their canoe into the river. They paddled to the anchored canoe, took one fish. Then they hurried back to the shore, hid their canoe in the brush as before. They hid themselves, hid good. They would now have food to eat.

The one man came from the water for the last time. He had two more salmon, large and fine. He got into his canoe and found one fish gone. Then that man stood up! He looked towards the land, but saw nothing. That man stretched out his arm, pointing up the river. That man turned slowly, sweeping the forest with outstretched hand. He turned until his arm pointed down the river. He found nothing. Then that man reached out his other arm, pointing down the river. Again he turned slowly! Slowly in the opposite direction. When his arm leveled directly at their hiding place, he stopped. That man stood looking! He had found them.

The man in the canoe now lifted the anchor-stone. He brought his canoe to the shore, got out on the land. He came to where the men were hiding. That man was big! Was strong! But he had a small mouth. He grabbed the three men and took them to his canoe. They could do nothing. He was stronger than all three of them combined. He got their canoe, tying it to his own. He took the stolen fish, placing it with those in his canoe. He shoved off from shore. The men said:

"He will kill us! We can do nothing! We will die!"

The Small Mouth hurried, paddled strong. The canoe went fast. It traveled as the fire-driven boat [steam boat] of the *Sho-yah-poo* [Suyapu, white men and women]. They approach a village on the river bank. The Small Mouth hallooed in a big voice:

"I have found a Big-Mouthed people! I have found a Big-Mouthed people!"

The villagers came to see. They all had only small round holes for mouths. Otherwise they were like the Indians of the *nChe-wana*.

The three men got ashore. They were very hungry, but saw nothing cooking to eat. The Small Mouths did not eat salmon. They threw the fish in a pile, waiting till the maggots grew. Then they ate the maggots. They knew not how to eat the salmon. They could not eat the salmon. The men asked by signs for a salmon. The Small Mouths signed back:

"You cannot eat the salmon!"

The men signed:

"We will show you how we eat salmon! We can eat the salmon!"

The Small Mouths gave them a salmon. The men baked it and ate it.

The three men learned the language of the Small Mouths. They were told of yearly battles with all kinds of water-fowl, ducks, geese, and all varieties. When spring came, they saw on an island, a great cloud of birds training ready for fight. They would fly in masses, wheeling, charging everywhere. The Small Mouths were alarmed! They made preparations for hiding, for getting under cover. The three men said to them:

"Let the water-fowls come! We will protect you! We will kill them!"

The men armed themselves with clubs. They got all ready for battle. It was to come soon, not long to wait for the big fight. One morning the birds came in great swarming waves, swooping down on the village. The men fought hard. They killed many of the fowls. But soon the air was filled with flying feathers. Down settled on the mouths of the Small Mouths, smothering them to death. They did not know how to save themselves, knew not how to brush the down away. The three men did this for them, saving many lives. The battle raged, but finally the invaders were driven off, beaten for a time. When they returned to the attack, the

Small Mouths had been taught how to protect themselves. They fought hard, and the birds were again put to flight after many had been killed.[6]

The three men had now remained with their strange friends more than one snow. They wanted to return home, but knew not how to get back over the long distance. The Small Mouths were grateful for what they had done for them. They said:

"We will take you back to your own country. We know where your people live. We will put you on the right way home. You must go towards the warm-land."

They now began preparing for the journey. Now the Small Mouths ate large quantities of the *Ahx-ahx* ["big end" or abalone]. Great piles of the shells were all around the village. Not the short variety, but shells of good length. The Small Mouths got this large size by diving for it in the sea. They sucked the insides from the shell which fitted their mouths so well. The three men asked for some of these shells to take home with them. They were told to take all they wanted. So they loaded their canoe with shells to take to their people, to be used as beads and ornaments.[7]

All ready, the three men started with their guides in a large canoe, their own canoe trailing at the stern. They were not allowed to help at the oars. The Small Mouths did the rowing. They were strong! They sent the big canoe fast, like the cedar tree had traveled. They went all the time. They did not stop for darkness. One morning they landed on an island. Here the Small Mouths said:

"We can go no farther! You must go alone. Go towards the warm-land to your people."

The three men were left there with their own canoe and shells. They did not know which way to go. They said:

"We will die! No use trying to get home! We will die here on this island!"

While they were talking, a whale came to them.[8] It spoke to them. It said:

"I know where you are from! I will take you back to your people. I will swallow you, swallow your canoe and take you home.[9] Do not be afraid! I will take you safely back to your own country."

The men said:

"All right! We will die if we stay here. We will take the chance with you."

So the whale swallowed the men. Swallowed their canoe loaded with the fine tusk-wampum. Swallowed them all safely in its stomach.

The whale goes during darkness and light, traveling fast through the sea. It speeds faster than any boat can go. It comes to the mouth of the *nChewana*. It goes up the river to near the village where the men live. There it set them ashore and told them:

"Go home! But leave the canoe and shells here where they are. Bring your people to see me. Bring all, but listen to my request. No woman or girl who is moon-sick is to come.[10] They must not come with the people, young or old. Go bring your people! Distribute the shells among them here."

The men went to the village, calling all the people together. They told them where they had been, what they had seen and how they had been brought back by the whale. They were to go now to see the whale, to talk with him. But no woman with moon-sickness could go. They must stay away.

So the people went. All the women wanted to see the whale. None of them would tell if she was unwell. All went. But the whale knew! When the people came in sight, the big fish knew. It dived! Was gone to be seen no more. It took with it the canoe loaded with the fine shells. All were lost.

52

Its-i-yi-i's Wife
Hemene Moxmox, Yellow Wolf (Nez Perce)
October 1924

ITS-I-YI-I [COYOTE] WAS traveling up the Snake River.[1] He stepped on Meadowlark's leg and broke it. Meadowlark cried with suffering, and said:

"There! you broke my leg. What you going around this country for?"

Its-i-yi-i made reply:

"Tell me what you know?"

Meadowlark answered:

"Lots of people have gone back towards the sunrise. You go over this mountain. A young woman is [there] sick."

Its-i-yi-i said:

"Tell me the truth, my aunt, and I will fix your leg."

Meadowlark replied:

"I am worrying about my leg. Fix it first and I will tell you."

Its-i-yi-i pressed the broken bones together. He said to his aunt:

"Stand up! Dance! How do you feel?"

Meadowlark stood up. She was afraid at first, but found her leg good and strong. She danced. She sang as she danced. She said to *Its-i-yi-i*:

"I am well! I feel all right in my leg. It is the truth! I tell you about the sick young woman."

Its-i-yi-i is going back towards the sunrise. He went over the mountain. He reaches Salmon River. He sees a tepee lodge. He said:

"That is what Meadowlark told me. A girl is there sick."

Its-i-yi-i struck his leg [penis?] and made young coyotes' "*wist-wist cau-cau*" to come out.[2] He left his children there, and went into the lodge. The sick girl said:

"I am worrying about the sickness I have. See if you can doctor me."

Its-i-yi-i replied:

"Yes, I can doctor you, I can cure you, if you will be my wife."

The girl answered:

"Yes, I will marry you. I have been worrying about this sickness."

Its-i-yi-i spoke:

"Wait! I will call for others to come here. There is a bunch of us."

Its-i-yi-i then stepped out the doorway and called to his children:

"Come over here and sing for me while I doctor."

They come. They enter the lodge where *Its-i-yi-i* and the sick girl are. He said to them:

"I am going to doctor for a little time. Do not say anything else."

Its-i-yi-i sees a piece of elk's horn in the sick girl's foot.[3] He knows that he can cure it in a few minutes. He sings his song:

"I am going pull it out! I am going pull it out! I am going pull it out! I am going pull it out! I am going pull it out!"

The helpers beat with sticks and sing, to lend strength to the doctor's words. *Its-i-yi-i* sees that the snagged foot is festered. The piece of horn will be easy to pull out. Then he sings:

"I am going suck it out! I am going suck it out! I am going suck it out! I am going suck it out! I am going suck it out!"

Its-i-yi-i then pulls the piece of horn out with his teeth. The young woman is dead [unconscious]. He blows his breath on her. Blows all over her.[4] She comes to life and feels better. *Its-i-yi-i* squeezes pus all out of the foot. He binds it up with a piece of deerskin with the hair on.[5] They are married, and they follow on the trail after the people who have traveled towards the sunrise.

In the evening, they see light in lots of lodges. There is another Coyote's lodge, and he calls out in the village:

"It is *Its-i-yi-i*! He cured the girl and has now come up with us. Better get ready, people, and we have a war dance tonight. Get ready!"

Its-i-yi-i paints the woman's face, combs her hair. He lets his wife sit behind him, where he sits beating the drum.[6] He leans back against her, while at the drum. He jumps up and dances for a while, then comes back, leans on his wife and beats the drum.

Eagle's son is watching *Its-i-yi-i*, and when he goes in the dance, the son said to Frog:

"You better go sit where *Its-i-yi-i*'s wife is sitting. Better go now."

Frog did as she was told, and young Eagle stole the new wife of *Its-i-yi-i*, and they went away. The dance is finished and the people all go home. *Its-i-yi-i* said:

"My wife, let us go home now."

Frog did not answer. *Its-i-yi-i* spoke again:

"You hear! My wife? Let us go home!"

Frog then made answer:

"Your wife is not here. I am your aunt. Somebody took your wife long ago."

Its-i-yi-i is then lonesome for his wife. Finally he said:

"Well, I will not be long like this. Human people will soon come, and other women will be here."

This was the rule made by *Its-i-yi-i* in the long ago, the Indian takes another wife if his own is stolen or leaves him.[7]

53

Ghue-ghue and *Pedt-jum*
Klickitat
1917

THERE ARE STORIES about *Ghue-ghue* [Raven], Crow, and all other kinds of birds, as well as animals, large and small.[1] All lived in one village and they had one big, high chief. This chief was controller over all in the village, all had to obey his word. That was the ruling, the law. Now all those birds and animals appear to have been people at that time, had language and talked same as we do. They still talk, can understand each other in everything. Some Indians can interpret their words.[2]

That big chief of the village had one daughter who grew to be a young woman. All the young men got eyes on that girl, the chief's daughter. She was good looking, handsome. Her father was rich. All wanted her. The best hunters, the bravest warriors, would like to have her.

Now *Ghue-ghue* thought that he was a progressive kind of man among the others. He was quite a hunter, could make his own arrow-heads and other necessary articles for hunting. He also controlled the *yahmas* [deer] and other game. *Ghue-ghue* thought that he had a good side-stand with the girl, a good standing with her father, the big chief.

But there were others who wanted the girl. *Speel-yi* (Coyote) thought that he was the one who could round with her, and *Pedt-jum* [Wild-Cat] thought that he could get round with the girl.[3] But *Pedt-jum* did not pretend that way. Nobody knew his mind. He fixed himself that he was an old man, fixed his face rough looking. But anything that he put on his face, meant something the future time.[4] For this reason he made himself to look old, to seem an old man. He would then be trusted anywhere in the village, without fear of his running away with the chief's daughter. But this same time *Pedt-jum* intended having the girl as his wife. *Pedt-jum* mounted up with everything to look like an old man, old and ugly. *Pedt-jum*'s mind was strong for the girl.

The chief's daughter had taken sick by this time. She was sick with *tahmahnawis* [spirit sickness], a secret medicine given by anything of a powerful nature. After she had been sick five suns, she heard the *tahmahnawis* songs. Then the big chief gathered his people, all who were in the village together. They must have a real *tahmahnawis* dance, that his daughter might become strong, become powerful.[5] That was just the thing for the young men. They said among themselves:

"This is the time we will run off with the girl, among the *tahmahnawis* dancers."

When the chief built the long-lodge for the purpose of the *tahmahnawis* dance, the same evening the dancing began. *Ghue-ghue* was there first of all the people. All came but *Pedt-jum*. He stayed in his own tepee, just to make the others believe that he did not care for the gathering, did not care about the dancing. But *Pedt-jum* was working all the time to get ahead of *Ghue-ghue*. He thought that he was strong enough himself to control all the hunting grounds, all the *yahmas*. It was he who could get the best of *Ghue-ghue*, the wise one. This was the plan of *Pedt-jum*, the cunning one.

That first evening after the people had entered the *tahmahnawis* dance-lodge, the chief counts them all. He must see if everybody is there before the dance begins.[6] They find that *Pedt-jum* is not there, is not in the gathering. They send after him, for him to join in the great dance. *Pedt-jum* tells them that he thinks too many are there, too crowded, that he might not do much for them if he was there. Then the people give up his coming.

The chief's daughter now starts her *tahmahnawis* dance. Then it was that *Ghue-ghue* was over all the young men, above all who wanted anything to do with the girl. Gifts are given to all the people attending the dance, presents as are usual in all *tahmahnawis* dances.[7] After dancing a few nights, they forget all about *Pedt-jum* being out from the rest of the people. They do not care for the old man remaining alone in his own tepee.

In the meantime *Pedt-jum*, too, thought that the people had forgotten all about him not being with them in the dance, so one night he went there. He slipped carefully upon the roof, looked in from peak of the roof. There he saw the girl, the chief's daughter. She was singing her *tahmahnawis* songs, the songs given her by her tah [spirit helper]. Unknowing, she looked up with mouth parted, singing her power-song. *Pedt-jum* on the lodge roof thought:

"This is the time for me to get the girl. This is my chance to get the girl for myself."

Pedt-jum now watched his chance and spat in the girl's mouth as she sang.[8] No one saw him do this. The girl herself did not feel anything. She did not notice anything from the roof. *Pedt-jum* got down and went back to his tepee. He was satisfied with his work. After five suns the dancing was finished.

Shortly after this, the girl had a baby born, a fine looking boy. The little boy cried for his father, cried all the time. The Chief asked his daughter to tell who the father was. The daughter could not reply until he had asked five times, asked the same thing over five times. Then the girl told him that she did not know how the little baby came.[9] She did not know anything about it. She could not realize how it was. The chief said:

"All those people were here doing the big dance. The baby will recognize its father. I know that it will recognize its father."

The chief now sent his men through the village to tell all the people to come to the dance-lodge. They came, all but *Pedt-jum*. He stayed in his tepee. He told them:

"It is no use for me to go to the dance-lodge. I have no show to get the girl."

But *Pedt-jum* knew that it was his baby. He knew how it was, but he kept still.

Ghue-ghue, *Speel-yi*, and the other young men claimed the baby was theirs. They did not think that it belonged to *Pedt-jum*. They said among themselves that *Pedt-jum* was [not] there during the big time, *tahmahnaw-is* dance. When the people had assembled in the dance-lodge, the chief spoke:

"Someone is father to this baby! And whoever is its father, must marry my daughter. You can all see that the baby is crying for its father. Each one of you men will have to go round and take hold of the baby. If he quits from crying, if he keeps quiet, that will prove who is the father. Each one of you pass by and take hold of him. Hold the baby in your arms."

Ghue-ghue was first. He had been around the girl more than any of the young men. He held the baby, but it kept on crying. It was not *Ghue-ghue* to be its father. Then *Speel-yi* held the baby. *Speel-yi* said:

"Let me hold the baby. I know that he will quit crying forever."

Speel-yi takes hold the baby. It does not quit crying. *Speel-yi* places his hand over the baby's mouth, shuts its mouth to keep it from crying. But the baby still cries. The chief said to *Speel-yi*:

"You better let the baby go! You will kill him!"

Thus everybody followed, all holding the baby in their arms. But still the baby cried, did not recognize any of them as its father. The chief said to the people:

"Now I do not know what to do about this. We have let everybody hold the baby, and nobody in this house is father of the baby. I think that we better go after *Pedt-jum*. Let him try holding the baby."

Others said to the chief:

"No use sending for *Pedt-jum*. He was not here during the dancing."

But the chief answered:

"Go after *Pedt-jum*! I want all to try!"

So they went after *Pedt-jum*, brought him to the dance-lodge. The baby was still crying; but when *Pedt-jum* stepped through the door-way, it calmed in its crying. *Pedt-jum* walked up to the baby took hold of it, when it stopped crying! It was quiet. The chief said:

"Well! *Pedt-jum* is the father of the baby. My daughter can be the wife of *Pedt-jum*."

The people all round said that they would have to punish the two.[10] *Ghue-ghue* said:

"We will have to leave them here. Let the two starve out alone."

The chief said the same. He gave orders for all the village to pack ready and leave that place. No food must be left. Nothing for *Pedt-jum* and his wife to eat. *Ghue-ghue* said:

"I am going to round up all the *yahmas* [deer] in all the hunting grounds. I will take them away so *Pedt-jum* can get no *yahmas*."

Everybody in that village got ready and moved to another place.[11] There was snow everywhere. After they had been left all alone, *Pedt-jum* and his wife said to themselves:

"Well, I guess we will have to live together."

Then *Pedt-jum* said to his wife:

"Do not feel troubled. We may live to the keeping of our lives some way, just as any one else."

Night came, the first night, and they both entered the one tepee. *Pedt-jum* said to his wife:

"You can stay on one side the fire; I will stay on the other side."

So they stayed through the night in that way. No bedding and hardly any covering. The girl was niece to *Ai-ai* [Magpie] and the aunt had left some food where her tepee had stood. In some way the girl knew that *Ai-ai* had left something there for her, and when the sun came she walked there and looked for it. She found it, found something to eat. A little of all kinds of food. After five suns living together, *Pedt-jum* said to his wife:

"I am going to make a sweat house, and I am going to sweat for five suns and five nights without coming to our tepee. I will take our little son with me, and we will sweat together. You must not come to see us.[12] You must wait till we come back ourselves, after sweating the five suns and five nights."

The wife agreed to mind what her husband told her, and then *Pedt-jum* took their little boy with him and made the sweat house. They went sweating, and when sweating, all the rough face of *Pedt-jum* came off. And every time he entered the sweat, he sweat off something, such as a buffalo robe, buckskin shirt, leggings and dresses. All kinds of fur skins and useful articles to wear. For a fact, he sweat out all of home needs. He sweat off one toenail for a peace pipe.[13] After all these things sweat off from him, he became a young man, and his son became a young man too. When they had gone out that first sun to sweat, the son was a little baby, but on the last day, the woman heard them talking like two grown people.

After the five suns and five nights sweating, *Pedt-jum* and his son came back to their home. *Pedt-jum* found his wife still there. He told his wife where they had been sweating, and for her to go bring everything that was there. She went, and saw all. Saw every kind of thing for their living. She brought them to the tepee. And what little food the *Ai-ai* aunt had left for her, became all that was needed. The next day *Pedt-jum* said to his wife:

"We will now go hunting the *yahmas*. We will find where *Ghue-ghue* has all the *yahmas* hidden away."

The woman fixes lunch and they go find the *yahmas*. They bring all the *yahmas* back close to their tepee home. The other people left no *yahmas*, were soon starving. Then *Ai-ai* came back to see how her niece and *Pedt-jum* were getting along. When she came near the tepee, she saw that they had everything, had plenty to eat. *Ai-ai* saw that *Pedt-jum* and his wife had everything needed. She stopped outside the tepee lodge. The niece saw her aunt, saw *Ai-ai*, and called her inside the tepee. She gave her all that she wanted to eat. She gave her all the food that she could carry, a big pack to take home with her. *Ai-ai* returned to her village that night, for the rest of the people were almost starving. She carried the food to her own hungry family. *Ai-ai* had many children to support, and *Ghue-ghue* could find no more *yahmas*. *Ai-ai* and her children ate at night. They began to grow stronger, while the other people were growing weaker each day.

Finally the chief thought that he would go see *Ai-ai*, and find out where she got her food. At last *Ai-ai* told all about how she was feeding her children. Then the chief sent *Speel-yi* to tell *Pedt-jum*, that they would all come back to live under him, make him the big chief over the village. *Pedt-jum* felt sorry for the people. He told them to come to him and he would give them all that they wanted to eat all the time. *Pedt-jum* told them that he would give them everything that they needed. The people came, and made *Pedt-jum* the big chief. This was how *Pedt-jum* beat *Ghue-ghue*, won from him the girl. This is how he destroyed the power of *Ghue-ghue*, in his holding all the *yahmas* in one place.[14]

Notes by McWhorter

In the lower reaches of "Grouse Canyon," Medicine Valley, Yakama Indian Reservation, there is an ancient flint chipping ground, alleged to be that of *Ghue-ghue*, the Raven. It is located on the main great Indian trail leading from the salmon fisheries at the Tumwater, on the *nChe-wana*. The warriors and hunters came to Raven for their arrow points and spear-heads. A decade ago the ground was thickly strewn with spalls, nuclei, and rejects, showing various stages of manufacture. But little now remains to designate this primitive workshop.

54

The Story of *Whe-amish* or *Chi-nach*
Mrs. Skouken John (Yakima)
July 1917

Just south of the village of White Swan, Yakima Indian Reservation, looms Whe-amish *or* Chi-nach, *the highest desert peak of the* Thap-panish *[Toppenish] mountain range.[1] The center of an interesting group of canyon-formed ridges facing north, it is peculiarly rich in Indian legend. The lofty summit is "vision" talismanic. It was there that* Sul-lil, *or* Suorl-lil, *the medicine man [Yakama holy man and Indian doctor], obtained his power of seeing the sickness within a human body.*

Whe-amish *[the mountain peak] was once a priest and the spiritual leader of the ancients, but being mortal he went astray. The total undoing of himself and his following was in the taking unto himself a new or second wife.* Chi-nach *means "married" more applicable to recent marriage. Overtaken in his wrong-doing* Chi-nach *and his household were transformed into this mountain.[2] The "old man" lies supine, staring into the north. At his left and facing him, reposes the new wife,* Ti-tuch-in's *hips," while on his right, with the papoose intervening, slumbers the old wife, her back turned in anger on her recreant spouse. However, there are different interpretations given this mountain "picture" as will be seen in the course of the legend. In June 1917 while exploring in the neighborhood, my Indian companion gave me this discourse:[3]*

"I DO NOT know this story in full, nor do I know of an Indian who does. The old people who could tell it have passed away. I will give you all that I know of it, and that is not much."[4]

"At that time *Chi-nach* was a leader of the old Indian religion [The Washani Religion], a good man. He taught good things to the people. The entire valley, from this Thappanish range to the Ahtanum ridge, from *Mool-mool* ["bubbling spring" or present site of Fort Simcoe] to the extreme lower reaches of the plain, was one continuous Long House, a big place for worship. Everything seemed good and the people were making progress to a higher life. But *Chi-nach* made a mistake. He took a new wife. The people on this Thappanish side of the valley were rather guilty, for they sided with him. They, as you see, retained their red color, but lost their white paint [they could not use one of the dual colors]. Along the other side of the valley and across the Yakima River, the people retained their white paint but lost their red color. They were opposed to *Chi-nach* taking a new wife."[5]

"At that time, had the old man done right, the people would have been taught a written language.[6] The big canoe wrecked on the Parker Bottom side of the valley was for carrying printed messages, same as mail. All the great Reservation plain was then covered with water, a lake. The people lived on the higher grounds, all around the water. One man was raising waterfowl on Thappanish Lake. All the young Indians were to be instructed and placed on ranches.[7] They were to be given some of the tamed waterfowl. But when *Chi-nach* took a new wife, everything went wrong, everything was quit. The man turned the fowls loose and they are still wild. All the people were changed into mountains and bluffs, some red, some white, just as you now see. *Chi-nach* has the worst color of them all, black. The mail-canoe drifted to the other side of the big lake and turned upside down where it now remains [as] a small hill against the mountain side. Between this canoe-hill and the Yakima River was the dance-ground of the worshippers. It was later used by the Yakimas."

"The school [Office of Indian Affairs School at Fort Simcoe] was to be at *Mool-mool*, where the *Pot-tee-mas* [carved or hammered marks] was located. *Pot-tee-mas* is a boulder which weighs several hundred pounds and has carved inscriptions on it. It is the story of *Chi-nach* and his wives written by themselves. No one now can read this history.[8] The boulder was through some mysterious power transported a considerable distance up the mountain side west of *Mool-mool*. It was moved after the wrecking of the great civilization, by *Chi-nach* taking a new wife."

"The last ferryman on the big lake was Sack. He was the only man who could manage a canoe on the rough waters. He carried people across from one mountain to the other."

After the disappearing of the water many bad and deadly beings [monsters and spirits] were left on the plain. No Indian dared venture there alone. Only large companies could cross the land in safety. Small parties of people were sometimes lost, never heard of again. Deer and antelope gradually invaded the waste and Indians, becoming more bold, crowded in, hunting the game in organized bands.

55

The Wrong of *Whe-amish*
Mrs. Skouken John (Yakima)
July 1917

WHEN THE OLD man, *Whe-amish*, goes to sleep, he lays down on his back with his face looking straight out.[1] He must not turn around, must not turn any way. You see his two wives, one on each side of him. One wife, the one on his left, is a Grizzly Bear. She faces the old man, her husband. The one on his right is his other wife, a Black Bear. She is lying with her back toward the old man and her child, which you can see, is between them. This wife is afraid of the Grizzly Bear wife and she wants her husband to protect her. This is why she has her back to him. *Whe-amish* likes his Black Bear wife, but does not like his Grizzly Bear wife. He cannot turn to Black Bear for fear Grizzly Bear will kill both of them. They lived there all the time but did not obey the law.[2] They must stay there always.

From this old story, some Indians took to the same way two wives. The same law is today, and when a man takes two wives, there is trouble. One watches the other and there is no good time or happiness. Jealousy rules and like the cold winds from the snow land, destroys the spirit of the warm heart. Bad things happen for all in that home. Only one wife is best, is enough for one man.

56

The Dead Canoeman of *nChe-wana*
Sitting Rock (Wasco)
July 1912

IT WAS IN the early times, in the days of the Animal People and near [present day] Lyle.[1] A man and wife were in a canoe on the *nChe-wana*. The man became sleepy. He said to his wife:

"Let me sleep on your lap. Do not be afraid if you [see] anything. Do not believe me dead if you see anything."[2]

The woman let her husband lay across her lap. He went to sleep. He was [appeared] dead. Soon worms began creeping from his shoulders, falling on her lap. Then the woman knew that her husband was dead. She pushed him from her lap. This brought the man from sleep (death). He said:

"Why did you do this? Why did you throw me from your lap?"

The woman made reply:

"You are dead! I was afraid!"

Then the man placed his wife on an eagle feather and threw her to a cave in a smooth cliff along the *nChe-wana*. The woman is still there, turned into stone.[3]

57

The Strong Boy of the Cascades
Che-pos To-cos, Owl Child (Wishom)
October 1923

TOS-CAS WO-HAH [LONG FOOT] was chief of the Cascades.[1] His village was where the Bridge of the Gods stood over the *nChe-wana*. A bad man, he had two hundred wives and he owned a big lodge.[2] Powerful and strong, his feet were half the length of a lodge-pole. Every evening he made smooth the sand all about his lodge, smoothed it down even and level. This so he would know if anybody came near his place during the dark. No tracks could be made there without his seeing them.

When any of his wives brought a baby, the chief would always ask which it was, a boy or girl. If a boy, he killed it. He was afraid the boy would grow up and become stronger than himself. If the baby was a girl, all was well. He let it live.

And the chief kept the sanded ground leveled all the time about his great lodge. Nobody could come without his seeing the tracks.

Ni-ti-it was one of the wives who came from the White Salmon. When her baby first cried, the chief asked her:

"What is the child? Is it a boy or girl?"

Ni-ti-it was afraid, for her baby was a boy. She answered:

"My child is a girl."

Every morning the chief examined the ground on every side his lodge to see if tracks had been made during the night. Two snows passed, *Ni-ti-it* keeping her baby hid all the time. One sun she said to the chief:

"My child wants to see my people. I want to take her to see my father and mother. To see all my people."

The chief was willing, and he said:

"All right! You can take the child to see your people."

Ni-ti-it was glad. She loaded five canoes with gifts and went traveling on the *nChe-wana*. She came to the White Salmon where her father and mother lived. She told them all about every thing, told how she had blinded her husband about her baby. She said:

"I want him to grow up a big boy. Big! Strong and powerful! I want to raise him here. I cannot keep him hid much longer."

Ni-ti-it remained with her parents where she could raise her boy in safety.

The bad chief still kept the sand smoothed and level about his lodge.

The boy grew up. His feet were an arrow's length longer than those of the old man, his father. The boy grew strong! Grew powerful with strength. He practiced his strength each sun. From morning till night he trained to be strong.

Between White Salmon and the Cascades beside the *nChe-wana* is a great rock. Larger than a tepee, it stands apart from the cliff, separated by a chasm. The boy placed this rock there. The boy stepped across the deep space and sat on the top of the rock, which is higher than the rest of the cliff. You can see this big rock. It is standing there to this day.

The boy was now big and strong. He went to the bad chief's lodge while it was dark, went inside the doorway. Then he returned to his mother's lodge at White Salmon. Daylight came. The old man going out saw great moccasin tracks in the leveled sand. Saw where they had entered his doorway, saw where they led away again. He measured the foot-marks there in the sand. Eh! They are longer than his own! The chief studied hard:

"Who has a longer foot than my own? *Ni-ti-it* lied to me that the baby was a girl."

The chief sent three best of his men to bring the boy. Sent three strong, powerful men! They went! When they got to the camp, two stayed in the canoe. The other one went to *Ni-ti-it*'s lodge. He entered the doorway and said to the young man:

"We want you! Come with us!"

The young man replied:

"No! I will not go with you."

The man went back to the canoe and told the two men:

"He will not come. We must go up and get him!"

The three strong men now go to the lodge. They say:
"We want you!"
The Boy is not scared! He is not afraid! He makes reply:
"No! I will not go with you!"
The three strong men take hold of the boy. They cannot handle him! He squeezes their arms in his hands and crushes the bones. He is powerful! Is stronger than all three of them. They leave him and return home. They say to the chief:
"We cannot handle him! He squeezed our bones and broke them."
The bad chief heard this, and said to his people:
"There will be war! Get ready to fight."
The chief and his warriors went in a hundred canoes. They had a big fight! The boy, alone, whipped them all. He crushed his father's bones with his hands. The chief and his warriors returned home to the Cascades.
The next sun the boy started for his father's place. He arrived there and called:
"Come out from your lodge, oh, Chief, and fight! It is your son who calls you!"
The chief is scared! He will not come out from his lodge. The boy enters the doorway, goes up close to his father. He takes hold of him, handles him easily. Handles him like a cradled papoose. When he gets him outside the doorway, he speaks:
"You will be chief no more! I am one chief! If you do not say you will not be chief, I know what I will do with you. I am going to be chief myself."
The old man asked the boy:
"What will you do with me?"
The boy made answer:
"I will not tell you! I know, only myself."
The old man then agreed:
"All right! I will give up! You can be chief! Do you take all my lodges?"
The boy answered him:
"No! Leave them here where they are."
Thus was the power of the bad chief of the Cascades broken. It was killed by the son whose life was saved in the lie told by his own mother. That lie was good.[3]

58

The Two Sisters and Their Star Husbands
William Poniah (Chehalis-Yakima)
December 1917

THERE WAS A tribe of Indians where lived two young sisters. The oldest was *Tah-pah-louh*. The younger was *Yas-lumas*.[1] Their mother told them to go dig *chah-kum* [an edible root]. The mother said:

"Go dig all day and stop there for the night."

The girls went digging all day and stopped there for the night. When they lay down to sleep, they looked up at the sky. The oldest sister said:

"I see two stars! They are not far apart. The smallest and red star, I wish would be your husband. The big bright star, I wish would be my husband."[2]

The two stars heard what the girl said, and when the sisters slept, unconscious, they came down and took them up to their own country. After they were brought up there, the younger sister began to wake up. But she could not open her eyes very well. There was something like wax in her eyes. When she woke up, she knew that she and her sister were in a strange place. She found that she was sleeping by the side of a man. She then lay down again and went to sleep. She said nothing, made no noise of any kind. When it came daylight, the man got up and built a fire. When the sisters got up, they looked all around. They did not know where they were. They were in a strange country. They thought about it, studied about their condition. The men knew their thoughts and said to them:

"It was your own wish! You wanted us!"

The man said to the oldest sister, said to *Tah-pah-louh*:
"You wished for him to be your husband! That is the reason we went down and brought you up here. Do not worry about anything any more. By your own wish, your own will, you became our wives. So do not worry! Here are things to cook with. Here is food to cook. Do not worry any more."

The girls then went ahead and cooked food. They had the same kind of roots as grow down here. When they were through eating, the men said:

"In a certain place you will find roots. Go dig them!"

The women went digging roots all day. The men went hunting. When evening came, the women returned home with lots of roots. The men brought in birds. The hunters had bows and arrows.

Down below the mother missed her daughters. She hunted for them but could not find them. She searched long. She had a great lamentation for her lost daughters.

The girls stayed all summer and all winter with their star husbands, and *Tah-pah-louh* had a boy baby. The women went digging every day and brought in lots of roots. The husband of *Yas-lumas*, was an old man. That was why her eyes were fast shut in the morning. She caught illness of the eye from her husband. The men said to the women:

"When you find a long root, do not dig it up. Break it off!"

The men told them this five times. *Tah-pah-louh* said to her sister:

"How is this? The men say do not dig the long roots all out."

Then the women laid plans to dig the long roots entirely out. They said:

"We might as well dig them all out."

Tah-pah-louh found a long root and said:

"I am going to follow it and dig it all out."

Tah-pah-louh followed the root and did not break it. When digging, she struck hard and pried with her digger. It went through the earth, and when she pulled it out, she felt a wind. A big wind came up through the hole made by the digger. *Tah-pah-louh* looked through with one eye and saw her own country.[3] The men were standing near and she shut the hole quickly. The men asked:

"What is wrong?"

Tah-pah-louh answered:

"Nothing! There is nothing wrong!"

The men were suspicious! They said:

"Where did the wind come from? We have no wind up here!"

The woman answered:

"I do not know! The wind just passed us here! I do not know where it is from."

When *Tah-pah-louh* said this, the men were satisfied and went away.[4] *Tah-pah-louh* stayed there digging roots. She said to her sister *Yas-lumas*:

"I know where the men brought us from! I know how we can get down from here, how we can get back to our own home again. We can gather bark from the hazel-nut brush all around here. I can braid it into a rope."

Then the women went home. The oldest said to her sister:

"We will start tomorrow doing that! We will start making the rope."[5]

The men came home, bringing birds and other game. The women cooked roots. They ate and slept. Morning came, and after they had eaten, the women went out and began braiding the bark rope. They peeled bark from the hazel-nut brush, *Tah-pah-louh* braiding the rope. With their power—thought—they made it to reach the earth.[6] Afternoon, they went digging roots. They worked fast and took the roots home. But there was not so many roots as before. Five times they did this. Five suns they worked in this way. The men said:

"How is this? You do not bring many roots! You used to bring lots of roots home."

Tah-pah-louh said to them:

"We are nearly done! We do not find many roots now."

This was how the women were delayed in digging roots. They were making the rope by which to escape.[7] They kept the rope hid all the time where the men could not find it. There was a big pile of that rope. Finally the women said:

"We are going to try this rope now."

Tah-pah-louh opened the hole and said:

"The wind does not come through any more."[8]

They tried the rope, let it go down. The oldest woman said:

"When the end of the rope hits bottom, when it hits the earth, its top will tip over."

But they could not make it tip over.[9] They could not reach the earth. They started making more rope. *Tah-pah-louh* said:

"When we reach bottom, when we reach land, we will be through. We will have rope enough."

Finally the rope touched bottom and tipped over. They knew that their work was done. It was now evening. *Tah-pah-louh* said to her sister *Yas-lumas*:

"After we eat in the morning, we will start down the rope. We will dig no more roots."

When they got there next morning, when they came to the hole, the oldest sister spoke to *Yas-lumas*:

"I will let you down first. When you reach the earth, jerk the rope so I will know that you are on the land. I will then let the child down after you, and when he reaches you, you take him."

This they did. *Yas-lumas* went down the rope first. When she felt the rope jerk, *Tah-pah-louh* sent down her baby. The baby was just old enough to crawl around. After sending down the child, the mother started down.[10] She plugged the hole so the men could not know where they had gone. When she reached earth, she found that they were where they had [dug] roots and camped when the stars came and carried them away.[11] The women hurried home. When they reached home, their mother was gone. She had died. The grandmother was still living, but she was blind. The grandmother was glad when she learned that her granddaughters had returned to earth and that they had brought the baby with them. From all parts of the country the people came to see the returned sisters. They had a big time! It was a big time that the people had. They swung on the hazel-bark rope. That rope remained there quite a while, hanging down from the sky.[12]

One woman who lived where the earth ends at the ocean found out about the women and the child. She was across the ocean but heard of the child. She studied out a plan and said:

"I better go over there. Somehow and some way I will go steal that baby."

That woman started on the journey to steal the baby. She traveled, and finally reached where the people were having the big time. She did not go where they were swinging on the rope. She went to the village camp, to the tepee where the blind grandmother was taking care of the baby. At the doorway she heard the grandmother trying to stop the baby from bad crying. She entered the tepee! The old woman was trying to get the baby to sleep. The grandmother was singing to it. The woman stole the baby and put fox-fire wood on the cradle-board. The blind grandmother did not know. She could not see.

The thief-woman started away, hurrying with the stolen baby. When she did this, the swing broke loose where the people were having the big time.[13] When the rope broke down, the mother knew that her child had been stolen. She ran to the tepee and heard what the old grandmother was saying. She saw that the old woman was singing, trying to make sleepy the rotten wood. *Tah-pah-louh* cried:

"Grandmother! The baby has been stolen!"

Tah-pah-louh ran back and called to the people:

"The baby is gone! The baby has been stolen!"

The mother felt badly and grieved for her baby. She thought:

"Somehow I may find that child again."

Tah-pah-louh then took the baby's *hopt-teen* [swatling] and wrung a few drops of urine from it. Out of this water she made some kind of a baby. She now had this new baby.[14]

All the people scattered, hunting for the lost baby. When they came back, they reported:

"Child not found! We have not found the baby!"

This was repeated. They again went out hunting but could not find the stolen baby. It was gone! Another would go looking, then come back and say:

"The child cannot be found."

Qash-qyah [Blue Jay] now said:

"I will try hunting for my grandchild."[15]

So *Qash-qyah* started hunting for the child. He hurried on the trail of the thief-woman. When he came to the [far] edge of the sea, where the sky opposes the sea, *Qash-qyah* studied and laid a plan. When the sky moved up and down opposing the sea when it opened, *Qash-qyah* darted from the opening. He went through, but the sky coming down nearly caught him. The sky rubbed his head. That is how Blue Jay got his top knot. It ruffled his feathers.

Qash-qyah crossed the sea, landed over the big waters. He knew the place where the child was. He found the stolen child who was sitting with his own baby. Had his own baby on the cradle board before him. He was now a young man. He was making something. It may have been arrow heads that he was making. *Qash-qyah* came near him and began making his loud noise. The man chipping his flints caught up a handful of the chips from the ground and threw them at *Qash-qyah* and said:

"Shut up! I am lost! I am feeling bad."

Qash-qyah said:

"Well my grandchild! I am looking for you and you threw dirt in my eyes."

Then the man caught *Qash-qyah*, opened his eyes and took the flint chips and dirt out of his eyes. He said:

"You are my grandmother."

Qash-qyah told the young man how he could go, how he might pass that place where the sky opposes the sea. But the man was in trouble. When the woman, his wife, went out to dig roots she left the baby right in front of him. If he stirred the baby would cry and she would know that something was wrong. The young man studied about this, studied all night. He thought it out that night. This red paint! He tied a small piece of it in buckskin. This he fastened to the bow on the cradleboard, close to the ear of the baby. He said to the paint:

"When the baby cries, say to him: 'My little son, do not cry!'"

He did that way. He tried it, and when he left it the baby began to cry. The paint said:

"My son! my son! keep quiet!"

The baby was quiet and the man thought:

"That is all right now. I got this lesson for him. I leave it for him."

The young man now took up his arrows and other things and put them in a pack. He got in his boat. He remembered all that *Qash-qyah* had told him about how to get away. He started and rowed his canoe as fast as he could. He came to where the sky was opposing the sea. When he arrived there, he watched! Watched it very closely. When the sky raised, he rowed his canoe fast. He passed. He was not caught by the sky as it came down.

We do not know how long it took him, but he at last reached this land. As he journeyed, he came to a place where there was a great monster [called] *Ah-yah-hos* [giant]. The young man paused before the *Ah-yah-hos* and said to him:

"You are not going to be this way. You are not to devour the people, but of course you are a monster."[16]

He continued on and came to another giant. The young man was the son of *Has-lo* [star], and he gave this *Ah-yah-hos* the same kind of talk. He said:

"You are not to be this way. You are not to devour the people, but of course, you are a giant."

The young man came to a river. He saw across that river a monster and he called to him:

"How did you cross over?"

The monster repeated his words:

"How did you cross over?"

The monster repeated every time what ever was said. He made no direct answer. The young man could not wade across, so he took off his clothing, put it on his head and swam across. When he reached the mon-ster, he asked him several questions. But the monster only repeated his words. So he killed him.

The man went on and came to another place, a village of the *Ah-yah-hos*. When he got there, the *Ah-yah-hos* tied him up. Tied him with thongs all over, up and down his limbs and body. But he held a small sharp flint in his right hand, close to his ear. Then he began cutting the thongs from his body, from his neck all down his body. He said to the *Ah-yah-hos*:

"You are not going to be this way. You are not to devour the people. You will be only a *met-klai*, a stomach worm [tape worm]."

Then he went on. He passed other *Ah-yah-hos* and killed them. To others he gave a discourse only. When he had passed all the way through; when he had followed the instructions of his grandmother, the *Qash-qyah*, he arrived at his mother's place. When he got there he found his brother whom his mother had formed from the wet of the *hopt-teen*. He told his younger brother:

"One of us must travel in the day time and the other in the night time."

He said to his brother:

"I will travel in the day time and you can travel in the night time."

Then the oldest brother started and traveled in the day time. But it got too hot and nearly roasted everything. That was him, the sun. Water got hot and nearly boiled. Then he said to his young brother:

"This is not good. You travel in the day time and I will travel in the night time."

So the younger brother traveled in the day time and it was only medi-um hot and about right. He is now the *Amm* [Sun]. The oldest brother travels in the night time. We call him *Al-lih* [moon]. *Al-hai-oh*, that son of a star and *Tah-pal-louh* is the moon. The sun is out of the *hopt-teen*. The sun and moon are brothers.

The broken rope where the two sisters escaped with the baby is still there. You can see it, a pile of white rocks at *Snoqualma* [Snoqualmie].

From the older sister and the star sprang the race of Chief *Weowikt* [Weowicht], the first root of the Yakimas. *Owhi*, the War Chief, and *Qualchen* [Qualchin], his son, were of this race.[17]

And the baby left by its father in the far away land where Blue Jay found them, grew up and married. His children are the white people. This is why the white people know how to steal. Their grandmother knew how to steal. She stole the baby of *Tah-pal-louh*, the golden boy from the bright star, the shining *Has-lo*. I have told you all the story.

Notes by McWhorter

A Klickitat version of the foregoing legend has it that the two sisters wished for the star-husbands five successive nights. The brighter of the stars proved to be the younger man who was accorded to the older girl in the wishing by her sister. The child was stolen by five Frog-People, sisters, who lived beyond the sea. (The Yakimas speak of these people—these women—as giants.) It took Blue Jay five days and five nights to go where the child was hidden by the Frog-Women. He got his blue color from coming in contact with the sky, where the sky and the earth comes together, where the earth moves up and down, as it appears on the horizon when gazing out over the ocean.

The flint-chips cast into the eyes of Blue Jay by the arrowhead maker caused the specks which are seen about the eyes of this bird to the present day. Blue Jay instructed the flint-chipper, who was a great hunter, to:

"Kill five deer and take the fat from around the kidneys. Cook it. Make it into five lunches. It will take five days to return, and I must fly, carrying you. When I become weak, you will place one of the lunches in my mouth. This will give me strength. I will grow stronger each time for the flying."

They started on their long journey, Blue Jay flying, carrying the boy. Once every day when Blue Jay grew weak, the young man would place one of the fat lunches in his mouth, renewing his waning endurance. On the fifth day, land was sighted, but Blue Jay was growing very weak. The boy placed the last lunch in the mouth of his benefactor, which strengthened him for a while. But Blue Jay was now extremely tired and in danger of dropping into the sea. Dipping lower and lower, Blue Jay at last reached land at the mouth of the *nChe-wana*, where he sank exhausted just at the ocean's edge. The boy hunted game and fed Blue Jay back to his full strength again.

After caring for Blue Jay, the young man came up the *nChe-wana*, killing monsters as he journeyed. He ended his work by slaying the mighty *Wun-un-pus-ye yuka*, the chief of all beavers. This legend has been fully set forth in The *Qui-yiah*, Five Brothers, but there are a few interesting variances in the version wherein the son of *Tah-pal-louh* and the star figures as the hero. Aside from a slight diversity in the pronunciation of the beaver chief's name, it may be noted that the monster beaver died in the *nChe-wana*, near Pendleton, Oregon.

The variety of bulrushes which were grasped by the hero in an attempt to save himself grow only in the Satus River country, where the course of the great beaver was stayed to such extent that the swaying back and forth of his body in the flood caused the crooked snake-like channel of the Yakima at this point. This last stream was at the time entirely created, its channel torn through the land by the mighty combatants.

All parts of the body were used in the creation of the tribes. The boy forgot the Sioux, and blood only remaining, he created them from the blood, throwing it far towards the sunrise. Thus the Sioux are a fierce and sanguinary people, always having their faces painted "red like blood," ready for war.

59

Spirit Costume of the *Ste-ye-hah mah*
Simon Goudy (Yakima-Klickitat)
1918

THERE WAS AMONG the Yakimas a young man poverty stricken and useless to his tribe.[1] Parents and all relations dead, he had no home. He traveled from place to place subsisting on the generosity of friends. If he ate out at one lodge, there were others where he might go. It is the Indian custom to turn none away without first supplying their physical wants. The young man was the Wanderer among the tribes.

The Wanderer came up the Yakima River to *Pah-qy-ti-koot* [four miles above Toppenish, Washington, on the Yakima Reservation].[2] There he saw five Indians disputing and contending among themselves. They were *Ste-ye-hah mah*, the Stick-showers. The Wanderer inquired the cause of their trouble, and one of them said:

"You see these clothes, these buckskins. We found them here. We cannot agree how to divide them. This man wants the coat, the shirt. This other man wants the leggings. This man here wants the moccasin while I want the head-dress. That man over there wants the entire suit. We cannot agree."

The Wanderer thought for a moment. He knew that the *Ste-ye-hah mah* were great runners. They were swifter than any other Indians. He said:

"Let me decide this for you! I will help you out."

The *Ste-ye-hah mah* replied:

"All right! We will let you manage it for us. You settle it for us."

The Wanderer rejoined:

"Yes! I will do this for you. All of you go down to *Ow-yah!* [Parker, Washington, on the Yakima Reservation]. Go to the big grease wood! Line up there for the race! The one who reaches here and puts his hand on the buckskins first, gets them. He will have the entire suit."

The *Ste-ye-hah mah* agreed:

"That is good! We will do as you say. You are wiser than we."

The five *Ste-ye-hah mah* then ran down to the big bush and were instantly coming like the wind. All touched the buckskins at the same time. The young man said:

"You will have to go farther in this race. Go down to the trail crossing. Run from there."

The *Ste-ye-hah mah* hurried to the starting place. It was out of sight, down the plain. They reach there! Now they are coming back! The young man watches the dust! The racers burst into view! They come like the deer! Five hands touch the buckskins at the same time. The young man laughs. He has never seen such running among the tribes. He said:

"You must go farther away. Go to *Luts-an-nee* [Red Willow]. Run from there."

The *Ste-ye-hah mah* are tireless. You cannot tire them. They race to *Luts-an-nee*. There is the returning dust cloud! They are coming fast! Fast as the hawk can fly. All five again touch the buckskins at the same time. The Wanderer laughs. He is surprised, but he laughs. He said:

"Go this time to *Cee-cee!* [Toppenish, Washington, Yakama Reservation]. Run from there! This business must be decided."

It is not long till the *Ste-ye-hah mah* are at *Cee-cee*, where the sand is not firm under the foot. Soon the swirling dust cloud is seen! The *Ste-ye-hah mah* are coming in a bunch! Five reaching hands touch the buckskins at the same time. The Wanderer is serious this time. He speaks:

"You have raced four times. None of you have won the buckskins. The fifth time must decide who is to have them. Go to *Pal-lah-^{h}lee!* [junction of the Satus and Yakima rivers]. Run from there."

The *Ste-ye-hah mah* are not tired. They hurry down across the desert to *Pal-lah-^{h}lee*. The Wanderer thinks:

"I will look at these buckskins. They appear good."

The young man examined the buckskins. He found them fine and showy. He thought:

"The *Ste-ye-hah mah* will not be back soon. My own garb is poor. It is about worn out. I will see if these will fit me."

He tried the buckskins, leaving his own on the spot where they had been lying. They fit him nicely. He thought:

"I think that I would like to have these buckskins. I wish that I could get away with them. But no! The *Ste-ye-hah mah* can run faster than any Indians of all the tribes. They are good trailers. Nothing can hide from them. They would catch me sure. I had better let them alone. I had better replace the buckskins, better not have anything to do with them. The *Ste-ye-hah mah* want these buckskins badly. Otherwise they would not race for them as they do."

While thus debating, the Wanderer saw the approaching dust-cloud. It was far down the desert but was coming fast. The five runners were as eagles flying. The young man had decided too late. He could not change the buckskins. Instantly in view, the *Ste-ye-hah mah* would be upon him would catch him. Scared! He stood aside from his discarded garb. There was no use trying to run away! No use hiding! The five *Ste-ye-hah mah* all touched the old buckskins at the same time. Then they saw what had been done. They began to accuse each other for the loss. They said:

"You did this! You wanted all the buckskins! All the dress! Now this Indian has stolen all of them! We will get nothing!"

"No! You caused it! You wanted the shirt!"

"No! It was you! You wanted the leggings!"

"Had you not contended for the head dress, we would now have the entire suit. It is your fault that all are lost."

"Why do you say that? It was you who wanted the moccasins! You would have the moccasins and now every thing is gone."

During this trouble, the Wanderer stood only a few steps away. None of the *Ste-ye-hah mah* seemed to notice him, did not look at him. He wondered why this was, why they did not attack him and take the buckskins. But no! They began to fight among themselves. The young man knew that they would fight till all were dead, killed at the same time. He decided quickly what he would do. He would get away with the suit! It was fine! He began to think what an impression he would make at the village with such buckskins.

So while the *Ste-ye-hah mah* were fighting to the death, fighting so equally matched that all would die at the same time, the Wanderer left. He went through *Pah-qy-ti-koot*, traveling north. He reached the village at the mouth of the Naches. A great tribal festival was in progress. He was soon surprised, disappointed that none of his friends paid any attention to him. His fine costume counted for nothing. He was hungry. He went from group to group where they were eating. He stood close to his best friend, stood in front of them. None noticed him. No one would look at him; no one would speak to him. A woman carrying food would have walked over him had he not stepped aside. He began to think, to wonder what was wrong. Maybe his friends did not want him. He went to different lodges. It was the same everywhere. Nobody noticed him. Then he remembered that the *Ste-ye-hah mah* had done the same way, had not noticed him. It might be the buckskins he was wearing? He would test it out.

Procuring some old buckskins, he went to the river. There under the bank he changed his costume. He hid his new buckskins and went back to the village. Immediately some of his friends called to him:

"Come and eat! You have been gone! For a long time we do not see you. Tell us what you know! What you have seen! What you have heard."

Yes! It must be the buckskins. Some great power in them. He sat down to the feast. He talked of his travels among the different tribes. He went to another group of feasters. As he approached, they called:

"You here? When did you come? We are glad! Come eat!"

It was so everywhere he went. He now understood that it was his *Ste-ye-hah mah* costume. That was the mystery. The buckskins must be a spirit suit, invisible. But he held his secret from his friends, from all the people.

The chief of the Yakimas had a daughter, a fine looking girl. All the young men wanted her for a wife. She was nice, good to look at. Her father, the chief, was proud, rich and haughty. He would not allow the suitors in general. The young man who would wed his daughter must first prove his ability to provide for her as the first woman of her tribe. He must show his strength and agility as a hunter, as a warrior. His prowess to protect her in danger. The daughter must marry, but marry well.

The chief had a high platform built in front of the Long, or Councillodge. Four posts were planted in the ground, the tops inclining inward. On these, a platform of sticks was laid. This platform was reached by a ladder made of cross poles tied to two of the posts. On the side facing this ladder, was a long level strip of ground, cleared of brush and stone. This track extended considerable distance to a mound, or natural elevation, where there was some brush. When all was ready, the daughter was placed on the platform in sight of all the lodges. A crier went the rounds of the village with this message:

"Young men! Hunters and warriors! Listen to the words of our chief! His daughter is now of the age to marry. She knows how to tan skins, how to make them into robes and clothing. She knows how to cook the *yahmas* and the *camas*. She knows how to prepare the different roots, how to cure the salmon for winter food. She will make a good wife, knowing how to care for the lodge and her husband's moccasins. But he who would marry this maiden must first prove his strength and courage. He must show his ability, his power to provide the game, the skins. He must be able to protect her from harm. Listen! To the young man who can run and leap over the girl seated on the platform, who can take from her hand the *sunny-kol-wash* [a tool used in working buckskin] in passing, will be given her for his wife. Listen! The chief will also bestow on the husband half of his wealth, half of his power as chief. The offer is to all, to all the tribes. Let runners be sent to the different tribes that they may come to the feast, take part in the sport. Let their young men enter in contest against our young men. In five days after all are gathered, the feasting, the contest will begin. Let the young men prepare their bodies, their minds for the great game. Let them make body and mind clean by fasting and sweat. I have spoken the message of our chief."

The village was all excitement. Swift runners were dispatched to the different tribes. It would take the Spokanes many suns to travel to the land of the Yakimas. The same could be said of the Umatillas and the *nChe-wana* tribes. All would come. The fame of the Yakima chief, the beauty of his daughter, was widely known. The feasting, the games and sports would last more than a moon. The young men of the village began to make ready for the contest. The body and mind must be made clean, made strong by fasting and sweating.

The chief selected a cook [male] to prepare the game food for the great feast. The young man who had the Spirit Costume joined the cook. He would help with the food. There he would find plenty to eat. The cook took him in. He helped with the cooking. He was content.

In the meantime, many of the young men attempted to leap the platform where each day the girl was seated. None could do it. They landed against the ladder-side and would fall to the ground. The people watched the sport and laughed. To leap that platform was impossible, beyond human ability. The chief had been cunning, had been wise.

One sun the Wanderer found near the village a great yellow dog. It was gaunt and weak from starvation. Wanderer hid the dog in the brush. He carried its food, stolen from the cook-lodge. Every sun he fed the dog, watching it grow in strength. He began to teach the dog to jump, to spring into the air. He taught it to spring higher and higher. He trained it to bear him on its back, to run, to leap over a high pole or other obstruction. In time it could leap very high, higher than the girl on the platform. The dog could do this with Wanderer on his back. This was good! The young man had a scheme! He said to the cook:

"I know how to win the girl! I can do it! I will win her! I will give her to you for a wife."

The cook was scared! He said:

"H-h-hu-sh! Do not let any one hear you say that! The chief will kill you if he hears you say that. The Chief is higher than we. His daughter must marry a great warrior, a good hunter. You cannot leap the platform. Do not speak of it again. It will make us trouble."

The suns went by. The feasting, the trial of leaping the platform continued. Many young warriors, many hunters had tried, but all failed. They only drew the laughter of their companions, the fun-making of the people. One sun the cook said to his helper:

"I am going to see the sport. The young Spokane warrior is to try the leap. I will see the fun, will see him fail."

The Wanderer said:

"I will be there. I will win the girl. I will give her to you. I do not want a wife."

The cook looked around. He said:

"H-h-hu-sh! Do not say such things! The chief will kill you if he hears your words."

The people all assembled to watch the Spokane's trial at leaping. He ran the length of the race path. He leaped higher than any of the other young men. But he struck the ladder, falling to the ground. He met with a big laugh from the crowd, a big fun-making laugh. Ashamed, the Spokane warrior left the space [place]. The people still laughed at him.

Eh! Every one is still. A great yellow dog is coming over the top of the mound. He is at the head of the track. All look! That dog is tall! Is slim! A fast runner! He comes down the track in a lope. He comes near the base of the scaffold. He leaps! Clearing the platform, passing over the girl's head. In the passing, a strange thing happened. The *sunny-kol-wash* disappeared from the girl's hand. The dog continued loping, fading in the thick brush near the river.

By the words of the chief, the girl had been won by the dog. She must become the wife of that dog. The chief questioned his daughter, how she had lost the *sunny-kol-wash*. She knew nothing. They had been snatched from her as the dog went over her head. She had seen no one, seen nothing but the dog.

The chief was scared! Was angry! He did not want his daughter to go to the dog. He was going to make a test of the mystery. That evening he announced that his daughter would sit on the platform the next sun, holding his own ring. It would be seen if the dog or evil spirit would come again, if he would meet this second trail.

The next sun the girl mounted the platform with her father's ring. The people line up in silence. Soon the same big dog appears over the top of the mound. That dog comes down the run-way in long, easy lopes. He makes no noise, does not bark. That dog leaps over the girl's head. The ring disappears as did the *sunny-kol-wash*. That dog lopes on towards the river, pursued by the people. They cannot find him. He is lost in the brush as on the day before. That dog is to be the girl's husband. The words of a chief must not be broken. But the father was not satisfied. He said:

"Tomorrow we will see about this strange business!"

The next day the chief called all the people together. He questioned each separately. He asked if anyone owned such dog as had been seen, if they knew of such dog. No one knew. Then the cook was called. He thought:

"Nothing will be lost if Wanderer loses his life, if he is killed. I will tell what I know about him feeding a dog. I will tell what he said to me about winning the girl."

The cook told all. Then the chief called the Wanderer. The young man said:

"The cook has talked with a straight tongue. I rode the yellow dog in the contest for the girl."

The chief said:

"Have you the *sunny-kol-wash*?"

Wanderer produced the *sunny-kol-wash*.

"Have you the ring?"

Wanderer produced the ring. The people saw them. They were the same that the girl had held in her hands, the same ones. The chief asked:

"Why were you not seen?"

Wanderer answered:

"The Spirit Costume! You cannot see me when I have it on."

The chief did not know. He asked:

"Where did you get it?"

Wanderer made reply:

"The *Ste-ye-hah mah*. Five of them fought. All were killed."

The chief again spoke:

"Where is the costume? Where is the dog?"

Wanderer answered:

"The brush at the river is thick. They are there."

The chief told him to go bring them. Wanderer went, followed by many of the people. He brought from the brush the buckskins, brought the big dog. All returned to the village. The Chief said:

"This young man must now prove his power, prove his words. If he cannot do so, he shall die by the arrow."

Then he said to Wanderer:

"Climb to the platform. Strip off your buckskins. Strip naked, then put on the Spirit Costume as I tell you."

Wanderer was soon on the platform. He stood naked, where all could see him. The chief commanded:

"Put on the Spirit Moccasins."

The young man did so. His feet disappeared. "Eh!" said the people. The chief spoke:

"Put on the leggings."

The young man did so. His legs disappeared. "Eh!" said the people. The chief ordered:

"Put on the shirt."

The young man did so. His body disappeared. "Eh!" said the people. There was one other piece of the costume. The chief said:

"Put on the head dress."

The young man did so. His head disappeared. "Eh!" said the people. The chief called to him:

"Are you there?"

The young man gave answer:

"Yes! I am alive! I am here!"

Then the chief told him to remove the costume. To begin with the head dress, then the shirt, the leggings. The moccasins would be last.

Wanderer removed the head dress. His head came to view.

He removed his shirt. His body was seen.

He removed the leggings. His legs were there.

He removed the moccasins. His feet were there. Wanderer stood, seen by all people. The Spirit Costume was no lie. Tears came to the chief's eyes. He had been beaten by the worthless young man, beaten by Wanderer. The girl thought:

"It is all right. I will be his wife. He is strong, is good looking. He has the Spirit Costume. He will get half of my father's property. He will be equal in power as chief."

The chief spoke to Wanderer:

"It shall be as I said. My daughter will be your wife. Half of all that I have is yours. Half of my power as chief is yours."

Wanderer spoke from where he stood on the platform:

"Tomorrow we will have a big feast. I will give the feast. After we eat, I will tell you my mind, what I will do."

The next day the people had the feast, a big feast. Then the young chief spoke:

"I will now show you my mind. You know me. I have no parents, no brothers, no sisters. I am nobody. I go from village to village, from tribe to tribe. I want no power. I do not want to be chief. I want to be free to go, free to do my work. You see this man here, this cook? He is a good young man, has good sense. There is nothing bad about him. I give him the girl for a wife. I give him all that the chief has given me. He will take my place as the new chief. You have heard my words."

So the cook got the girl and all the property that went with her. Then her father gave his son-in-law the balance of his wealth. He could not let the worthless young man outdo him in gifts. The old chief was now without anything, poor, without power. He lived with his daughter and her husband. He had fallen to the level of the poorest of his tribe, while the poor cook had risen to the highest chieftaincy of the Yakimas.[3]

Wanderer, with his dog and Spirit Costume, now started to visit the Spokanes. Reaching the *nChe-wana*, he had no way of crossing. He found a nugget of gold on the shore. He picked it up. It spoke to him:

"Keep me! I will be your wife. When you want anything, when you are in trouble, shake me. I will change into a woman, your wife. I will always help you."

Wanderer shook the gold. All at once it became a beautiful young woman, standing by his side. She showed him a canoe. He crossed the *nChe-wana* in the canoe. The young woman changed back into a gold nugget, which he placed in the bag at his belt. He went on. In time he arrived among the Spokanes, at the Spokane Falls. He stopped there. He saw a large canoe fastened to the bank of the river. On the island was a lodge with five partitions, five rooms. The lodge, like the canoe, was fastened, locked. All the doors in the five partitions were fastened tight. The canoe and all the doors could be unfastened only with some implement, something like a key. The chief of the Spokanes was rich, was powerful. In the last of the rooms was his own ring. To the man who could unfasten the canoe, cross to the Island, pass through the five doors and bring out the ring, he would give his daughter as a wife. He would also give with the girl, half his wealth, half his power as chief. None had been able to do it. Many young warriors from the different tribes had come and tried. The girl was good looking, was industrious.

Wanderer stood on the banks of the Spokane, clothed in his Spirit Costume. He was going to win the daughter of the Spokane chief. He took the gold nugget from his belt-pouch. He shook the nugget. A young woman stood at his side. She gave him the instrument for unfastening the canoe. He crossed the island. There his *tahmahnawis* [spirit or medicine] wife gave him the implement with which to unfasten the five doors of the lodge. He secured the ring. He refastened the doors, returning to the other side of the river. He secured the canoe as he had found it. Removing his Spirit Costume, he took the ring to the chief, claiming his daughter, claiming half his wealth, half his power as chief. The chief did not believe him, did not believe that he had rode in the canoe, that he had unfastened the five doors. He asked Wanderer how he had done it. Wanderer answered:

"I am from the *Yah-ha-kimas*. It was I who leaped the platform where the chief's girl sat, leaped it after all your young men had failed. I have the Spirit Costume. You see here my big dog. I also have a gold wife to helps me in all my troubles."

The chief said:

"Let me see this gold wife."

Wanderer shook the nugget. A fine looking girl stood at his side. She dazzled the eyes of the chief. He could not look at her. He covered his eyes, turned his head away. He was beaten. He gave Wanderer his daughter, half his wealth, half of his power as chief. Wanderer in turn gave all to a poor, but honest young man. Then the chief gave to his new son-in-law, all of his remaining wealth. The Yakima must not outdo him in gifts. Thus the big Spokane chief lost all of his power. He was a poor man. He now lived with in son-in-law and daughter.[4]

Wanderer went on to other tribes. He continued tearing down the class-power of the big chiefs.[5] He continued creating chiefs from the lower ranks, from the honest poor. He broke up the bad class-chieftaincy. After that any one could be chief who was capable, who was honest, who was brave.[6]

Notes by McWhorter

Some storytellers say that this legend is given as occurring in the Kittitas country. This is not unusual. Often the same story is fitted to conform with the immediate surroundings of the different tribes. This is especially true of the creation legends. *Ow-yah* is located at present day Parker on the Yakima Indian Reservation. No particular meaning to the name has yet been discovered. It may be derived from *wow-yah* (whipping), such as chastising a child.

Luts-an-nee is the name of the red barked bush of the willow family, found along the sloughs and water courses. Its berries, an acrid, grayish cluster-fruit, is used as food. It is more in favor with the older people. *Cee-cee* means "sand that breaks under the foot." It is the name of the country where Toppenish now stands, about four miles below *Pah-qy-ti-koot*, Yakima Indian Reservation. *Pal-lah-*^{h}*lee* is a place name where the Satus River empties into the Yakima River, about thirty miles below *Pah-qy-ti-koot*. *Sunny-kol-wash* means "cutting with two knives." The primitive [*sic*] Indians manufactured crude scissors from two ribs of the buffalo or moose, a two handed implement used by the women in tailoring buckskins [today the term primitive is derogatory to Native Americans, but McWhorter means Indians living prior to white contact, living without manufactured tools].

In the Feast of The New Food, the game-food is all prepared by men. No woman is supposed to take any part in it. Her care is the roots and the herbs which she has brought in from the hills as her contribution to the yearly tribal invocatory thanksgiving. An aged woman is the authority for the legend that two strange children, brother and sister, appeared on the Island at Spokane Falls, which figures in the text. From these children sprang the Spokanes. According to the Pon de Relle legend, Spokane signifies "children of the sun" or "sun children."

60

How *Its-i-yi-i* Lost Immortality to the Tribes
Hemene Moxmox, Yellow Wolf (Nez Perce)
7 August 1924

THERE WERE TWO brothers living together. *Its-i-yi-i* (Coyote) was the oldest and *Teli-pah* (Fox) was the younger.[1] Coyote had a daughter. He sent his daughter up the canyon. *Hemene* (Wolf) was there hunting. The daughter went to get bones where the deer was killed by *Hemene* to make the soup. The daughter's name was, *Tomy-e-too-le-nicht*.

It was late in the fall. Ice was over the creek. It was early morning when the daughter goes to the creek for water. She sees in the water, every morning, trout, steel-head and other fish, all strung on a hemp string. She gets them and takes them home every morning. Coyote told his daughter:

"Take them out and throw them away. I do not like winter salmon."

Otter was fishing there [at the creek]. He would like to marry Coyote's daughter. But Coyote did not want her to marry Otter. That was the reason he told her to come away [from the water]. In the morning when she comes from getting water at the creek, she goes up the canyon for bones. The wolves were five brothers. They said:

"We have been skinning here yesterday. The bones are gone. Somebody might be picking them up. Who are taking these things? Maybe Coyote's daughter is taking them. We will lay [in wait] for them, for who is taking these things."

The Wolves chased a big buck to the same place and killed him. Where shot with bow and arrow, the oldest brother lay an arrow on top of the dead deer.[2] Then the wolves hid in there [in brush] and lay for whoever comes. They see Coyote's daughter coming up [the canyon]. The Wolves say:

"That is what we thought! It was her taking the bones."

Coyote's daughter walks up to the deer laying there. She said:

"Thank you! My father will feel welcome [grateful] to see this fresh deer."

The Wolves get up. The girl gets ashamed. Next to oldest Wolf said:

"Do not get ashamed. Do not get bashful. If you want the whole deer, my brother will have to pack it for you."

The girl said:

"Yes, I want to take him home."

Wolf then told his older brother:

"You better take him home for her."

The older brother packs the whole deer. He gets right to the lodge of Coyote. He throws the deer down. That makes a noise, for Wolf is panting, tired. Coyote hears the noise. He is lying in the lodge sick. The daughter comes in. Coyote asks her:

"What you drop outside?"

She told him:

"One man was packing a deer for me. He killed the deer."

Coyote asked her:

"Who is the man?"

She answered:

"I do not know him."

Coyote said:

"How many of them?"

The daughter answered:

"Five of them."

Coyote thinks that it must be *Hemene*. He told his daughter:

"Get ready and go with him [the man]."

The girl thought:

"Whatever my father tells me, I will do it."

The man [had] left. She follows after him, follows his trail. She got up with him at their camp. She stays off from the brothers at a distance. The youngest brother was sent to see who she was. She was quite a ways from the camp. He spoke to her:

"What you doing?"

She answered:

"The man packed the deer for me. My father told me: 'You better follow him, better go with him.'"

The younger brother goes back to the lodge. He tells the older brother: "Her father told her to come. She comes for good to our lodge."

All the brothers are glad. That brother got married: got a cook for them.

Next morning the brothers left the woman in the lodge and went out hunting. Wherever Coyote has his lodge, they drive five big deer there. They kill the deer right in front of the lodge, not far away from the door. They had only a little ways to go and said:

"We will take the deer and pile [them] in front of the door."

Coyote told Fox:

"What is making noise outside? Better look!"

Teli-pah sticks his head outside. He looks back at Coyote and said: "We got five big bucks lying outside here. Five of them."

Coyote told his partner:

"You better go out and skin them. You take one and I will take four."

The Otters were setting traps for the girl, with strings of fish. Every morning they find the fish way down the creek in the drift. Every five days the *Hemene* brought dried meat to his father-in-law, Coyote and Fox. Otter did not yet know the girl was married to *Hemene*. He was still putting fish in the hole in the ice for her. When he comes back, the fish is still there. She was not taking the fish. Fox was going after the water all the time. The girl was not going there any more.

Early in the spring, the Otters set traps for the girl. They wanted to know if Coyote's daughter got the fish.

Otter told Meadowlark:

"Auntie, I guess you know something. Better tell me. I broke your leg. Tell me and I will fix your leg for you."

Otter fixed her leg. Meadowlark said:

"I cannot tell you any thing. She is married, that girl. What you put fish in the water hole for? Coyote does not like you. That is the reason he threw the fish in the creek."

Otter got mad. He knows where the Wolves stay. He goes to their camp. They make pitch-kindlings. Stick it all over outside of the lodge. They burn the lodge, and all the five brothers and the wife, Coyote's daughter, were burned up.

Towards morning, Coyote was lying close to the fire in his own lodge. He does not know. He never saw the Otters come into his lodge.

When Coyote looked up, he saw Otters standing there, dancing, making noise: *chu! chu! chu!* Coyote said:

"What you do here? Go out!"

Coyote got a stick. He again said to the Otters:

"What you dancing around here for?"

The Otters run away for a little while. Then they came and danced again in Coyote's lodge. Coyote gets mad. Always gets mad at the Otters. He said to them:

"You people stink full of fish. I do not want you here! I do not like the smell of you. You better go out of here."

It is about daybreak. Coyote hears laughing outside. He hears his daughter laughing. When his daughter laughed, she said:

"Where are you?"

Coyote answered:

"What? What you want, my daughter?"

The daughter answered:

"Otter got jealous and burned us up. We are going where there are lots of people. Going up to *Ah-kum-ke-ne kah* (land above or land high up)."

Coyote said to her:

"You better tell me truth. What you are saying? Let me know."

She answered him:

"We are going up to *Ah-kum-ke-ne kah*. Where lots of people are. My husband has gone already. You better burn that beaded buckskin bag. I want to take it with me."[3]

Coyote said:

"You better tell me what you want me to do."

She told him:

"I cannot tell you anything else. Otters were jealous. They burned us up. I am in hurry! Better burn the beaded bag and I will go."[4]

Coyote said to his daughter:

"I am going too."

His daughter told him: "You cannot go the way you are. You cannot go alive to *Ah-kum-ke-ne kah*."

Coyote cried. He said:

"How am I to make living here? I get lonesome!"

His daughter answered:

"If you want to go with us, you better burn yourself up. Kill yourself. Then you can go."

Coyote thought to go with his daughter. He would throw himself in the fire and burn himself. He did this. He suffered! He was out of con-scious[ness]. He was jumping around. He does not know anything. He throws himself in the fire again. He dies. He follows his daughter and the others. He looks at them from where he is following. He is with the com-pany. They had lots of fun where they were going.

Coyote went away, then came alive again. When he came to self, he was on the ground. He heard his daughter and others laughing overhead. They were going towards the Above. He called to his daughter:

"I am going [with you] anyway!"

She answered him:

"If you say so, if you are going, then come ahead."

Wherever Coyote hears the laughing, hears the noise, he follows in that direction. When they get to the Happy Ground, Coyote was nearly there too.[5] His daughter called to him:

"My father, Coyote, we [have] got here."

Coyote asked:

"What you say?"

She answered:

"I said [that] I am telling you. Lots of people here having fun. Can you not hear them?"

Coyote answered:

"I am very glad we are here. You told me it was quite a ways, but I have been here before."[6]

His daughter told him:

"You will see them. You are nearly on [to] the place now."

Coyote looks. He sees lots of people when he got up to *Ah-kum-ke-ne kah*. Indians were playing the bone game. Indians were having a war dance. They were having another dance—the circle dance. A chief called to all the dead people:

"Keep quiet, keep quiet! I am going to tell you something. I will let you know. I will let you know that Coyote has come to the Above, alive. He is *eli-whe-emch* [half-cooked]."

The chief made lots of fun again. Let the people know that Coyote is alive among them. Coyote stayed with [a] bunch of war dancers. People are all dressed Indian way, buckskin suits. Coyote had lots of fun. Women hugging him around. Coyote looks around. Lots of tepees, lots of lodges. Lots of people everywhere. Coyote saw nearly daylight [com-ing]. He said:

"This woman has never forgot me. I used to run around with her [on earth]."[7]

Coyote sees it is just daylight coming. Sees boys and men sleeping. He will get in the middle [of them] and sleep. He sleeps till about midday. Then he wakes up. His face is covered with blanket. He thought:

"I am sleeping on [in] long-house."

Coyote uncovers his head. Sees no tepees, no lodges around there. He thought:

"Where [have] the people moved?"

Coyote looks around. Nothing in where he is sleeping. He thought to urinate. Then a bunch of women laugh. They say:

"You urinated on somebody."

Coyote does not see anybody. He gets ashamed, covers his head. Then Coyote walked. The women laugh again. They say to him:

"You are going out at back end of the tepee. You go out at the other end of the tepee."[8]

Coyote was bashful and said:

"What is use for me to look for door. I cannot find it! I am going through anyway."

Coyote understands very well. He marked and located the doorway and goes out every day. His daughter told him:

"Do not stay with the people in the tepees all day. You will break the tepees and everything up. Go out in the shade some place."

Coyote made answer:

"I did not do this for [on] purpose, did not break tepee [on] purpose. I get up in sleep and this what happens at times."[9]

His daughter said:

"Coyote, I am going to tell you. You are not going to stay very long in this world. I will let you know. You are going to stay here five days. You will then go back home where you came from."

Coyote made reply:

"What do I go back home for? I will be lonesome, there alone."

His daughter answered:

"Do not say it like that! You will know when you arrive back home."

Coyote answers his daughter:

"I am going back home, I think."

His daughter said:

"I will let you know when I tell you, you are going back. Tomorrow, in the morning, you will go back home. When you get there, I will let you know what to do. I will come see you tomorrow morning."

Coyote told her:

"I do not think I will get lazy, and I will go 'back home.' [But] I am going have lots of fun [now]. Never see these many people any more."

Just from dark Coyote stayed in the war dance all night. In the morning his daughter came and told him:

"You are going home this morning."

Coyote's daughter had a package about this size about this long (here the narrator folded and rolled a hand-towel, making a package about eight inches long and about three inches in diameter, using this in demonstrating the daughter's instructions to her father). It was buckskin-wrapped. It was tied at each end with long strings, just long enough strings to pack. She said to Coyote:

"I am going tell you. You going pack this. You going home. Do not unpack this. Just keep on packing it. This pack, do not ever take off (your back). When laying down to sleep, let it be on you. Do not take it off if you get tired. Five days you will be going. Five mountains you are going travel over. You must pack this. The last mountain you go over, at the foot of the last mountain when crossed, you can unpack it. If you hear whispering, talking or laughing, do not turn round. Keep on going! I am telling you facts. If you get tired, do not turn round. Just lay down and sleep, but do not look back."

Coyote told his daughter:

"I do not think I will get tired. Pack is too small. I walk all day with it on my back. Too small!"

His daughter answered:

"Believe me! Do not you take the pack off. When you get over the mountain, you can take it off."

Coyote said:

"I will not get tired with this little thing. I will take him [it] off after I pass over last mountain."

His daughter told him:

"You going now."

Coyote said:

"Yes, I am going right now."

He put the pack on [his back] and he went. He went, left that place. Coyote got right at foot of the first mountain. Goes over the mountain. Second mountain, he goes over. Third mountain, climbs nearly to summit. Pack kind of feels heavy. Fourth mountain, going up. Feels pretty heavy![10] At foot of this fourth mountain, over this fourth mountain, pack is pretty very heavy. Coyote lays right down, the way he is going, and sleeps. The fifth mountain, he is starting up. Nearly to top of summit, nearly all in. He hears whispering! Hears laughing, at his back. Almost turns around! But he remembers his daughter, and he keeps his mind and does not turn around.

Coyote is now tired down. Nearly at top of mountain, all tired out. It is just like a great, heavy load, his small pack. Coyote thought:

"The last mountain, my daughter told me, I do not have to turn round. I think here is where I turn round."

Coyote throws his pack and turns around. He sees his daughter and a great lot of people. His daughter says to him:

"Now you have done wrong! What you had to pack were the people you had fun with in *Ah-kum-ke-ne kah*. You were taking them back [to] where you came from. We part now! You will never see me again! You see this bunch of people? They are now going back where they were, where you found them in Above. Coyote, had you carried the pack as I instructed, the people in future would die only to be in the grave-ground for two or three days, when they would have come to life never to die again. You were taking these back not to die again. You have done great wrong. Had you made it over the last mountain, it would have been good work. From now on, the people will die for good. They will not now return. That is where you done wrong! We are going back right now."

Coyote cried, cried, cried! He cried five days. Then he quit. He thought:

"I am not only one to feel bad over it. Not very long and another people will be in this world. The daughter or son to [will] die, the parents will cry five days, feel bad. Then they will forget it."

That is old custom. We follow it. Child dies, we cry five days. About five graves [generations] back, was when the world changed. Now, away back, like we are making. It is still ahead of me. I remember this story as told me by the old people. This end of it. The young people, people still back to come, will see this story of long ago.[11]

61

How Coyote Lost Immortality to the Tribes
Anonymous

COYOTE WAS LIVING around here somewhere. He felt sad because so many of his people were dead.[1] Every day he cried, longing to see his kindred who were in the Spirit Land. Coyote thought over this. He decided to go see the First Man, who lived far towards the sunrise, beyond five mountains. He started traveling, looking to the morning sun, until the five mountains were crossed. There he found the First Man, the Ruler of all. He said to the Ruler:[2]

"Many of my people are dead, gone from me. My heart is sad! I cry every day because I cannot see my people, my friends who are gone. I want my people with me again. I have come far to tell you that I am crying for my people, to ask that you let them go back with me to live. I am lonely! I want my people with me always."

Five times Coyote asked this of the First Man. When he asked it the fifth time, the First Man answered:

"All right! I will let you take your people back with you, but you must do as I instruct you. You must make no mistake!"

When Coyote said that he would follow instructions, the First Man took a small piece of deerskin and placed a bit of the spirit of each of all the dead in it and tied the bundle securely. He gave the pack to Coyote and said:

"Take this with you to your home beyond the five mountains. Do not untie it till you reach your own country. All your people will then be alive to be with you forever. Do not loosen the deerskin until you have passed the five mountains."

Coyote was glad. He made promise:

"I will do as you tell me. I know the law of the five mountains. I am lonely for my people."

Coyote took the pack and started on his return home. His heart no longer felt poor, for he would now see all his friends and brothers. They would be with him always. He was happy as he traveled towards the sunset. He sang because of his happiness.

Coyote crossed one mountain on the trail. He crossed two mountains, three mountains. After a time, he had crossed four of the mountains on the trail. As he approached the fifth and last mountain, he heard a great noise. It seemed many people talking, shouting, laughing, singing old-time songs, songs that Coyote had heard before. He stopped surprised. He listened! Yes, he knew those songs, those voices. Some of the singers were his kindred. Friends who had been gone the many snows. Coyote said to himself:

"I want to go where those people are, my friends, my brothers, my sisters. How can I get there? How can I go? I want to see my friends now; I want them with me now! I do not want to wait till I pass the last of the five mountains."

Coyote then untied the pack. When he did this, the spirits all flew back to the First Man, back where they had been, towards the sunrise. Had Coyote waited till he crossed the fifth mountain, the spirits when liberated would have remained with him. The dead people, all of them, would have returned to life and lived always. But because Coyote did this, because he did not do as told by the First Man, all Indians are now short-lived, must die before growing very old.

It was thus that Coyote lost immortality to the tribes.[3]

Notes by McWhorter

Still another version of the foregoing legend is that Coyote, on his way back home and after crossing the fourth mountain, was met by *Tech*, the black stink-bug, who threatened him with death unless he untied the bundle given him by the First Man. Coyote, in fear of his life, unfastened the pack, with the disastrous results as depicted.

Still another portrayal has it that it was *Tis-kai*, the skunk, who intercepted the returning Coyote, with threats caused him to loosen his precious burden, permitting the spirits to escape. This happened while Coyote was climbing the fifth and last mountain.

Tis-kai was a malicious medicine man who killed with his stink-poison all who opposed him. He inquired of Coyote what his pack contained and was informed that it was filled with costly things with rare objects. *Tis-kai* demanded that it be untied that he might see its contents. This Coyote refused, but when menaced with death, complied.

Coyote's dead wife and children were in the bundle, and when it was opened, they, with the other spirits, rushed out, singing songs not of earth. They bade him goodbye, as they vanished back over the trail towards the sunrise.

Poor Coyote now went crying, wailing in grief, his heart more lonely than ever. He had lost perpetual earth-life to his people.

62

Coyote's Big Mistake
Burning Bush (Klickitat)
5 February 1911

IT WAS NEARER the beginning, before man came to this earth that there lived a great Coyote Chief.[1] He was ruler of all the land; ruler of everything that lived. He thought himself the bravest, the wisest of all and that everything was afraid of him.

This big Coyote Chief had one daughter whom he loved above everything. It made no difference that the young men were in love with her. Coyote would not let her marry, would not let her leave him. One sun this daughter grew sick and died.

It was the custom of that time, that when anyone died to let them lay for five suns, then step over the body five times, when [then] they would return to life. So when his daughter died, Coyote thought to wait five suns, when life would be restored and she would be with him as before.

Now this old Coyote Chief used to fall asleep, at which time he would die and sleep for five suns, talking with his spirit-powers, communicating with his secret *tah*.[2] This he did when his daughter died, awaking on the fifth sun. While thus sleeping, he saw that which was in the future snows events to come with the dawning suns [he dreamed]. He called the people together, telling them of his message. He said:

"A new people are coming. Strange, and different from us, they will be a higher race. The earth is to be changed and made better."

But on this fifth day, Coyote's daughter did not get up. The old Chief then knew that something was wrong, that his daughter was dead beyond life.

He went to the mountains crying, calling to his daughter. He sought lonely places, rolling on the ground in grief. Among the cliffs and dark woods, he wailed in agony. For five suns Coyote did nothing but cry and call to his daughter. Then on this fifth sun, he heard her voice calling to him, telling him to come up to the highest mountain, to the top where she would talk to him.

Coyote was now glad. He climbed to where his daughter had directed, high and solitary. There she met him and told him not to cry for her. She said:

"I am in a good place; I am not dead. There is no trouble where I am, no distress of any kind. It is a fine country, always light with no darkness. The spirit life is best. Do not cry. It hurts me!"

But Coyote was lonely. He asked his daughter to return to earth and be with him again. He had been sad since she left him. Finally she told him that if he would do as she directed, she would come back and be with him always.

Coyote promised, for he was glad that his daughter would never again leave him. She then gave him a pack, telling him that it contained Life. She said:

"You must carry this on your back to the valley where you live. There you can untie it, and all those who have died will return to life and live forever. You must not look back on the trail. No difference what you may hear, what sounds come to you, you must keep going and not turn or look back."

Coyote took the bundle and promised his daughter that he would not look back nor stop until he reached home. If he heard anything, if strange and mysterious sounds of any kind or noise followed him, he would pay no attention, but keep on going. Nothing could stop him or make him look back over the trail.

With his pack, Coyote started for the valley where he lived. His heart was light, for now his daughter would be with him always. But as he walked, the pack grew heavier, ever more heavy. He drew near his home, traveling down into the valley. He heard strange murmurings back of him, coming with the air. He did not stop, did not look around. He hurried, for he was nearly home. Only a short distance more, when he would be at the doorway of his lodge.

Back on the trail, Coyote now heard the musical murmur growing. Louder, still louder it came. Voices were in that place, now laughing, talking, singing. Heavier grew the pack and Coyote was becoming very tired. But he did not stop; he did not look backward over the trail.

The strange noise-sounds were taking form. *Eh!* That was his daughter's voice! She is singing as in other suns.

Staggering under his load, Coyote stopped, listening. He turned and looked everywhere. He could see nothing! Could only hear his daughter's song among the many other voices.

Lonely to see his daughter, Coyote stood considering what to do. Why should continue farther? Why not see what was in the pack, why it was becoming so heavy? He thought to let everything out of the bundle. He was so near home.

Tired and not wanting to wait longer to see his daughter, the old Coyote Chief untied the pack. Loosening it, he beheld the people long dead. He saw grass growing from cavernous eyes, ears, nostrils, and mouth. The dead were all about him! He saw his daughter, who looked at him pityingly. She said:

"Oh, you made big mistake! I told you not to stop, not to look back, but carry the pack home. You made big mistake! These people will now go back to their graves. Had you not opened the pack, had you done as I told you, they would all have come back to life. They would have lived here forever. This earth would have seen no more dying. But now the new people who are coming as you saw in sleep-vision, will die as have the first, the older kinds of people. You made big mistake! I am going now. Goodbye!"

With this, the dead people all vanished, returning to their graves. Saddened by what he had done, poor Coyote cried, cried, cried! He would see his daughter no more in this life.

63

How Coyote Moved *Pah-to* and *Tahoma*
Anonymous
No Date

COYOTE RULED ALL the land. His headquarters were at the bridge crossing the *nChe-wana*, which afterwards broke down, forming the Cascades.[1] Coyote had a wife and daughter. The daughter was single, had no man. Coyote was anxious to marry her to some good man, one who had plenty of food, plenty of skins for robes and clothing. With his wife and daughter, Coyote set out traveling. They came to the Klickitat country, where Goldendale, Washington, now stands. There he wanted to find a man for his daughter. The people said to him:

"Go see our chief. He has plenty of everything, is a great man."

Coyote asked:

"Who is your chief?"

They told him:

"*Pah-to*."

So Coyote left his wife and daughter with those people and went to see Chief *Pah-to* who then stood where Goat Rocks now stands. *Pah-to* was a great big mountain, larger than now.[2] All about were plenty of berries, some roots and lots of game. Coyote said to *Pah-to*:

"What would you like? Would you like to marry my daughter?"

Pah-to made reply:

"No! I have one girl, one girl I am going to marry. You are too late."

Coyote then said:

"All right! That is what I wanted to find out. You will not get any roots. I will also stop the salmon at *Weep-ne-tash* ["falling down," or the Falls of the Big Klickitat River]. You cannot be so great."

Pah-to asked:

"What do you mean?"

Coyote made reply:

"I am ruler of this country. I am chief. You are not going to have so much. You are not going to be so great."

Pah-to laughed. He laughed loud and long. He said:

"All right! If you think that you control me, go ahead."

Coyote made answer:

"Yes! I will show you what I can do. I know what is on my mind, what I will do."

Then Coyote moved *Pah-to* south, dividing the mountain, leaving Goat Rocks undisturbed. Since then *Pah-to* has had berries and game, but no roots nor salmon. Had Coyote not moved *Pah-to*, that mountain would be colder than now. Goat Rocks are colder than *Pah-to*. Wind blows ice across the summit of the peak. Before the division, that was the main mountain. That is why it is so cold there.

Coyote now went back to Klickitats and got his wife and daughter. They came to the Yakima River in the Yakima country, up the Yakima River to the lakes, Kachees and Keechelus [headwaters of the Yakima River in the Cascade Mountains]. There he left his wife and daughter. He heard of *Klum-tah*, found out about Chief *Klum-tah* [a mountain northeast of Mt. Rainier], who had lots of berries. Coyote thought:

"I better go see him. He might buy my daughter, might marry her."

But when Coyote got there, he found that Chief *Klum-tah* had another woman, had already bargained for a wife. The chief had fish brought him from the [Puget] Sound, up the Puyallup River by the father of the girl he was to marry. Coyote asked *Klum-tah*:

"Would you like to marry my daughter?"

Klum-tah answered:

"No! I already have a girl."

Coyote then said:

"All right! That is what I wanted to find out. You go ahead! Marry the girl. All that you will get is a poor salmon, nothing else but a certain kind of salmon."

Klum-tah said to Coyote:

"What you mean?"

Coyote told him:

"You know that I am ruler of this country. All you will get is a certain kind of salmon. It will be the *um-to-li* [fall run of salmon], the poor salmon. You will not get the fat *qee-nut* [spring run of salmon]."

The big chief laughed. He said to Coyote:

"All right! If you think you control me, go ahead. Do so."

Coyote made reply:

"Yes! I am controlling you. You will get *um-to-li*, nothing more. You will get no berries. Only *um-to-li*."

Coyote now did a big work. He took part of *Klum-tah* and turned it west. This part is now Tahoma. He left *Klum-tah* where it was, where the main mountain always stood. Tahoma was the chief part of the mountain *Klum-tah*, and if it had not been for Coyote, the two would now be the largest of all mountains. Not many berries about Tahoma, the richest of berries are with *Klum-tah* [where they] were always. No salmon except the *um-to-li*, the poor dog-salmon, comes to Tahoma, comes up from the west side. This was the ruling of Coyote.[3]

Notes by McWhorter

Weep-ne-tash means "falling down" or "sloping down" and it is the Falls of the Big Klickitat River. The name applies to the peculiar formation of the falls, the undulating sweep of the water. Salmon do not pass these falls. None are found in the upper waters of the streams in the Mt. Adams watershed.

Klum-tah: means "head." A mountain perhaps fifteen or twenty miles northeast of Tahoma [Mt. Rainier]. The Indians speak of it as a part of Tahoma. Before the division by Coyote, the entire mountain was *Klum-tah*, the greatest of all mountains.

Um-to-li or *M-to la* means "slacking-back" or signifying "old age." This name is given the *qee-nut* (royal Chinook) the largest of salmon, during the fall season when they spawn. They are the dog-salmon of the whites. The *qee-nut*, when it comes up the *nChe-wana* in June, is fat and highly prized for the flavor of its flesh. The characteristic of the fish, according to the Indians, is that it enters some deep hole in the rivers at or near the small stream where it is to spawn and remains there until October, when it leaves for the spawning grounds. They are caught in Lake Keechelus in that month. At this stage the fish is poor, "humped-back, crooked nosed and with long teeth." This, the Indians say, is the only salmon that Tahoma gets. They are dried and smoked by the Indians for winter use. When the female is caught, filled with eggs, the heavier or thick part of the back is cut away, leaving the thinner sides and belly with the eggs.

64

Pah-to, the White Eagle
December 1924

I WILL TELL you this Indian story. It is about one mountain the Sho-yah-poo calls "Mount Adams," a no-sense name.[1] The old name is of the Thappanish people. The mountain belonged to them, and was called: *Thappanish cli-mi Pah-to*. But now this name can be headed for all the Yakima, made up of many different tribes and bands.

Wasco, now called "Mount Hood," is a mountain in Oregon.

There was another mountain, *Wak-soom*, one time the summit of the Cascades. *Pah-to* stands beyond *Wak-soom* and towards the sunset of the present summit.

These three mountains had one husband, *Pos-twa-nit*, the Sun. Every time Sun came driving the darkness, he would strike *Wak-soom* first, greet her first. *Pah-to* saw all this and became jealous.[2] She made up her mind to destroy *Wak-soom*. So *Pah-to* came over in the night and killed her, beat her down. She then took all the game, the deer, the elk, the bear, and salmon belonging to the dead wife, took the berries and the best roots and left *Wak-soom* dead and of but little concern.

After that time, Sun coming with the morning, strikes *Pah-to* the first thing. This was good! It was what *Pah-to* liked of her husband.

Seeing this, *Wasco* became jealous. She made a strong mind to kill *Pah-to*.[3] It was just before daylight that *Wasco* came with a great war club and other weapons of fighting, and there was a big battle. When Sun came up from the far away, *Pah-to* was dead all torn to pieces. I do not know how it happened, but *Pah-to*'s head was broken off and scattered from there to Fish Lake. To this day that is a hard country to travel. *Wasco* took everything from *Pah-to*, game, fish, berries and roots. Left *Pah-to* sitting there headless, with no sort of life. Like *Wak-soom*, *Pah-to* was now no longer a producer of life. Not growing foods, *Pah-to* had lost her usefulness to the world, was no longer of any importance.

The Great Maker was a witness to all this, saw what *Pah-to* had suffered. He knew that which was coming. He beheld the new people who yet unborn, were awaiting the final preparation of the land for their reception, and He took pity of them.[4] He restored *Pah-to* to life and brought back to her all the game, salmon, berries and roots. These are all found there to this day. He gave to *Pah-to* a head to replace the one lost. This head was *Quoh Why-am-mah*, the great White Eagle, sent down from the Land Above.

Pah-to was now a powerful Law standing up towards the sky and was for the whole world. Once dead, but returned to life, that Law was divine. Coming from the great Giver, that Law was immortal. Wisdom was that of the White Eagle to watch and guard the entire world. Life was in the white bosom growing life for all foods that the people to come might eat and have strength. The White Eagle said:

"I want two children to sit by me, to watch towards the sunrise. I will send them to every part of the world, to observe how everything is going on. They will bring me word of what they see, of what is being done. I will regulate and control everything in the whole world."

So, this was the way that the Great Maker sent White Eagle to be the head of *Pah-to*. A Law standing high for all the world. The two children were given, and White Eagle declared:

"Whatever the Great Maker has done, I know. Women will born children. There shall be death; there shall be sorrow everywhere. When the children grow up, these shall be chiefs and rulers in the land. But *Quoh Why-am-mah*, will care for them all. The center of power, the head of the Law is in me. I will send my children all over the world, to take up and report to me what is going on. My power, my Law is stronger than all the people who shall ever live."[5]

Thus it was that *Thappanish cli-mi Pah-to* was killed and then restored to life again. The White Eagle-head, coming down from Above, holds a great spirit power. Life dwells there. Life is in the water flowing down from many caverned ice banks.

Facing the sunrise, the two young eagles sit at either side of White Eagle's top-most crown. *San-we tlah*, the "Speaker," is on the right, towards the Northland. *Kay-no klah*, the "Overseer" or "Manager," is at the left, towards the Southland. They are watching everywhere, going everywhere. Flying over all the world, they bring back news of what is being done. Nothing can happen without their seeing. Nothing ever escapes their sharp vision.

This is why we want *Pah-to* within our own reservation boundary. That mountain belongs to us. A witness to our treaty with Governor Stevens, White Eagle, ever points upward to the Great Maker who heard the promises of that treaty. Standing high among the clouds, White Eagle is always first to be greeted by the Sun. The berries, the game and fish of the mountains and streams, were created for us, who are the first real people of this country.[6]

This is why I do not like to see the *Sho-yah-poo* climb *Pah-to*. Young Indians used to go to the top, but they made no wrong. All that *Pah-to* has, all her foods are free. This is why I always give freely, why I feed the hungry without pay. It is the Law, the white Law, lifted high where it is painted by the Sun and blanketed by the clouds. A gift from the Great Maker, the foods planted for His children must all be free.

Notes by McWhorter

Thappanish means "sleeping down" or "sloping down," a place-name descriptive of the upper desert confines of Toppenish Creek, the recognized home of the Thappanish sub-tribe of the Yakimas. The mountain *Pah-to*: "standing up." was claimed by these Indians, hence the suffix, cli-mi: "belonging" to; "ownership," "property" of.

Some of the original of the fourteen bands and tribes composing the reservation Yakimas, have entirely disappeared, amalgamated, or [been] swallowed up by the more virile and stronger of the tribes. The Thappanish family possesses some distinctive characteristics from Yakimas proper.

Pos-twa-nit literally means "parting friends remember [each other]" or "parting friends do not forget [each other]."

Notes

Introduction

1. Eugene S. Hunn with James Selam and Family, *Nch'i-Wana, "The Big River"*:
Mid-Columbia Indians and Their Land (Seattle: University of Washington
Press, 1990), 228–68.

2. Clifford E. Trafzer and Richard D. Scheuerman, eds., *Mourning Dove's Stories*
(San Diego: San Diego State University Press, Publications in American
Indian Studies, 1991), 49–68.

3. Ibid., 3, 5–6; the original source is "Educating the Indian," in Mourning
Dove's Autobiographical Manuscript owned by the family of Geraldine
Guie, Yakima, Washington. The editor of this volume and Richard D.
Scheuerman were given a copy of this manuscript by Geraldine Guie and all
of the stories Mourning Dove was editing at the time she became ill in 1936.
Hereafter cited as Mourning Dove's Manuscript.

4. Virginia Beavert, ed., *The Way It Was: Anaku Iwacha, Yakima Indian Legends*
(Consortium of Johnson O'Malley Committees of Region IV, Washington:
Franklin Press, 1974), iii.

5. Ibid., xi; Document 520A, L.V. McWhorter Collection, Manuscripts,
Archives, and Special Collections, Holland Library, Washington State
University, Pullman, Washington. Hereafter cited as McWhorter Collection.

6. Nelson A. Ault, ed., *The Papers of Lucullus Virgil McWhorter* (Pullman:
Friends of the Library, State College of Washington, 1959), 2.

7. Steven R. Evans, *Voice of the Old Wolf: Lucullus V. McWhorter and the Nez Perce
Indians* (Pullman: Washington State University Press, 1996).

8. L.V. McWhorter, *Yellow Wolf: His Own Story* (Caldwell, Idaho: The Caxton
Printers, Ltd., 1940), 13.

9. McWhorter was such a powerful advocate of native peoples that officials of
the Office of Indian Affairs at the Yakama Agency kept a special file on him
simply entitled "L. V. McWhorter." This file contains correspondence dis-
crediting McWhorter, letters written by superintendents at the Yakama
Agency. See McWhorter file in Papers of the Yakima Agency, National
Archives, Pacific Northwest Region, Record Group 75, Seattle, Washington.

10. Ault, *Papers of Lucullus Virgil McWhorter*, 2.

11. Ibid., 2, 5–8.

12. Hunn, *Nch'i-Wana*, 230.

13. Andrew George, oral Interview by Clifford E. Trafzer, Richard D. Scheuerman, and Lee Ann Smith, 15 November 1980, Yakama Reservation, editor's collection.

14. Ibid.

15. Ibid.

16. Ibid.; Clifford E. Trafzer and Richard D. Scheuerman, *Renegade Tribe: The Palouse Indians and the Invasion of the Inland Pacific Northwest* (Pullman: Washington State University Press, 1986), 135.

17. Jane B. Katz, ed., *This Song Remembers: Self Portraits of Native Americans in the Arts* (Boston: Houghton Mifflin Company, 1980), 190.

18. George, interview.

19. Ibid.

20. Ibid.

21. Beavert, *The Way It Was*, xi; Helen H. Schuster, *The Yakima* (New York: Chelsea House, 1990), 14; Trafzer and Scheuerman, *Mourning Dove's Stories*, 2. See "Tepee Life," Mourning Dove's Manuscript.

22. Beavert, *The Way It Was*, vi.

23. Gerald Vizenor, *Manifest Manners: Post Indian Warriors of Survivance* (Hanover, Conn.: Wesleyan University Press, 1994): 96.

24. Trafzer and Scheuerman, *Mourning Dove's Stories*, 2; "Tepee Life," Mourning Dove's Manuscript.

25. "Educating the Indian," Mourning Dove's Manuscript; Trafzer and Scheuerman, *Mourning Dove's Stories*.

26. Trafzer and Scheuerman, *Mourning Dove's Stories*, 2.

27. Ibid., 3; "Tepee Life," Mourning Dove's Manuscript.

28. The program at the Yakama Nation Cultural Center was sponsored by the tribe and the Washington Historical Society in "commemoration" of the Oregon Trail and its impact on the region.

29. Steven R. Evans, telephone conversation with author, 24 August 1994, editor's collection.

30. Ibid.

31. Ibid.

32. Mourning Dove to McWhorter, 1918, as quoted in Dexter Fisher, "Introduction," *Cogewea* (Lincoln: University of Nebraska Press, 1981), viii. See also Trafzer and Scheuerman, *Mourning Dove's Stories*, 7.

33. Evans, telephone conversation.

34. The quotes are from Alanna K. Brown, "Looking Through the Glass Darkly: The Editorialized Mourning Dove," in *New Voices in Native American Literary Criticism*, ed. Arnold Krupat (Washington, D.C.: Smithsonian Institution Press, 1993), 278.

35. Evans, telephone conversation

36. Ibid.

37. McWhorter, *Yellow Wolf*, 283–92.

38. Reader's report by the University of Oklahoma Press of Clifford E. Trafzer and Richard D. Scheuerman's *Renegade Tribe*.

39. Paula Gunn Allen, "Bringing Home the Fact: Tradition and Continuity in the Imagination," in *Recovering the Word: Essays on Native American Literature*, ed. Brian Swann and Arnold Krupat (Berkeley: University of California Press, 1987), 563; Paula Gunn Allen, ed., *Spider Woman's Granddaughters* (New York: Fawcett Columbine, 1989), 5.

40. Beavert, *The Way It Was*, 211–12.

41. George, interview.

42. Andrew George to Clifford E. Trafzer, 29 March 1987, editor's collection.

43. Clifford E. Trafzer, "Washington's Native American Communities," in *People of Washington: Perspectives of Cultural Diversity*, ed. Sidney White and S. E. Solberg (Pullman: Washington State University Press, 1989), 1–23.

44. McWhorter, *Yellow Wolf*; Lucullus V. McWhorter, *Hear Me, My Chiefs!* (Caldwell, Idaho: The Caxton Printers, Ltd., 1952).

45. Trafzer and Scheuerman, *Mourning Dove's Stories*, 7.

46. Ibid., vi-vii, 6–8; Mourning Dove, *Co-ge-we-a, The Half-Blood: A Depiction of the Great Montana Cattle Range* (1927; reprinted as *Cogewea*, with an informative introduction by Dexter Fisher, Bison Books, Lincoln: University of Nebraska Press, 1981.) Alanna K. Brown of Montana State University has led the literary criticism of McWhorter regarding his work with Mourning Dove. Her recent scholarly works include "Looking Through the Glass Darkly," 274–90; "The Choice to Write: Mourning Dove's Search For Survival," in *Old West-New West*, ed. Barbara Howard Meldrum (Moscow: University of Idaho Press, 1993), 261–71; and "The Evolution of Mourning Dove's Coyote Stories," *Studies in American Indian Literatures* 4 (summer/fall 1992): 161–80. Brown is considered the leading scholar of Mourning Dove's literature, including Mourning Dove's work as a storyteller who preserved

the oral traditions of Okanogan people of Washington and British Columbia.

47. Although there is no evidence that McWhorter deleted mention of bodily functions from the stories he compiles, he may have never composed the original text as he heard it or decided not to record stories that were sexual in content. Certainly the people shared stories of love and lust as well as those that dealt with bodily functions, and McWhorter would have heard these stories. He likely decided not to deal with them in his own representation of Plateau people.

48. See "Battle of Cold Wind and Chinook Wind" in this volume.

49. Andrew George to Clifford E. Trafzer, 29 May 1987.

50. Gerald Vizenor has often explained that story is an essential element of native culture, and he made this statement in Santa Fe, New Mexico, at an event sponsored by the Santa Fe Indian college.

51. Robert Ruby and John Brown, *Dreamer-Prophets of the Columbia Plateau* (Norman: University of Oklahoma Press, 1989), 3–26.

52. Mary Jim Interviews by Clifford E. Trafzer and Richard D. Scheuerman, 1 May 1977, 2 April and 17 November 1979, 25 April 1980, Yakama Reservation, editor's collection.

53. Ibid.

1. *Alo-quat* and *Twee-tash*

1. Although McWhorter does not identify the tribal origin of this story, it is Yakama and shared by many Sahaptin-speaking tribes including the Palouse, Cayuse, Nez Perce, Umatilla, Walla Walla, and Wanapum.

2. Ahtanum Creek flows out of the Cascade Mountains, through the Yakama Reservation, and joins the Yakama River near Union Gap, Washington.

3. Five is the primary sacred number of Plateau Indians and many native people of the Northwest. According to Mary Jim, a Palouse Indian elder presently living on the Yakima Reservation, the number five is sacred because humans have five fingers on their hands, and the right hand is used in prayers which conclude with a person exposing their right hand with palms out and fingers extended to send prayers and receive the power of creation. The number five is fundamentally important in the stories and in the lives of Plateau Indian people today.

4. The basic law created in this story is that each day on earth, we will have one day and one night. This is a fundamental law of earth, the result of the struggle between Grizzly Bear and Frog.

2. How Coyote Killed Sun

1. This is a Nez Perce story told by *Hemene Moxmox*, Yellow Wolf, a nephew of *Hinmahtooyahlatkeht* (Thunder Rising Over Lofty Mountains) or Chief Joseph. Yellow Wolf was a young man during the Nez Perce War of 1877 and became a war chief during the conflict. Yellow Wolf was a close friend of L. V. McWhorter, and together they wrote a classic book on Northwestern Indian history, *Yellow Wolf: His Own Story.* All of the native words in this story are Nez Perce. Yellow Wolf argues that "Every old story is Coyote." I believe he is trying to convey that the oldest stories among Plateau Indians involve Coyote (*Its-i-yi-i*), who is the major actor at the time of creation but also one of many characters. The story describes the transitional period from the time of Plant and Animal people to the time when humans arrived in the Northwest. The plants, animals, stars, monsters, mountains, rivers, etc., all interacted and intermarried, conversing with each other before humans arrived.

2. Coyote is not the only character who makes "laws" by which plants, animals, and nature will function, but he is a principal actor and creator. In many Northwestern Indian stories, Coyote is a hero who works for the benefit of the larger community and one who is always concerned about establishing rules and continuing creation for the good of human beings who will arrive on earth. Coyote sets things in motion or changes things, usually for the good of human beings, and his actions are a part of contemporary native society on the Columbia Plateau.

3. In this story Coyote sets out to change the creation so that Sun will not continue to kill Plant and Animal People, the *Wah-tee-tash.*

4. Coyote kills the son of Sun and in so doing creates death and rebirth, creating a law that will be positive and of benefit to the Plant and Animal People as well as the "different people" or human beings who were coming to the earth. Coyote set Sun "in the sky all the time."

5. It is against the law for Coyote or humans to eat human meat, although at this time, Porcupine had dried human meat for consumption. Most often in the texts, Monsters eat humans. In this story, Coyote is the protector of humans from Sun and Porcupine.

6. Note that the story refers to the coming of humans, because the action of the story occurs during the time when plants, animals, and geographical features interacted to prepare the earth for humans.

3. Legend of the Great Dipper

1. This is a Wasco story and the words are Chinookan. The five Wolf Brothers are important characters in many Northwestern tribes, including diverse Indians speaking many different languages.

286 ◉ GRANDMOTHER, GRANDFATHER, AND OLD WOLF

2. Coyote is a creator in this story, establishing the stars and planets in the universe. In this way, Coyote created the laws of the cosmos for all time. Notice that Coyote has five quivers of arrows.

3. Coyote established the law creating the Big Dipper as well as other celestial formations. He also told the story of how these stars were created so that people might know of the historical process that put into motion this part of the creation.

4. Coyote placed all the stars and planets in the sky. This places plants, animals, rivers, mountains, and humans in direct relationship with the cosmos through Coyote and his creative work. The word of this creative activity is the story, and these are sacred texts.

4. How Beaver Stole Fire

1. The quest for fire is a common theme in Native American stories and those of peoples throughout the world. Coyote is generally the hero of native people of the Columbia Plateau, but in this story Beaver and Eagle are the central characters. Still, Coyote suggested that the people make an arrow ladder from earth to the home of Fire People in the sky. This story establishes the law that earth should have fire.

2. The men referred to in this part of the story are Animal People, and they had a history before the arrival of humans.

3. The wren is a small bird, but is a major hero in this story. Wren shoots the arrows, creating the arrow ladder that provided Beaver access to the Land of the Fire People. Wren works for the good of the community.

4. Buffalo lived on the Columbia Plateau in prehistoric times, but there were no buffalo native to the region. However, Plateau Indians traveled by foot to the Buffalo Plains to hunt the shaggy animals. When horses arrived on the Northwest Plateau in the middle of the eighteenth century, Plateau Indians increased their hunting. Buffalo is a character that is familiar to the native peoples of the Columbia Plateau.

5. Ropes made from hazelnut trees are common in the stories of the Columbia Plateau. The Indians used the plant and wove it into their stories.

5. Boy Hero and Cannibal

1. This is a Wishom or Wishrom story which McWhorter entitled "Wishom Legend." I gave the story its present title. The story deals with a fundamental law that humans should not be eaten. The boy introduces a new diet to a cannibal to establish a law that was and is followed by Plateau Indians. Notice that the hero carries five quivers of arrows.

2. Only monsters ate humans, and it is unacceptable behavior among Plateau Indians to eat other humans.

3. Another law among Plateau Indians is giving gifts, because generosity is greatly respected. Creation was a gift as were the many laws given to the people so that they could live on earth. Give-away ceremonies were and are common and a person is expected to give and share.

6. *Iques* and *Twee-tas*

1. This is a Yakama story with Sahaptin words. McWhorter used both *Twee-tas* and *Twee-tash* to describe Grizzly Bear, and I have kept standardize his spellings to *Twee-tash*.

2. The *Pa-loute* is the bone game of Plateau Indians. The game is an integral part of native culture of the region, and the gambling occurs during the night when people sing and call on the power to defeat their foes. Some people purchase love medicine to aid them in the Bone Game, since love and gambling are similar activities—both are games of chance. See Clifford E. Trafzer and Richard D. Scheuerman, eds., "Learning Love Medicine," in *Looking Glass*, ed. Clifford E. Trafzer (San Diego: San Diego State University Press, Publications in American Indian Studies, 1991), 142–56.

3. Note that the number five is employed in the Bone Game.

4. Notice the continual use of the number five, a sacred number among Plateau Indians.

7. The *Qui-Yiah*, Five Brothers

1. This is a Yakima story provided by Simon Goudy. The influence of McWhorter's voice is not as pronounced in this story as in others.

2. Consultation is important in decision making among many native people, particularly Indians of the Columbia Plateau. Councils and discussions are common in many stories, as people work collectively to discuss different points of view.

3. Note that the youngest brother is important in the council discussion and the opinion of the younger people is valued by older people. This is the law.

4. In this story, it is obvious that the youngest brother has superior knowledge to that of the older brothers.

5. The plant that saved the boy was an elder, an older plant person who is portrayed as a grandparent.

6. The ancient people mourned their dead, establishing a law that is repeated in other stories.

7. The story is pre-Christian, and in this story the rib is used to create the people of the Puget Sound. The shortest rib was used to create the native people of the Kittitas country.

8. The *Pushwanapum* are Stoney Rock People, the northern and smaller branch of the Yakima tribe. McWhorter spells the name *Pishwanapums*.

9. The *Qui-yiah* state that they were making the earth ready to receive Indian people, and the Five Brothers determined to hide when humans arrived. The spirit of the brothers is alive among traditionalists today.

10. Five Brothers live in Lake Keechelus, Washington. This is a sacred place to many Plateau Indians.

8. Battle of Cold Wind

1. This is a Wasco story told by one of the Grandmothers. Her name was Ana-whoa or Black Bear, the most elderly person of Wasco descent in 1917.

2. The voice is that of *Ana-whoa*, not McWhorter.

3. Chinook Wind is represented by the number five.

4. Notice that the feather dropping is a sign.

5. Native people of the Columbia River ranked Sturgeon among the Salmon People.

6. The hero is a man or man-like person.

7. In this version, the Cold Wind wrestles, but in other versions, the Wolf Brothers wrestle. Notice the important help that Chinook Wind receives from women.

9. Coyote and *Lalawish*

1. The story is shared by many Sahaptin-speaking Indians from the Columbia Plateau. The words are Yakama and Klickitat.

2. Coyote was concerned that the *Qui-yiah*, five dangerous and powerful brothers, not live in Lake Keechelus. He was committed to have the *Qui-yiah* live elsewhere in order to protect the Indians when they arrived in the land. The law was that the Five Brothers would never live in Lake Keechelus.

3. Coyote is considered a powerful chief, a leader with powers over the Salmon People and others, including humans. His power is not static but dynamic, and Coyote remains a powerful person today.

4. Coyote's five sisters are *Wiwlú-wiwiú* or Huckleberries. They live in his stomach, and they are smart. Their intelligence surpasses that of Coyote, but they are always reluctant to tell their brother anything, because he always listens and learns from them before claiming he already knew something.

5. Notice that the great leader, Coyote, needs advice, and he knows that he can receive no better advice than that of women, his own sisters. The point is that all important leaders need advice, and it is the wise leader who accepts advice.

6. The message is that we should be wise and resourceful, and in this way, we can be fed.

7. There is no salmon run into Toppenish (Thappanish) Creek because Coyote deemed it so. Coyote created this law at the time of creation.

8. The law established by Coyote was influenced significantly by the groups he met along the river systems of the Plateau. Those people who treated Coyote well, giving him food and wives, received salmon and fisheries. Those who did not treat Coyote well did not receive fish or fisheries.

9. Coyote created the first fish nets, but it is unclear if he taught them how to make many kinds of fish nets or just the dip net. Coyote created the path of the salmon, fish traps, waterfalls, and spawning grounds. For an excellent discussion of the salmon run and the construction of a fish net by James Selam, see Hunn, *Nch'i-Wana*, 121–27, 148–55.

10. Battle of the *Atteyiyi* and *Toqueenut*

1. "The Battle of the *Atteyiyi* and *Toqueenut*" is a shared story of the Klickitat, Cascade, Wishom, and Wasco tribes of the Columbia River. The phrase, "In that day," refers to the time of creation when the Plant and Animal People interacted intimately with nature before the arrival of humans. This was the time when the Animal People or *Wah-tee-tash* created the law, a time that is recreated with each telling of the story.

2. *Speel-yi* is a common term among the tribes of the Columbia Plateau for Coyote. The Yakama call Coyote *Speelya*. Also, note that the *Toqueenut* are also called *Qeenut*.

3. One of the messages of the story is for humans to face their enemies, to be strong and brave in the face of adversity.

4. While one must be courageous in the face of grave difficulties, one must also be alert and intelligent.

5. Even the hero, Coyote, can make mistakes but in this story, he recognizes his mistake. This is not always true in reference to Coyote, just as with all humans.

6. Grandmother of the young *Qeenut* represents the significance of elders within native societies of the Northwest. The role of elders is and was very important, and most individuals treasured and respected the knowledge of elders.

7. Notice that young *Qeenut* lives in a tipi, just as Indians of the Columbia Plateau (but not the Northwest Coast) once did. The young *Qeenut* is very human in character.

8. Here the storyteller laments the passing of his or her elders who lived in mat lodges and tipis. Like many Indians living in the twentieth century, the storyteller regrets the loss of culture, history, and people once known.

9. The wild rose bush was and is used to sweep down graves and caskets to ward off ghosts who might harm the dead. In this story, the rose bush was used to protect *Wenowyyi* and to aid him in his fight.

10. Notice the help *Wenowyyi* received from females including his grandmother and aunt. In addition, through her death, *Wenowyyi*'s mother gave him a special birth that set the action into motion that would result in his challenge of the *Atteyiyi*. Women play a significant role in the stories.

11. A common theme is found in this passage. In Native American stories in general and Northwestern stories in particular, the more a character fights an enemy the stronger the character becomes. *Wenowyyi* became stronger the more he fought the *Atteyiyi*.

12. Notice that the writing here is from the oral tradition. The sentences are choppy and direct in presentation. The story at this point reads like a told and heard story. The voice is that of the storyteller.

13. This is an interesting phrase, acknowledging that whites want records of historical events. Yet the Indians believe this story to be historical, one of the episodes in their historical past. The oral tradition and this document serve as a testimony of Native American society prior to white contact. Indians traditionally believe that all of the events described in this story actually occurred. See Clifford E. Trafzer, "Grandmother, Grandfather, and the First History of the Americas," in *New Voices in Native American Literary Criticism*, ed. Arnold Krupat (Washington, D.C.: Smithsonian Institution Press, 1993), 474–87.

14. It is a law that people must share their food and bounty.

15. The law regarding the victory cry began before humans arrived, and it is still a part of Northwestern Indian culture.

11. How Coyote Destroyed the Fish Dam

1. This is a Wishom version of a common story shared by many Indians of the Columbia Plateau. Most of the words found in this story are Chinookan, although the word *nChe-wana*, "Big River," is a word shared by many native people for Columbia River. McWhorter almost always uses this word for Columbia River, except in the Nez Perce stories. The *Yuka-mah* are beaver, and they are the main characters in this story. They act in the same role as the *Tah-tah Kleah* in other versions of this story. This is a Wishom version of the fish dam story that establishes the law that salmon and other fish should not be dammed but allowed free access to swim up the rivers. There are similarities between this story and others, including Coyote's Huckleberry Sisters who teach him how to catch fish in the sand. For information on the Wishom or Wishram, see Robert H. Ruby and John A. Brown, *A Guide to the Indian Tribes of the Pacific Northwest* (Norman: University of Oklahoma Press, 1986), 268–70.

2. Like chapter 7,"The *Qui-yiah*, Five Brothers," where the youngest brother is wise beyond his years, the youngest sister of the *Yuka-mah*, is also wise. It is not uncommon in Northwestern Indian stories that younger, smaller, weaker, insignificant characters teach a lesson or become heroes. This is to teach that everyone is important within the community, and anyone can contribute significantly to the well-being of the group.

3. The five wooden hats are described in other versions of this story as wooden spoons or ladles. The point of the passage is that one must be prepared for the work they wish to accomplish, just as Young Chinook Wind prepared for his battle with the North Wind Brothers in a previous story.

4. The work of Coyote to break the fish dam and release the fish is executed for the benefit of the Animal People. It is not done for the glorification of Coyote, but for the good of the community, that is, the people who live—or will live—in the inland Northwest. All of the major heroes of Northwestern Indian stories work for the good of others, not on their own behalf. This is the law and the traditional lesson taught to children. Spiritual leaders, civilian leaders, war chiefs, and others were expected to act for the benefit of the whole group, not themselves.

5. As in the story of Young Chinook, the main character—in this case Coyote—becomes stronger with adversity. Northwestern stories graphically point out that life is full of adversity and that humans should engage in life which includes conflict and growth as a result of struggles. This is the law.

6. The law established at the time of creation required that fish should not be dammed but allowed to swim upriver to spawn. This law predates white law and the advent of dams on the Columbia River and its tributaries. It is an important aspect of contemporary law involving Indian fishermen who catch fish, in part and traditionally, for the benefit of the community and who participate in communion ceremonies with the salmon through First Salmon Ceremonies.

7. Coyote refers to Salmon as "my make" which in English means the ones I have released, allowed to live, and guided up the rivers to spawn.

8. The stories are filled with spoken and heard words that McWhorter and other writers have difficulty committing to paper. The mark of great storytellers is the ability to make animal sounds or those of erupting volcanoes, raging rivers, or cold north winds. Facial expressions, varying voices, tones, and body movements are all elements of storytelling that are difficult or impossible to convey in written words. But the words have power in transmitting a portion of the story, the essential body of the narrative.

9. The salmon sacrifice themselves for Coyote. The fish give of themselves because this is the law. The concept of sacrifice is important, because in making the journey upriver, the salmon sacrifice themselves as a means of recreating the cycle of life.

10. In previous versions, the five Wolf Brothers blew sleep medicine at Coyote which put him to sleep so the Wolves could do their work. In this story, the Wolves put Coyote to sleep. The inconsistencies are typical of oral storytellers as versions of stories exist among different storytellers, particularly if they are from different tribes, languages, or regions.

11. The best choke cherries grow along the Columbia River at this place as a result of Coyote's law.

12. Owl Child is reluctant to tell us that Coyote's sisters live in Coyote's stomach and that they are Huckleberries. This is typical of a storyteller who leaves out details that they do not want to share with non-Indians.

13. In the first version of this story, the Wolf Brothers are eating venison. In this version of the story, the Wolves eat eggs. Nevertheless, this fact does not change the themes of the story. The difference represents the way in which the story was passed along from generation to generation within particular tribes.

14. Coyote created the fish run, the routes traveled by the salmon, the river falls, and fish traps for the benefit of Indians who would come to the region after the time of creation, the time of the *Wah-tee-tash* or Animal and Plant People who once held sway on earth.

15. The issue here of different nets and spears refers symbolically to diverse tribes and bands who spoke many dialects. Most Indians were multilingual and could converse in the sign with native peoples of the Rocky Mountains and Buffalo Plains.

16. The law discussed here is that there would be no salmon in Toppenish Creek. This law is mentioned in different versions of the story.

12. *Speel-yi* and the Five Sisters

1. This is the only version of the fish dam story that contains this information about the deer hunter who tricked the greatest trickster. The story is Klickitat. *An-nee-shiat*, the storyteller, grew up on the Columbia River, not in the Yakama country. McWhorter refers to her as "Grandmother."

2. Notice the use of English in the phrase, "made rain to come." This is English with native usage by *An-nee-shiat*. The entire story contains a great deal of Indian discourse, provided by an elder who lived her life along Columbia River.

3. Coyote controlled the weather. This was one of his many powers. In the various versions of this story, Coyote threatened his Huckleberry Sisters with rain, hail, and wind that would destroy them.

4. Coyote leaves one activity and begins a serendipitous adventure to see what he could find. It appears that Coyote was thrown into his adventure with the *Weet-weet-yah*, the Five Cliff Swallow Sisters.

5. Although the text does not suggest that Coyote knew about the Five Sisters, Coyote built the baby basket and "packed in like a baby" for a purpose. This is different from other versions where Coyote planned to trick the sisters who had dammed the fish.

6. In the previous versions, Coyote finds the fish dam near the Cascades of the Columbia River. In this version, Coyote floats in the basket into the Pacific Ocean and travels south. The Klickitat live so close to the Cascades that their version of the story had to extend west from their homeland into an area far from their homes.

7. There is no mention in this version that a fish dam existed, but the Cliff Swallows controlled all the fish in a lake and would not share them. It is also worthy of note that the Five Sisters were Cliff Swallows, not the *Tah-tah Kleah* Sisters or the Five Beaver Sisters.

8. In this version, the youngest sister realizes that the Cliff Swallows raise Coyote as a brother. In previous versions, he was raised as a child.

9. As in previous versions, the youngest sister realizes that the "baby" is trouble. In this case the youngest sister identifies the baby as Coyote.

10. Will Rogers, the great Cherokee humorist and actor, once commented that experience is what you get when things do not turn out the way you planned. In this case, the youngest sister knows that Coyote is pretending to be a baby, but she is willing to allow her sisters to experience their decision to keep the child and raise it as their own brother. The result was an "experience" that is shared in story by native peoples to this day.

11. This is the only version that contains the use of eel's tail as a pacifier for Coyote.

12. The use of the term canal is either the voice of McWhorter or the storyteller, both of whom were influenced by the canals built by non-Indians in the Northwest. In this story, Coyote has to prepare before opening the lake and permitting the fish to escape.

13. In this version, Coyote does not make wooden spoons but he takes spoons belonging to the Five Sisters. Notice that during the day Coyote is a man.

14. The broken digging stick is a sign, one which alerts the Five Sisters who respond to the sign. Native Americans in the Northwest watch for signs, and some people today heed the signs.

15. Coyote creates the law that the fish will leave the Pacific Ocean and travel into the inland rivers and streams.

16. As in other versions, the law that Coyote establishes is that the fish should not be contained in such a way that they cannot have free access to swim upriver. By establishing this law, Coyote was preparing the earth for the

arrival of humans. Coyote worked for the benefit of the larger Northwestern community and became a Salmon Chief, leading the fish upriver.

17. In this story Coyote called the salmon out onto the gravel. In previous versions, Coyote called the salmon out onto the rocks.

18. In other versions Coyote's five sisters are identified as Huckleberry Sisters. In this version they are not identified.

19. In every version of the story Coyote threatens his sisters with rain, hail, or wind which can drive huckleberries from the bush, smash, and ruin them. After the sisters are threatened, they always give Coyote advice—advice that the hero claims he knew all along.

20. In other stories the Five Wolf Brothers used sleeping medicine to put Coyote to sleep, but in this version they wished him asleep.

21. This story differs from other versions. In this version Coyote changes the hair of the wolves. In past stories, Coyote transforms the shape of the wolf, including their ears and snouts.

22. The fleas referred to in this account are females. This is the only version that mentions fleas.

23. The ritual described here is very unique. It established a law that a male should act as a clown at the beginning of the salmon run and that the person must act out his clowning as prescribed by Coyote on *Skein* Island. Coyote created a good fishery at this place, a fishery that was "for all people."

24. The law provides for many methods of catching fish—nets, gaff hooks, spears, etc. This is important today, verifying the Native American legal claim that they traditionally caught fish in many ways, not just with pole and line.

25. Coyote created the law that the Wenatchee fishery would be for all people but that the people would take fish on the west side of Columbia River, the present-day site of Wenatchee, Washington.

26. Coyote's daughter is a big rock in the river, because she "rules" the region. Coyote's daughter was a chief, the major leader in the area.

27. It is common knowledge among diverse Native Americans in the Northwest that Wenatchee was *the* place for young couples to meet and court. This is a joyous and sacred place along Columbia River.

28. Because of the bluffs above the Columbia River, the camping area was very narrow. Many tipis once lined the Columbia River at Wenatchee during the fishing season.

13. *Tah-tah Kleah*

1. Although the title indicates that this is a story from the Mount Shasta area of northern California and southern Oregon, the words used are Yakama, not those of the *A-Juma-We, Atsuge-We,* or any other native group in the region. This is a story that became common among the tribes of the Northwest Plateau, although William Charley, a Yakama elder, argues that the origin of the story is Shasta, not Yakama. This is interesting because the Yakama and other tribes of the Columbia Plateau share a belief in the *Tah-tah Kleah.* This is evident in story number 16 about *Sho-pow-tan.* One of the *Tah-tah Kleah* died in the Yakama country south of Toppenish, and her remains can be seen today. This is a sacred but dangerous site. The last creation referred to in this passage indicates the time that Indians arrived on the Columbia Plateau, after Coyote had set the creation into motion and had started establishing the laws. The last creation was a time when humans, plants, animals, mountains, rivers, etc., began their relationship together. The first creation is the time before humans and the second creation occurred after the arrival of native people.

2. There are two *Tah-tah Kleah* in this story, but in others there are five. This may distinguish the origin of particular stories about the *Tah-tah Kleah,* because five is the sacred number among Plateau Indians. According to Andrew George, a Palouse Indian *Twati* or doctor, Coyote told two *Tah-tah Kleah* to stop eating humans and they starved to death in Yakama country. See George interview. See also Helen H. Schuster, "Yakima Indian Traditionalism: A Study in Continuity and Change" (Ph.D. diss., University of Washington, 1975), 154–55.

3. In other versions there are five *Tah-tah Kleah,* the Five Monster Sisters of the Lower Columbia River.

4. Notice that Indians specifically are actors in this story, because it occurred after the last creation.

5. Baskets are sacred objects to the native people of northern California. Many native people from this region believe that at the time of creation the Creator placed a basket in Mount Shasta so that it could send positive action around the world. The basket and mountain are sacred, and as a result, Native Americans in northern California and southern Oregon oppose plans of the United States Forest Service to clear-cut portions of Mount Shasta for ski runs and allow building of a large ski lodge on the side of the mountain. This would be a violation of the law and a desecration of the sacred basket that lives within the mountain.

6. The reference here is to a higher power, a creator. It is not common, however, in the stories for Grandfathers and Grandmothers to mention the Creator or the higher power. The names used by various Indians for the Creator were

and are known to traditional speakers, but they do not often or readily speak these sacred words. Readers should know that the people believe in a superior being, but they do not often refer to this power. Instead, they speak often of the Creator's earthly actors, particularly Coyote. It is through their sacred action that the world began and laws created. The Creator is called *Saghalee Tyee* (Our Father), *Nami Piap* (Elder Brother), *Impeish* (Creator), *Honyawat* (Creator).

7. In a letter to me dated 18 May 1994, Eugene S. Hunn stated that "The Great Horned Owl is indeed a portent of death." Sahaptin-speaking people say that "The call of the owl is interpreted . . . as: *pá-tkwa tan-a* [has eaten] *taníshin* [arrowhead + subject suffix] X; 'Arrowhead [I believe, a symbol of death] has eaten X, ...with X the name of the victim." See also Schuster, "Yakima Indian Traditionalism," 440.

8. A child's fear of monsters and behaving correctly to prevent monsters from taking them, is a common theme in Native American oral tradition. For example, Hopi people of the Southwest fear ogres who were created by Two Hearts, evil humans who made the monsters in order to eat children and prolong the lives of evil humans among the people.

14. Coyote, His Son and Salmon

1. This is a Yakama version of Coyote and the fish dam. It begins in a unique way with Coyote's son and seven wives.

2. Notice that the grandmother in this story is a provider and a key character.

3. Coyote teaches through his positive and negative actions. This action took place at *Skein*, a site on the lower Columbia River near the Cascades.

4. As in a previous version, the broken digging stick is a sign that something is wrong.

5. Note that the sequence of telling about the wooden spoons is almost an after thought in this version of the story. In the earlier versions Coyote dealt with the spoons as he prepared to dig the dam. The different sequence does not change the meaning of the story, but in the earlier versions Coyote is concerned about getting prepared to do his work, anticipating an attack by the sisters.

6. The significance of the number five is clear with repetitions of five, five sisters, and five digging sticks.

7. The word choices in this story seem more like McWhorter, particularly his use of "wallowed in the sand."

8. The story is the history of why there are no salmon found in Toppenish Creek in Central Washington.

15. Coyote and Two Sisters

1. This is a Wasco Indian version of the Coyote and fish dam story. The words are Chinookan.

2. In this version of the story, the oldest sister is wise, warning the others not to raise Coyote as their baby.

3. Coyote is represented as a changer, one who can easily change from being a baby to being a man.

4. This is similar to another version where the two sisters are Cliff Swallows. The law is that the Cliff Swallows shall move up the Columbia River ahead of the Salmon. They are the "sign" that the Salmon People are making their way inland from the Pacific.

5. This is the only version of the story with the no-mouth people who receive a mouth from a cut of Coyote's knife.

16. *Sho-pow-tan* and the *Tah-tah Kleah*

1. This is a Sahaptin story and most likely *Tamwash*, the storyteller, was Yakama.

2. For a brief discussion of owls, see note 7 in chapter 13.

17. How *Speel-yi* Tricked *Tah-tah Kleah*

1. Because of the words used in this story, it was determined that this was a Yakama story. The original title provided by McWhorter was How *Speel-yi* Tricked the People Devouring *Tah-tah Kleah*, and it was shortened for this presentation.

2. In most Native American stories the point is made that people should be wise, intelligent, and active. Knowledge and mental development are traditional virtues of native people, and the stories of the Northwest encourage people to think and act on behalf of the community.

18. Battle between Eagle and Chinook

1. This is a Wasco story with a Chinookan-speaking version of the story of the Five Wolf Brothers and Young Chinook Salmon.

2. The horn of the mountain sheep was used to make a short but powerful bow. In order to make this bow, the horn had to be split. The horn was also used to make spoons, but in either case, it was difficult to split.

3. *Lalawish* is a word for Wolf that is shared by many people living in the mid-Columbia River region. Some Palouse use the word as well, although some Palouse who once lived near the junction of the Columbia and Snake rivers used a term that sounds more like *Harlish* to describe Wolf.

4. This story is composed of a few distinct stories that are woven together so they flow. Included here is a version of the canoeman story in which he asks his wife not to fear his death even though worms seep out of his nose, mouth, and eyes. The story also contains elements of other tales.

19. Coyote's Adventures

1. This is a story heard by McWhorter, possibly at a powwow or rodeo, and recorded later. It is a story shared by many Sahaptin- and Salish-speaking Indians, although McWhorter did not know or did not record who told him the story. It is clear from the narrative that the major voice is that of McWhorter, and the run-on sentences—rather than choppy sentences—indicate that it is his retelling of the story. Still, the body of the story is authentic and very much in keeping with traditional stories of the Northwest Plateau tribes.

2. Fox is the brother of Coyote, and he is also a trickster. Notice here that Fox agrees to be Coyote's dog in order to effectuate the trick.

20. How Coyote Trapped Wind

1. This is a Klickitat story, although McWhorter does not identify the storyteller.

2. Coyote is working on behalf of the people who are being killed.

3. Coyote uses the mountain pass, an element of nature, to subdue another element of nature, the wind.

21. How Coyote and Wood-Tick Took the Sweat

1. McWhorter accompanied some Yakama and other men on a hunting trip in April 1921. This trip was the source of storytelling, and McWhorter did his best to collect and preserve the stories told in this hunting camp. McWhorter was known for his note taking, and he probably took notes of the stories after they were performed for the group around a fire. Some of the stories taken in this encampment are identified by tribe, while others are not. This is a Yakama story, although McWhorter did not identify the storyteller. McWhorter may have forgotten who gave this particular story, or he chose not to identify the storyteller but simply provide the story. Some of the text reads as if it is McWhorter's voice, while other parts of this story sound very native.

2. For an excellent discussion of the *Whe-acht*, see Hunn, *Nch'i-Wana*, 264–68.

3. There is evidence here of the storyteller's voice, in spite of the fact that McWhorter recorded this story in a hunting camp. Notice such phrases as "Coyote promises to be good, to do not wrong, do no bad things" and "Soon pretty hot! Grease drops down from *yahmas* ribs."

4. The sweat lodge is sacred to Northwestern Indians. It is connected to the earth and creation. Eating in the sweat lodge is inappropriate behavior. Moreover, Coyote's idea to kill another person is not correct behavior and demonstrates a misuse of the rite that connects humans to the spirit world. The fact that Coyote made his plan to commit murder in the sweat lodge is abhorrent behavior and should never be contemplated by humans. Through his negative example, Coyote teaches.

5. The repetition of words, and the redundant nature of the phrases here are indicative of oral storytelling.

6. Reference is made to hell, and this is a Christian influence. Coyote's wife monitors his behavior, one of the many duties of wives.

22. How Coyote Was Cheated by *Cusho*

1. The idea that Coyote had a "book" is modern and not traditional. Although this story follows a traditional narrative, the subject is modern, that is, post-contact. The influence of whites is obvious in this story about Pig. Coyote represents Native Americans and Pig represents whites. Native stories are dynamic, not static as usually presented by scholars. The story is an example of cultural change and mediation.

2. Pig is a white person, one who is materialistic and greedy. Once he gets the book, he gets everything. Pig eats all things, and as a result, Coyote (Indians) becomes poor, broke, always broke.

3. The explanation that accompanies the end of this story is not a traditional method of ending a story. It is rare for storytellers to explain their stories, because the point is to make the mind of listeners work and think. The ending here might have been that of the storyteller or McWhorter.

23. How *Speel-yi* Was Tricked by *Too-noon-yi*

1. This is a Wasco story with Chinookan words.

24. How *Speel-yi* Was Tricked by *Ots-sp-yi*

1. The storyteller is not identified in this story, and it is likely a shared story of many tribes and bands. Most of the words used in this story are Sahaptin. The story was probably told by a Yakama person.

25. How *Speel-yi* Tricked *Twee-tash*

1. This is a Yakama and Klickitat story. The words are Sahaptin.

2. Coyote calls on two of his five Huckleberry Sisters who live in his stomach. He often consults them for their wise counsel, but in this case he asks them to act as his dogs.

26. How *Speel-yi* Was Tricked by *Schah-sha-yah*

1. This is a difficult story to identify. *Speel-yi* is a common term for Coyote used by many Indians of the Columbia Plateau, including Sahaptin- and Chinookan-speaking peoples. I was unable to find the word, *Schah-sha-yah*, which McWhorter identifies as Fish Hawk. Perhaps this is a personal name of the Fish Hawk in this story.

27. How *Iques* Stole the Favorite Wife of *Enum-klah*

1. This is a Sahaptin story, and given the fact that it was recorded at a Yakama hunting camp, it is likely a Yakama story.

28. How Coyote was Changed into an Eagle

1. This is a Yakama story that McWhorter recorded during his hunting expedition of April 1921. McWhorter does not use native words in this story, and the entire text reads as if McWhorter wrote the account after the hunt. The voice is that of McWhorter, a storyteller in his own right. The outline of the story is true to Northwestern Native American oral tradition, but the details that a native storyteller could have brought to the tale—including the use of native words—are missing.

29. *Isti-plah*

1. This is a Klickitat story given to McWhorter by a famous Klickitat chief who became the head of the Yakama Nation. The Klickitat once lived along the Columbia River and its tributaries. This is a story shared by Sahaptin- and Chinookan-speaking Indians, and this is a version left by a Sahaptin-speaker.

2. In this story, Coyote is a hero who works on behalf of the people.

3. It is unusual for Native Americans of the Columbia Plateau to state that humans are "a higher people." At the time of the second creation, humans appeared on the earth, after the *Wah-tee-tash* or Animal People had made the earth ready to receive these new people. The word choice regarding a higher people may be McWhorter or Waters, both of whom were influenced by Christian beliefs.

4. The law as established during the time of the *Wah-tee-tash* was that *Isti-plah* would not be allowed to swallow up humans. This law remains in effect today.

30. *Ne-siwa-nu-way-pah-cin*

1. This is a Nez Perce story given to McWhorter by his good friend, Yellow Wolf. This is a Nez Perce version of the story in chapter 29 about *Isti-plah*. For another version of this story, see Clifford E. Trafzer, *The Nez Perce* (New York: Chelsea House Publishers, 1992): 18–19.

2. This Nez Perce version is very similar at this point with the story about *Isti-plah*, only this version occurs in the heart of the Nez Perce country near Kamiah, Idaho, not the Columbia River.

3. As in other versions, The Man (Coyote) is a hero working on behalf of the community, not for his own individual benefit. The law is that humans should work on behalf of their group, not for their own selfish interests.

31. *Nihs-lah*

1. Notice that McWhorter entitles this story, "A Legend of Multnomah Falls." This is because there are many stories about the falls and several versions, including one posted today at Multnomah Falls, Oregon. This particular story is Chinookan and was provided by *Ana-Whoah* (Black Bear), who was a Wasco Indian. The story was given to McWhorter in September of 1911, and at that time the storyteller told McWhorter that her mother had given the story to her nearly 100 years before. *Ana-Whoah* heard this old story around 1815.

2. Once again, Coyote calls on his Five Huckleberry Sisters who live in his stomach, although the fact that they are Huckleberries or that they live in his stomach is not disclosed by the storyteller.

3. Coyote is presented as a culture hero, one who protects the people and mirrors his positive traits of being helpful rather than being destructive.

4. Most of the Indians who lived on the Columbia River near its mouth with the Pacific Ocean were Chinookan-speaking Indians. Nevertheless, the Wasco were sometimes enemies with the Chinooks, Clatsops, and other Chinookan-speakers. See Clifford E. Trafzer, *The Chinook* (New York: Chelsea House Publishers, 1990): 13–23.

5. Note that the gender of *Nihs-lah* is male. In the stories of the Northwest Plateau, the gender of the monsters is often given. For example, the monsters who dammed the Columbia River preventing the salmon from traveling upriver were female Beaver, Cliff Swallows, or *Tah-tah Kleah*.

32. Coyote's Attempt to Circumnavigate the Land

1. This is a Sahaptin story and the words are those of the Klickitat.

2. *Wah-yah-mah* is the Klickitat word for Eagle and is spelled in this form by McWhorter. Eugene Hunn indicates that Bald Eagle is *Kamamul* and Golden Eagle is *Xwaama*, "High Above." The character in this story is Golden Eagle.

33. How *Its-i-yi-i* Was Thwarted in Attempt to Change the Course of the *In-che-lim*

1. This is a Nez Perce story given to McWhorter by Chief Joseph's nephew, Yellow Wolf.

2. Notice that throughout this story and the others attributed to Yellow Wolf that the voice is distinctly that of the famous Nez Perce warrior.

3. Yellow Wolf meticulously tells us the names of a host of edible roots which were so important to the Plateau Indians for food. For the best discussion of the significance of roots among the native people of the region, see Hunn, *Nch'i-Wana*, 103–9, 170–77.

34. Coyote and Crow

1. This is likely a story shared by Indians of the Columbia Plateau and the Puget Sound. The voice is that of McWhorter, not a native storyteller. McWhorter probably heard this story at a powwow or rodeo and composed the essence of the story after it had been given to him. Notice the sentence structure compared to the last story, and note that no Native American words are used in this text.

35. Battle between Eagle and Owl

1. This is a shared Yakama-Klickitat story that was likely told among many diverse groups on the Columbia Plateau. The native word *Amish*, used for owl, is not found among the many entries for owl in Hunn, *Nch'i-Wana*, 322–23. This may be this particular owl's name.

2. To make oneself clean is to take a sweat bath so that the person is clean in mind, body, and spirit.

3. The granddaughter does not follow the instructions of her elder, and an unfortunate drama unfolds between two powerful forces. The law is to obey the wise counsel of parents, grandparents, and tribal elders.

4. When the bow broke, Eagle knew that this was a sign that something was amiss. This is similar to the fish dam story when the digging stick broke and the sisters hurried back to their home to learn what was wrong.

5. The law is that Owl is supposed to serve others, but he broke this law when he neglected his duties to flee with the girl.

6. This incident is similar to the story of Coyote carrying meat tied with deer intestines rather than rawhide or other rope.

7. Notice here that the storyteller says that Owl is of a lower class. This may be McWhorter's interpretation of what was said, but traditionally there were different classes of people, known for their abilities as medicine people, warriors, doctors, hunters, etc. Even though Owl is of a lower class, he had tremendous power which can be used to do evil. The Owl was someone to fear and with whom to reckon even though he was of a lower class.

8. It is important to know what is ahead, particularly as one prepares for battle. A fight is not something to face unprepared, and so Eagle prepared in order to have an advantage.

9. Thinking collectively is a virtue and planning is important.

10. The law of the sweat lodge is that people inside the lodge must make the sound so that anyone outside might open the flap. This is the law.

11. Evil is destroyed in the sweat lodge, and fire in this case serves a positive end even though it can be destructive.

36. Eagle and *Tis-kai*

1. This is a Klickitat version of the previous story, "Battle between Eagle and Owl," which was told to McWhorter by Simon Goudy (Yakama-Klickitat).

2. In this version of the story, *Tis-kai* (Skunk) is the keeper of the camp, and he has powerful medicine.

3. This account is similar and different from the "Battle between Eagle and Owl." One of the similarities is the reference to using a rope to bring home the deer and Eagle's interest in investigating secret activities within the lodge.

4. Eagle uses an arrow to set the girl's mind straight. Not only was she deceived by *Tis-kai*, but she was under his magical influence. She was not thinking and acting in the same manner that she had when she lived with her grandmother. Eagle exorcised the negative power of *Tis-kai* and put her in line with a right-thinking person. That is, the girl realized she had been sent by her elder—who knew what was best for her—to marry Eagle, not Skunk.

5. Bullets are not traditional among the Indians of the Columbia Plateau, but a material item introduced by *Suyapos* (white people). Notice how the story is dynamic. The storyteller, Blazing Bush, uses the modern term, bullet, to convey an idea of the awesome power of *Tis-kai*'s poison. This is common among Native American storytellers today who use examples from the present to illustrate old ideas. Although it changes the details of the text, it does not alter the theme and focus of the story.

37. How Young Eagle Killed *Pah-he-nuxt-twy*

1. This is a Wishom story, and the native words used in the tale are Chinookan.

2. Notice that the youngest son of Eagle is much like Young Chinook Salmon. After the tiny Salmon returned to the Pacific Ocean, his Grandmother took him in and trained him so that one day he could face the Five Wolf Brothers and the Five North Wind Brothers who had murdered his father, mother, and tribe. In order to do this, Young Chinook Salmon worked out physically every day, pulling up trees, throwing them like spears, and twisting them apart. Each day these young characters worked at making their bodies physically fit so that they could meet the challenges set before them during their lives.

3. This passage offers another similarity to Young Chinook Salmon. As in the other story, Young Eagle travels the same trail as his father, resting where his

father had rested and camping where his father had camped. In both the Young Chinook Salmon and Young Eagle adventures, the younger persons are better prepared than their father. They are more aware of what dangers lie ahead and are better able to deal with the situation. The message is obvious. Parents, grandparents, and elders should prepare children better than they had been trained, and the elders have an obligation to inform, train, and counsel the young so that they may deal successfully with the challenges that they will face in life.

4. This story deals with an important law concerning gambling. Although gambling is a serious and widely accepted element of traditional Native American culture on the Columbia Plateau, players of the bone game or gamblers of horse races, foot races, or canoe races, were not permitted to kill someone over the event. Gambling and gaming is not worth the loss of human life, and gambling events played for such high stakes as one's life was not tolerated. Thus, it was against the law to have a contest within one's own tribe or band that would result in the death of another person.

38. How a Waterball Was Made

1. This is a Wishom story that deals with a human event that occurred after the time of the second creation—after the arrival of humans. It is a story that deals with three powerful men who use their medicine or spirit power to do unusual things. Such people existed among all of the tribes of the Columbia Plateau where men and women both had (and have) extraordinary power to create lightning in closed buildings, make eagle feathers stand on quills and dance, converse with animals, etc. Such men and women are greatly respected among the Indians of the region because of their ability to use positive and negative power.

2. When this man was a boy, he received his spirit power from Seal. Traditionally, when boys and girls were between ten and twelve years old, elders left them alone in isolated places so that young persons could receive their power. Waterbugs, wolves, bears, trees, rocks, clouds, fog, and other elements of nature could speak to young persons, sing to them, teach them. Spirit helpers remained with people throughout their lives. Spirit power remains an element of Plateau Indian culture, and some people still have spirit helpers in their lives. In this story, Owl Child reveals that the man who could make the invisible waterball had received Seal power when he was a boy, and that is how he was able to create the waterball.

39. Girl Rock

1. Billie White Thunder was Yellow Wolf's son who grew up primarily on the Colville Indian Reservation, not the Nez Perce Reservation. This is a Nez Perce story, a story shared by the Salish-speaking Indians of the Colville

Reservation, although it may have been a story told by Nez Perce people prior to their forced removal to the Colville Indian Reservation. Like Chief Joseph, the government of the United States forced Yellow Wolf and his family onto the Colville Reservation in north-central Washington and would not allow Joseph's family to return to the Nez Perce Reservation in Idaho. Following the Nez Perce War of 1877, Gen. William Tecumseh Sherman exiled those Nez Perce who had fought in the conflict to Fort Leavenworth, Kansas. When the army transferred control of the Nez Perce and their Palouse Indian allies to the Office of Indian Affairs, the Interior Department moved the people to the Quapaw Agency and then to the Ponca Agency of Indian Territory (present-day Oklahoma). The Nez Perce and Palouse called Indian Territory *Eekish Pah*, the Hot Place. Nearly all of the former participants of the Nez Perce War remained in Indian Territory until 1885, when the government removed them to the Northwest. All of the Indians believed they were returning to the Nez Perce Reservation in Idaho, but when the train arrived at Walula Junction, government agents sent Joseph, his family, and more than half of the people to the Colville Reservation. Yellow Wolf and his family moved onto the Colville Reservation at Nespelem, Washington. Billie White Thunder grew up on this reservation, and was influenced by the stories of the Salish-speaking Indians he grew up there.

2. This story is influenced greatly by McWhorter's word choices, and his voice is seen throughout the short presentation. The Nez Perce call Coyote *Its-i-yi-i* (Imitator) while the Salish-speaking people on the Colville Reservation call Coyote *Sme-ow* (Important) or *Sin-ka-lip* (Coyote). The Salish word for Kettle Falls is *Swah-netk'* (Big Water Falls).

3. White Thunder provides a brief version of a common story told among the Salish-speaking Indians of the Northwest. The story involves Coyote's incest with his daughter and her death as a result. The law offered in this significant tale is that incest is prohibited. See Trafzer and Scheuerman, *Mourning Dove's Stories*, 51–68.

40. How the Mountain Broke

1. The words used in this story are Sahaptin, and this story is probably Yakama.

2. The worship mentioned is the *Washat*, a ceremony that has its origins in the *Washani* religion. The reference to *Pom-pom* (drum) is an important part of the ceremony. Some Indians of the Northwest call the *Washat* faith the Seven Drums Religion because of the use of drums. Although McWhorter or the storyteller used the term Dreamer to describe the "priests," many contemporary Indians of the region feel that the term Dreamer is derogatory, preferring the term *Washat* in reference to the dance and faith of the people.

3. The words and phrases of this story appear to be those of McWhorter, not a native storyteller. Although the story is native in origin and outline, such phrases as "aflame with ripping tongues of lightning" do not sound traditional or in the English dialect of Northwestern Indians. This is a reconstruction of a traditional story by McWhorter.

4. This is McWhorter's spelling of the Sahaptin word for Rattlesnake. Hunn spells the term, *waxpus*.

41. Bridge of the Gods

1. This is a Wasco story, and the words used in the tale are Chinookan, but a Palouse Indian named Mart Jim, who was born at the village of *Tasawicks* on the Snake River and grew up speaking the Palouse dialect of Sahaptin, knew the word *Hal-ish* and used it in reference to the Wolf. She identified the son of Palouse Chief *Tilcoax* as *Harlish Washomake* (Wolf Necklace). It is a shared word among the Palouse and Wanapums who lived on or near the banks of the Columbia River.

2. In this story, Thunderbird has made the law, not Coyote, and *Hal-ish* determines to challenge the law.

3. Wolf is a powerful character in Northwestern stories, and Wolf is generally connected with cold, northwesterly winds, snow, and ice.

4. In this story, Wolf is acting as a hero on behalf of the larger community, because one must stand against laws that are not created for the good of the people. Thunderbird tried to limit the movement of the Animal People, so Wolf and the other heroes of this story challenge the law to permit access to this region for the humans who will come into the region. The events discussed in this story occurred during the first creation before humans.

5. Like the other heroes, including Wolf, Grizzly Bear, Cougar, and Beaver, Coyote's oldest son (actually a total of Five Coyote Brothers) declares that the law is wrong and that he will challenge it. Thus, in this case Coyote will break the old law of Thunderbird that limits movement of the people and create a new law that will permit the movement of people beyond the five mountains.

6. Notice that Coyote's son is Five Coyote Brothers, because five is the sacred number of the Plateau Indians, and such power is needed in this drama to break the law of one as powerful as *Noh-we-nah klah*, Thunderbird.

7. The elder Coyote was wise and intelligent. He knew things through his experience and knowledge. Native peoples respected such elders and listened to their wisdom.

8. In the Northwest, the native peoples had a traditional belief in a Higher Being or Creator. The Plant and Animal People as well as mountains, rivers,

rain, fog, etc., were all actors in the creative drama that set the world into motion. Coyote, for example, is not a god, but Coyote is the active creator on earth on behalf of that which is more powerful. Native Americans in the Northwest, as well as in many other regions, do not worship Coyote but respect the Hero, Trickster, Imitator, Changer for the positive and negative forces that Coyote brought to this earth.

9. Historically, and in documents, literature, film, and other media, native people are sometimes portrayed as being uncaring, unfeeling, stoic people. This traditional text provides a window of opportunity to see that Indians mourned their dead in a caring, loving fashion. In this case, Coyote laments the death of his sons.

10. Coyote visits "The Great Man" in order to get a new law, because he knows that the law originates with the The Great Man or Creator, not with the *Wah-tee-tash*. Coyote acts for the good of the community and for humans who will arrive on earth one day.

11. The thunder voice of Coyote is a sign, and it is symbolic of a higher law at work on earth. Coyote is given the power to create the thunder voice to strike fear into the heart of Thunderbird.

12. Prayer is important to many Native Americans, and this is no less so of people in the Northwest. Indians prayed long before the arrival of the *Suyapos*, or white people, and the text points out clearly that "Coyote prayed again to the powers of *Wha-me-pom-mete* to help him one more time."

13. When canoes passed under the natural bridge, no one was permitted to look up at it. The reason is clear. The Bridge of the Gods was a sacred place, too powerful for people to study with their eyes. Such natural wonders, including mountains, rocks, and areas, are not to be violated by humans with their eyes or their feet. Some such sites today are sacred to native peoples but they are not supposed to touch, see, or walk upon such places. For example, the site where one of the *Tah-tah Kleah* died near present-day Toppenish, Washington, is considered a sacred place, but people are forbidden to walk onto the area that holds the monster's remains or to touch the rocks that compose the remains. This, however, is a powerful place where individuals go to pray or leave offerings.

14. The Man Above made a new law, permitting the five mountains to make great noises, shake the earth, and strike fear into the hearts of people (through volcanic activity and earthquakes), but the five mountains would never again have the power they once enjoyed. This was the new law.

15. The statement here by *Ana-whoa* is significant. She states that she was never "to tell all the story, not even to my own children." The story was too sacred to be heard in its entirety, but the storyteller broke with tradition to share the

story with McWhorter. She wanted the story recorded for all time, and she wanted the story recorded correctly so that it would not be forgotten.

42. Spalding Memorial Rock

1. This is a Nez Perce story shared with McWhorter by *Heyoomyummi* (Woman Grizzly Bear) whose English name was Susie White, and her mother, *Pe-nah-we-non-mi*, who was born in the early nineteenth century.

2. The use of the term Governor is probably that of *Heyoomyummi*, who drew on modern-day terminology to convey a major leadership position within the group. In the early twentieth century when McWhorter recorded the story, the term "Chief" was misused often to refer to any Indian male. The storyteller used the word Governor to ensure that the listener understood that this was a real leadership position.

3. McWhorter always spelled the Clearwater River as the Clear Water. I have kept his spelling, although it is not used today.

4. *Heyoomyummi* is poking fun at whites who often called Native Americans "heathens." She uses the story to turn the tables on *Suyapos*, saying that it is whites, not Indians, who are unholy. This is also a common theme of McWhorter, one that was vigorously supported by the traditional elements of the tribes, including people who rejected Christianity.

43. Big Skukum Inlet

1. This is a Nisqually Indian story from the Puget Sound of Washington. I have purposely included it in this collection to illustrate that such stories from another region of the Northwest were told on the Columbia Plateau. The Indians did not live isolated lives before the arrival of the horse. Plateau Indians traveled to the Coast, Puget Sound, Rocky Mountains, Great Plains, and California. Native peoples from these regions traveled to the Columbia Plateau. People traded, married, fought, danced, and sang with each other. They also learned each other's languages and shared stories. The story of Big Skukum illustrates the cultural sharing between the Plateau and Puget Sound Indians.

44. Origin of the Name *Lapwai*

1. Many Wounds (Sam Lott) was a close friend of McWhorter through Yellow Wolf. He was a warrior during the Nez Perce War of 1877, and he worked with McWhorter and Yellow Wolf on their famous collaborative book, *Yellow Wolf: His Own Story*.

2. *Lap-lap* on Lapwai Creek may have been the only place in the region where numerous butterflies landed in the moist sand and flapped their wings, but I have seen such a place on the Snake River below the confluence Salmon

River just above Lewiston, Idaho, where the butterflies congregated and flapped their wings while remaining quietly in a shady, cool, and sandy spot on the banks of the river.

45. Coyote and Flint

1. Because of the words used in this story, it is identifiable as a Salish story, but the text reads like McWhorter's voice. Still, this is a story shared by Salish-speaking Indians of the Columbia Plateau.

2. The word *squ-stenk* is Salish for Coyote's medicine, his spirit helper, and his unique power. For an example of a Salish story that emphasizes Coyote's *squ-stenk*, see Trafzer and Scheuerman, *Mourning Dove's Stories*, 82–91.

46. Octopus and Mink

1. Puyallup Indians from the Puget Sound intermarried with various Indians on the Yakama Reservation and their tribe is found in the Yakama Censuses, 1880–1930 and in the Death Certificates, 1888–1964, National Archives, Pacific Northwest Region, Seattle, Washington, Record Group 75. Like the previous story of the Big Skukum, this story was collected by McWhorter and is included because of the sharing of stories among various tribes of the Northwest.

2. The story explains the law regarding "batting" appearing in the Puget Sound when the tide is in.

47. How Deer Stole Rabbit's Coat

1. This is a Yakama story, and the word, *whe-acht* (sweat lodge) is a Yakama word.

2. Using the sweat lodge is a holy act, one that is not generally associated with trickster activities.

48. How Ant Came by His Small Waist

1. This is a Yakama story. Unfortunately, neither the storyteller nor McWhorter gives us the "rules" to be followed "for a time of five suns."

2. The people once had an opportunity at the time of creation to have plenty of deer meat, hides, sinew, etc., but this original law of plenty ended when a rule was broken. This can be compared to the eating of the apple by Eve, the breaking of the law which had consequences.

3. Coyote broke the rules, but the storyteller does not tell us about the rules or which ones Coyote violated.

4. Because of Coyote's negative actions, deer came alive and ran off. Thus, Coyote's negative act created negative and positive results. It was negative

310 ● GRANDMOTHER, GRANDFATHER, AND OLD WOLF

because the people would not automatically get everything from the deer they needed, and it was positive because the deer was set free and humans could hunt them.

5. The law is that ant shall have a small waist. As a result of Coyote breaking the rules and the deer coming alive, the ant received a small waist for all time.

49. How Blue Jay Outwitted Dog Seal

1. This is a Tulalip story from the Puget Sound that was known by Plateau Indians. There were and are no seals in the inland Northwest, but Native Americans living on the Columbia Plateau had knowledge of seals through stories and travels to Puget Sound and the Pacific Coast.

2. Blue Jay is a well-known character in the stories of Northwestern Indians.

3. Northwestern Indians do not consider the method used by Blue Jay to be "cheating." Rather, it is seen as "being smarter than what you're doing." That is, Blue Jay used intelligence to outwit Dog Seal.

50. Raccoon and Grizzly Bear

1. This is a Yakama and Klickitat story with Sahaptin words.

2. The use of hazelnut to make ropes is common among Northwestern Indians, and the point of creating rope from hazel nut is used in other stories. In chapter 4, "How Beaver Stole the Fire," and chapter 58, "The Two Sisters and Their Star Husbands," a hazelvine rope is made for travel from earth to sky. The rope was sacred, an umbilical cord carrying the characters to their rebirth on earth. The cord petrified into a rock formation that exists today as a sacred place.

3. Notice that Raccoon planned ahead as he faced *Twee-tas* so that he could defeat his adversary.

4. The statement, "I had better throw him out" is an example of the storyteller or McWhorter carefully avoiding the earthy expressions that might have been used to describe *Twee-tas* defecating *Kah-las*.

5. This passage suggests the lesson that it is all right for one to feel good about oneself, particularly if the person has acted positively on behalf of the community.

6. The song sung by *Kah-las* has five stanzas because five is the sacred number of Northwestern people.

7. Grandmother acts contrary to tradition, violating the law of the sweatlodge. That is, grandmother made a "home" or sweat lodge where she stored and ate meat, laughing in the lodge. The sweatlodge is a sacred dwelling, a deity that must not be violated.

8. Although McWhorter does not identify the storyteller—which may have been the wish of the native person—the storyteller comments that he is giving the story to McWhorter "for the foreign nationality [whites] which has come, that the whites may know the learning of the Indian, may know the wisdom of the race that they have destroyed."

51. Small Mouthed People

1. This is a Klickitat story, and the words found in the text are Sahaptin.

2. Plateau Indians living along the Columbia and Snake rivers often took wood out of the rivers and used it for fuel. They also took entire trees that had been uprooted during rain storms or as a result of spring runoffs. The tree mentioned in the story was probably a cedar tree which could be dug out and used as a canoe.

3. The three men were no match for the tree which had a mind and spirit of its own. The tree symbolizes the strength of nature over man, a circumstance that is law to Northwestern people. Often humans believe themselves to be in control of their lives, but nature has great power over them. In this story, the three canoemen are caught in an adventure that they had not planned or desired. Such is the way of life and one of the teachings of this unique story.

4. The tree is a participant and central character in this story. It is uprooted but still it has life, spirit, direction, and intelligence.

5. The law required that this tree go to this place and stand up again and grow. In this way, this type of tree was planted in this far-off place, the place of the Small Mouthed People.

6. As a result of their positive action on behalf of the Small Mouthed People, the three Indians from the Columbia River established a law at the time of the second and last creation. The law was that no longer would the birds attack the Small Mouthed People. The Small Mouthed People might have learned how to eat salmon from the three canoemen, although this is not clear from the text.

7. Plateau and Coastal Indians valued abalone shells which were traded and shared. Shells connected the people living in the two culture areas.

8. The law could have been established that whales would travel up the Columbia River as a result of this adventure with the three canoemen. But as a result of the actions of men and women, whale rarely travels up the Columbia.

9. The three canoemen enter the belly of the whale and go underwater. They return to their people transformed by their experience and help establish a new law when they disobey the rules established by whale.

10. Moon sick or monthly is the term used here for menstruation. The Indians ignore the wishes of whale and visit him. As a result, Whales do not travel up the Columbia River.

52. *Its-i-yi-i*'s **Wife**

1. This is another Nez Perce story given to McWhorter by Yellow Wolf.

2. It is unclear to me whether or not Yellow Wolf actually said that Coyote struck his leg to produce children. It makes sense that Coyote struck his penis, and leg may be a euphemism for penis. Generally Native American storytellers do not avoid references to sexual acts, bodily parts, or biological functions. But McWhorter recorded this story in 1924, a time when he worried that the public, readers of his book, would object to such topics. He was also concerned that non-Indians might consider Indians to be uncouth, uncivilized, and non-Christian "savages" who dealt openly with such base subjects.

3. Most Northwestern native people believed that enemies within the community could "witch" another person by placing foreign objects into a person's body which would cause illness or disease. Indian doctors or medicine men and women used their positive power against the negative power of one who sought to hurt or kill another by extracting the foreign objects by pulling or sucking them from their patients. Some Northwestern Indians still hold with these traditional beliefs.

4. Coyote used wind power to revive the woman and restore her health. Wind is a powerful natural wonder that contains both positive and negative power. In this case, Coyote used the power in a positive manner to restore life and good health.

5. Indian doctors on the Columbia Plateau relied and rely on spiritual power, including prayers and songs, as well as practical knowledge of medicinal plants and the biological workings of the body.

6. Drummers are usually men but women may support a drum by standing behind the seated men who are drumming. Women sing, bring water, or act as back rests for drummers.

7. The law is that an Indian male should not be alone but should marry another women if his first wife dies or leaves him for another man.

53. *Ghue-ghue* and *Pedt-jum*

1. This is a Klickitat story, and the native words are presented in the Sahaptin language.

2. Animal People talk, have power, and are related to humans through the experience of the second creation. Some people can converse with animals,

hear their words and understand their stories. Animal People can and do give messages to humans.

3. *Pedt-jum* wanted to "get round" with the girl which means that Wild-Cat wanted to have a relationship with the girl.

4. The law is that for all time Wild-Cat would look mature, old, and fierce— even young Wild-Cat looked fierce.

5. The girl had spirit sickness which resulted from her own spirit quest. During her vision quest a power appeared to her, sang to her. The spirit that came into her life as a result of the quest was so powerful that it had made her ill with spirit sickness. The girl had to be cured by a powerful medicine man or woman. Otherwise, she could have died. For this reason, her father and family hosted a major ceremony to bring out the spirit sickness. Although such ceremonies are not common today, in the early twentieth century they were common. This is the ceremony mentioned in the text.

6. During the ceremony, the entire community appears to give their support to the one who is stricken with spirit sickness and to support her family. The event is major and costs a great deal. Friends and relatives within the community donate food and money to help support the family.

7. During the ceremony the family of the girl has a "give away" in which a speaker for the family calls out the names of individuals who have helped or who are important to the family. The person comes forward and is given something of value as a gift—skin, blanket, beadwork, feathers, money.

8. Spit has power, and in this case it has the power of semen. During this contact of spitting into the mouth of the girl, *Pedt-jum* symbolically has sexual intercourse with the girl and she becomes pregnant with his child.

9. It is a common theme in Native American stories that women become pregnant through someone's power or unknown power, rather than sexual intercourse. Sometimes women become pregnant through the power of the Creator and give virgin birth. This is found in oral texts and predates the arrival of whites.

10. The girl is not punished for becoming pregnant, which is the result of a natural act. Rather, she is punished out of jealousy.

11. The story is similar to those told by Mourning Dove, a Salish-speaking storyteller from the Colville Reservation. See Trafzer and Scheuerman, *Mourning Dove's Stories*, 29–43.

12. For a contemporary discussion of sweats, see Hunn, *Nch'i-Wana*, 264–68.

13. This is symbolic of the fact that the sweat of our bodies produces the things necessary or desirable in our lives.

14. The law is that Crow can no longer control Deer, and no one is to horde the animals and not permit them to be available for the hunt. Crow's law of controlling all the Deer was broken by Wild-Cat. When whites invaded the inland Northwest, they had a different view of laws involving fish and game. These laws are in conflict with those of Native Americans nearly everywhere. Whites do not understand the first law of the Americas.

54. The Story of *Whe-amish* or *Chi-nach*

1. This is a Yakama story, and the native words used in the text are Sahaptin.

2. The law is that more than one wife is acceptable but multiple wives cause problems and divisions within the household. This is the point of the story.

3. The reference to "different interpretations" sounds very much like McWhorter and not a traditional Indian storyteller like Mrs. Skouken John.

4. Notice that John tells McWhorter that "I will give you all [of the story] that I know of it, and this is not much." When storytellers such as John shared their stories with McWhorter, they understood that he could write them down and preserve them. The intent of the storyteller was to preserve the tales and share them through the written word.

5. The division of the people in this part of the story is symbolized by the colors of red and white. Such divisions among tribes and bands that are distinguished by colors is not uncommon. Muscogees of the Southeastern portion of the United States had Red Villages and White Villages, people who were more war-oriented and people who were more peace-oriented. The people in the Yakama country split over the issue of whether or not *Chi-nach* should have one wife or two and their stand on this question was expressed in paint and color.

6. In this passage there is mention of printed messages. To my knowledge, this is the only story from the Columbia Plateau that mentions "written language." Petroglyphs and pictographs are found throughout the region, however, the reference may be to the many etchings and pictures found in the region. Clearly the storyteller is informing us that these are much more than "rock art," for they are "printed messages."

7. The use of the term, "ranches" is modern, since there were no ranches in the Northwest prior to the 1750s when Plateau Indians acquired horses from Shoshones of the Rocky Mountains, introducing horse herds to the Columbia River region. Before the arrival of whites into the region, Indians became stock raisers on a large scale, conducting selective breeding and producing fine horses known as *cayuses*. These may be the ranches referred to in the text, although John may have used a contemporary word to describe the point of her story.

8. In this text the storyteller wishes to convey that Indians had a written language prior to white contact, but "No one now can read this history." John not only tells us that the ancients had written languages but that "history" was written on the rocks. The drama described in the text is considered history by native peoples, a point disputed by some academic historians but unchallenged by most native people.

55. The Wrong of *Whe-amish*

1. This is a continuation of chapter 54, told the same month as the previous story but likely a different day. Elements of the first story seem to have come to mind after the first telling. In this story, John provides details that were absent from the first story.

2. The law was for *Whe-amish* to have one wife because two wives cause trouble and divide people.

56. The Dead Canoeman

1. This is a Wasco story in the Chinookan tradition.

2. The point of the story is one of obedience, hearing verbal instructions and following through with that which is told to you. In some ways, the Canoeman story is similar to the biblical story of Lot's wife.

3. The stone woman is a symbol of the law of obedience.

57. The Strong Boy of the Cascades

1. This is a Cascades Indian story, originally told in the Chinookan language of the Cascade people. This version of the story is told by a Wishom storyteller who also spoke a dialect of the Chinookan language. This story was shared by many peoples living along the Columbia River.

2. The leader of the Cascades, Chief *Tos-cas wo-hah*, was considered a bad sort because he had more than 200 wives which caused friction among the people. He took wives from many different tribes, and he murdered all of his own male babies. He was considered a monster, and his behavior teaches us not to be like him.

3. The mother told a good lie, one which was spoken to save the life of a child. There are times when a lie is positive and of benefit to others.

58. The Two Sisters and Their Star Husbands

1. This is primarily a Yakama story that explains the origins of the *Weowicht* family, one of the foremost families of the Columbia Plateau. Chief *Weowicht*, who lived in the late eighteenth and early nineteenth centuries, was a direct descendent of *Tah-pah-lohu*. He had several wives and many children by these wives, including Chief *Teias* and Chief *Owhi*. *Weowicht* had

a daughter named *Kamoshnite* who was the sister of *Owhi* and *Teias*. She was also the mother of Chief *Kamiakin*, one of the most famous Yakima and Palouse leaders of the mid-nineteenth century. *Owhi*'s son, *Qualchin*, was also a famous war chief during the Plateau Indian War, 1855-1858. All of these historical figures were related to *Tah-pal-louh* and her son, the son of the star men. Today, descendants of these people, living primarily on the Yakima, Colville, Coeur d'Alene, and Warm Springs Reservations, believe that they are related to the famous star man who was once married to *Tah-pah-lou*. This is a very serious and important story among the extended family of *Kamiakin, Owhi, Teias, Qualchin*, and *Weowicht*.

2. According to Emily Peone, a descendent of *Kamiakin* who lived on the Colville Reservation, the two stars were Venus and Mars. The girls traveled to Venus.

3. The wind that enters the star world is symbolic of consciousness, an awakening that the girls are away from home and want to return.

4. Emily Peone said that these two women were intelligent and persuasive, just as women are today. They convince the star men, without great difficulty, that nothing is wrong in spite of the big wind.

5. The rope will serve as a link between two worlds, and it symbolically serves as a birthing path that enables the two women to be reborn among their own people after their transformation in the star world. It also serves as a link between the star men and the baby who becomes the patriarch of the *Weowicht* family.

6. Once again the hazelnut rope plays an important role in a story. Through the thought, vision, and work of the women, the rope reached the earth. Native Americans in the Northwest do not believe that the rope was simply a symbolic representation of the path of the women and baby back to earth. They believe that the rope existed and that there is physical evidence of the rope in a major rock formation, the petrified rope.

7. Note that there is a voice change here from Poniah to McWhorter. A phrase such as "by which" sounds more like McWhorter than the native storyteller.

8. The wind did not come through any more because the women were not conscious of their situation.

9. The storyteller is not speaking metaphorically. Northwestern Indians contend that the rope existed and that they literally attempted to have it reach the earth.

10. The hazelnut rope served as an umbilical cord, linking the mother earth with the reborn children who had been transported to the star.

11. The women returned to the center of the earth with the baby. They returned to the origin site of their adventure after being transformed by the star men, particularly with the birth of a child.

12. Northwestern Indians, particularly descendants of *Weowicht*, believe that all that is presented in this text is historical and a part of tribal history.

13. The broken rope is a sign that something is wrong, and it is common a event in native stories. In this case, the broken rope indicated to the mother that someone had stolen her child.

14. A liquid portion of the star baby, its urine, creates a new kind of baby that becomes part of the family.

15. In this case, Blue Jay, who is often the trickster, becomes the grandparent and hero who hunts for the stolen baby.

16. Blue Jay creates a new law, through his words destroying the negative in *Ah-yah-hos* and instilling the giant with positive. Blue Jay commands that the monsters stop devouring people. In this way, Blue Jay helps make the world ready to receive humans who will not want to be eaten by monsters.

17. Neither Poniah nor McWhorter mention that the story also is related to the *Kamiakin* family. For a discussion of the family, see Trafzer and Scheuerman, *Renegade Tribe*, 43–44, 199.

59. Spirit Costume of the *Ste-ye-hah Mah*

1. This is a Yakama story which contains Sahaptin words. The voice in the first paragraph seems to be McWhorter. After that, much of the voice is that of Simon Goudy.

2. Wanderer could be Coyote, because the main character is certainly like the trickster. But this story is one that originated during or after the second creation when human beings, not just Animal and Plant People, inhabited the earth.

3. In Northwestern Indian culture, it is important to give, and the more one gives, the more important he or she is within the community. [The people of the Northwest Plateau did not have elaborate potlatches like the people of the Northwest Coast,] but they did have—and still have—major ceremonies in which individuals have give-aways to honor friends and relatives. A person's power and class is exhibited by their generosity in gift-giving.

4. The chief understood the significance of giving, and so he gave away everything to his new son-in-law and daughter. He may have been a "poor man," but he was recognized within his society as an important person of a high class because of his generosity.

5. The use of the phrase, "class-power of the big chiefs" is unusual, and I do not believe this is the voice of Simon Goudy. Although the idea might have been his, the use of the word—class— is very much like that of McWhorter. Notice the use of the word, class, in this story and the fact that the story was collected in 1918. McWhorter may have been influenced by Marxist writings and revolutions in foreign lands.

6. The law would be that chiefs would not be hereditary but based on ability. Leaders had to be capable, honest, and brave. Most important, they had to earn and keep the respect of the band, the group of men, women, and children who permitted a person to be chief.

60. How *Its-i-yi-i* Lost Immortality

1. This is a Nez Perce version of the story regarding Coyote and death. All of the words are Sahaptin in the language of the Nez Perce.

2. The Wolf hunters honored the Deer and thank it by placing an arrow on top of its body.

3. In order to take the buckskin bag, the Coyote's daughter instructs her father to burn the bag so it may travel to the spirit world.

4. Coyote's daughter is on her way to *Ah-kum-ke-ne kah*, the land above, which is another word for the term "heaven." The Nez Perce and other Indians of the Columbia Plateau had a belief in an afterlife long before the arrival of whites, as evidenced by this and other oral stories that predate Christians.

5. The reference to "Happy Ground" is probably McWhorter's, not Yellow Wolf, although the old warrior may have used it, having heard other people refer to *Ah-kum-ke-ne kah* as the "Happy Hunting Ground."

6. Coyote stated that he had been in the Land Above before. His origin is with the Creator and he had been a part of the spirit world before he was part of the physical world.

7. Coyote loves women, and even in *Ah-kum-ke-ne* he finds time to court a woman that he had known on earth. It seems that nothing could stop Coyote's sex drive, not even death.

8. The activity on another plain is invisible to Coyote because he is not dead. Coyote was only half-dead and deals with his daughter as if he were in a dream.

9. The discourse in these passages sounds very much like Yellow Wolf, and McWhorter successfully captured the way in which Yellow Wolf told him things in broken English. The statements here are consistent with notes written by McWhorter when he interviewed the great warrior for *Yellow Wolf: His Own Story*. The original notes are located in Manuscripts, Archives, and special collections, Holland Library, Washington State University.

10. The bundle that Coyote carries becomes heavier and heavier which is symbolic of one who is carrying back to earth the souls of the dead. This is a weighty matter of great significance, and the storyteller expresses it through the burden that Coyote is carrying.

11. Yellow Wolf gives the story to McWhorter so that "young people, people still back to come, will see this story of long ago." Yellow Wolf was keenly

aware of the dramatic and disastrous cultural change that had been forced on his people by whites, and he told McWhorter his stories as a matter of preservation for future generations of Nez Perce.

61. How Coyote Lost Immortality

1. This is a Salish, Chinookan, or Sahaptin version of the previous story. It is impossible to know, since McWhorter does not tell us and because so many people living on the Columbia Plateau share this story. Notice that this story uses no Native American words. It is likely a story that McWhorter heard at a powwow or rodeo, a version that differed from the story he received from Yellow Wolf. As a result of the differences, he composed this story. The voice is that of McWhorter but the story is that of Plateau people.

2. Yellow Wolf's version of this story is more exact, more detailed.

3. In the original manuscript, McWhorter did not include notes, but he did include portions of another version. I considered making this another story, but there was not sufficient material for a full story. For this reason, I created another section of Notes by McWhorter to discuss the other version. For a concise and readable synthesis of the various versions of this story, see Nashone, *Grandmother Stories of the Northwest* (Newcastle, Calif.: Sierra Oaks Publishing Company, 1987), 36–39.

62. Coyote's Big Mistake

1. This is a Wasco version of the story about Coyote and death, and it was given to McWhorter by Burning Bush, a Klickitat Indian storyteller who knew this version of the tale. McWhorter recorded this version of the story in 1911 and that of Yellow Wolf in 1924. It is different in some respects from Yellow Wolf's version, but the basic idea remains the same. Coyote's action lost the people immortality.

2. Burning Bush was Klickitat and spoke Sahaptin. He used the Sahaptin word, *tah*, to describe Coyote's power.

63. How Coyote Moved *Pot-to* and *Tahoma*

1. The Cascades were located near present-day Stevens, Washington, on the Columbia River. Coyote is considered a chief and leader who has great power.

2. *Pah-to* (also spelled *Pot-to*) is a mountain, and at the time of creation, such mountains could be chiefs. As a result of the power of *Pah-to*, ("Standing High" or "Snowcapped," Mount Adams), the mountain, like *Tahoma* (Mt. Rainier), is a sacred place. The story ties native people of the Northwest to such sites, and there still remains a close relationship between this sacred mountain and people living on the Yakama Reservation.

3. This is a story that creates law as established by Coyote who determined where the salmon would travel and which salmon would go to which geographical location and at what time of year. Coyote has the power to separate mountains which explains the movement of geographical formations.

64. *Pah-to*, the White Eagle

1. This is a Yakima story with Yakama words. I chose this story to be the last of this volume because of the message of the story, the law and the spirit. Jealousy and mean-spirited acts are destructive to those who commit such acts. The Creator saw the negative deeds and ultimately forgave them, bringing a rebirth or law that stands to this day. In a way, the story is one of death and renewal. The law stands mighty over the Yakima Valley, a constant reminder of a higher order that controls the lives of many native people today. This law is everlasting, the result of a higher power, not human beings.

2. The law is that one should not be jealous since it often results in hatred and death.

3. The phrase, "made a strong mind," sounds native, and I believe the voice here is that of the storyteller, not McWhorter.

4. The voice here is that of McWhorter.

5. The strongest law is that of Creative Power, not that of humans.

6. The voice may be that of McWhorter or a Yakama person, both of whom knew that the mountain was rightfully in the Yakama country. Notice that the narrator does not say that the Indian people *own* the land, since no one can *own* a part of creation. Rather than a piece of property that is owned, the mountain is law, and this distinction separates native philosophy from Western philosophy.

Bibliography and Suggested Reading

Books and Documents

A Primer of the Yakimas. Toppenish, Wash.: Yakima Indian Agency, 1962.

An Illustrated History of Klickitat, Yakima, and Kittitas Counties. Spokane, Wash.: Western Historical Publishing Company, 1904.

Ault, Nelson A., ed. *The Papers of Lucullus Virgil McWhorter.* Pullman: Friends of the Library, State College of Washington, 1959.

Ballou, Robert. *Early Klickitat Valley Days.* Goldendale, Wash.: Goldendale Sentinel, 1938.

Bancroft, Hubert Howe. *History of Oregon.* 2 vols. San Francisco: The History Company, 1988.

————. *History of Washington, Idaho and Montana.* San Francisco: The History Company, 1988.

————. *Native Races of the Pacific States of North America. Vol. 1.* San Francisco: The History Company, 1986.

Beal, Merrill D. *"I Will Fight No More Forever: Chief Joseph and the Nez Perce War."* Seattle: University of Washington Press, 1963.

Beavert, Virginia. *The Way It Was: Anaku Iwacha, Yakima Indian Legends.* Consortium of Johnson O'Malley Committees of Region IV Washington: Franklin Press, 1974.

Bierhorst, John. *The Red Swan.* New York: Farrar, Straus, and Giroux, 1976.

Bischoff, William N. "The Yakima Indian War: 1855–1856." Ph.D. diss., Loyola University of Chicago, 1950.

Brown, Mark H. *Flight of the Nez Perce.* New York: Capricorn Books, 1971.

Brown, William Compton. *The Indian Side of the Story.* Spokane, Wash.: C.W. Hill Printing Company, 1961.

Bunnell, Clarence O. *Legends of the Klickitats.* Portland, Ore.: Metropolitan Press, 1933.

Burns, Robert Ignatius. *The Jesuits and the Indian Wars of the Northwest.* New Haven: Yale University Press, 1966.

Caduto, Michael J., and Joseph Bruchac. *Keepers of the Faith.* Golden, Colo.: Fulcrum, 1988.

Clark, Ella. *Indian Legends of the Pacific Northwest.* Berkeley: University of California Press, 1953.

Cline, Walter et al. *The Sinkaietk or Southern Okanogan of Washington.* General Series in Anthropology, no. 6. Menasha, Wis.: George Banta, Publishing Company 1938.

Curtis, Edward S. *The North American Indians*. Vols. 7 and 8. Norwood, Mass.: Plimpton Press, 1911.

Desmond, Gerald R. *Gambling Among the Yakimas*. Washington, D.C.: Catholic University of America Press, 1952.

Doty, James. "A True Copy of the Record of the Official Proceedings at the Council in the Walla Walla Valley, held Jointly by Isaac I. Stevens Govn. and Supt. W.T. and Joel Palmer, Supt. Indian Affairs, O.T. on the part of the U.S. with the Tribes of Indians Names in the Treaties Made at that Council, June 9th and 11th, 1855." National Archives, Record Group 75. Washington, D.C.: Records of the Bureau of Indian Affairs. Available on microcopy T-494, Roll 5, Item. 3.

DuBois, Cora. *The Feather Cult of the Middle Columbia*. General Series in Anthropology, no. 7. Menasha, Wis.: George Banta Publishing Company, 1938.

Edmonds, Margot, and Ella Clark. *Voices of the Wind*. New York: Facts on File, 1989.

Erdoes, Richard, and Alfonso Ortiz. *American Indian Myths and Legends*. New York: Pantheon, 1984.

———. "Chief Joseph and the Red Napoleon Myth." Master's thesis, Washington State University, 1969.

Evans, Steven R. *Voice of the Old Wolf: Lucullus Virgil McWhorter and the Nez Perce Indians*. Pullman: Washington State University Press, 1996.

Fahey, John. *The Kalispel Indians*. Norman: University of Oklahoma Press, 1986.

Gibbs, George. *Indian Tribes of Washington Territory*. Fairfield, Wash.: Ye Galleon Press, 1972.

Gidley, Mick. *With One Sky Above Us*. Seattle: University of Washington Press, 1979.

Haines, Francis. *The Nez Perces*. Norman: University of Oklahoma Press, 1955.

Howard, Oliver O. *Nez Perce Joseph*. Boston: Lee and Shepard, 1881.

Hines, Donald M. *Ghost Voices*. Issaquah, Wash.: Great Eagle Publishing, 1992.

———. *Magic in the Mountains*. Issaquah, Wash.: Great Eagle Publishing, 1993.

———. *Tales of the Okanogans*. Fairfield, Wash.: Ye Galleon Press, 1976.

Hunn, Eugene S., with James Selam and family. *Nch'i-Wana, "The Big River": Mid-Columbia Indians and Their Land*. Seattle: University of Washington Press, 1990.

Josephy, Alvin M. *The Nez Perce Indians and the Opening of the Northwest*. New Haven: Yale University Press, 1965.

Katz, Jane B. *This Song Remembers: Self Portraits of Native Americans in the Arts*. Boston: Houghton Mifflin Company, 1980.

Lyman, W.D. *History of the Yakima Valley, Washington, Comprising Yakima, Kittitas and Benton Counties*. Chicago: S.J. Clarke, 1919.

Lyman, W.D. *The Columbia River: Its History, Its Myths, Its Scenery, Its Commerce*. New York and London: G.P. Putnam, 1909.

Marriott, Alice, and Carol K. Rachlin. *American Indian Mythology*. New York: Crowell, 1972.

———. *The Continued Crime Against the Yakimas*. Yakima, Wash.: The American Patriot 1916.

———. *The Crime Against the Yakima*. North Yakima, Wash.: Republic Works, 1913.

———. *The Dicards, by He-Mene Kawan: "Old Wolf."* Yakima, Wash.: Self Published, 1920.

McWhorter, Lucullus V. *Hear Me, My Chiefs!* Caldwell, Idaho: The Caxton Printers, Ltd., 1952.

———. *Tragedy of the Whak-Shum: Prelude to the Yakima Indian War, 1855–56; the Killing of Major Andrew J. Bolon*. Fairfield, Wash.: Ye Galleon Press, 1958.

———. *Yellow Wolf: His Own Story*. Caldwell, Idaho: The Caxton Printers, Ltd., 1940.

Miller, Jay, ed. *Mourning Dove: A Salishan Autobiography*. Lincoln: University of Nebraska Press, 1990.

Mourning Dove. *Coyote Stories*. Caldwell, Idaho: The Caxton Printers, Ltd., 1933.

Nashone, *Grandmother Stories of the Northwest*. Newcastle, Calif.: Sierra Oaks Publishing Company, 1987.

Pandosy, Marie C. *Grammar and Dictionary of the Yakima Language*. Translated from the French by George Gibbs and J. G. Shea. NewYork: Cramoisy Press, 1916. Reprint, New York: AMS Press, 1970.

Phinney, Archie, ed. *Nez Perce Texts*. New York: Columbia University Press, 1934.

Ramsey, Jarold, ed. *Coyote Was Going There: Indian Literature of the Oregon Country*. Seattle: University of Washington Press, 1977.

Ray, Verne. *Cultural Relations in the Plateau of Northwestern America*. Los Angeles: Southwest Museum, 1939.

Relander, Click. *Drummers and Dreamers*. Caldwell, Idaho: The Caxton Printers, Ltd., 1956.

———. *Strangers on the Land*. Yakima, Wash.: Franklin Press, 1962.

Richards, Kent D. *Isaac I. Stevens: Young Man in a Hurry*. Provo, Utah: Brigham Young University Press, 1979.

Rigsby, Bruce J. "Linguistic Relations in the Southern Plateau." Ph.D. diss., University of Oregon, 1956.

Ruby, Robert, and John A. Brow. *A Guide to the Indian Tribes of the Pacific Northwest*. Norman: University of Oklahoma Press, 1986.

———. *Dreamer-Prophets of the Columbia Plateau: Smohalla ad Skolaskin*. Norman: University of Oklahoma Press, 1989.

Schuster, Helen H. "Yakima Indian Traditionalism: A Study in Continuity and Change." Ph.D. diss., University of Washington, 1975.

————. *The Yakimas: A Critical Bibliography.* Bloomington: Indiana University Press, 1982.

Slickpoo, Allen P., Sr., and Deward E. Walker, Jr. *Noon Nee-Me-Poo (We, the Nez Perces): Culture and History of the Nez Perces.* Lapwai, Idaho: Nez Perce Tribe of Idaho, 1973.

Smith-Trafzer, Lee Ann, and Clifford E. Trafzer. *Creation of a California Tribe.* Newcastle, Calif.: Sierra Oaks Publishing Company, 1988.

Splawn, A.J. *Ka-mi-akin, Last Hero of the Yakimas.* Portland, Ore.: Stationery and Printing Company, 1917.

Swadesh, Morris. "Cayuse Interlinear Texts." Unpublished Manuscript. American Philosophical Society Library, N.D.

Thompson, Stith. *Tales of the North American Indians.* Bloomington: Indiana University Press, 1968.

Trafzer, Clifford E., and Richard D. Scheuerman, eds. *Chief Joseph's Allies.* Newcastle, Calif.: Sierra Oaks Publishing Company, 1992.

————. *Renegade Tribe: The Palouse Indians and the Invasion of the Inland Pacific Northwest.* Pullman: Washington State University Press, 1986.

Trafzer, Clifford E., and Richard D. Scheuerman, eds. *Mourning Dove's Stories.* San Diego: San Diego State University Press, Publications in American Indian Studies, 1991.

Trafzer, Clifford E. *The Chinook.* New York: Chelsea House Publishers, 1990.

————. *Death Stalks the Yakama: Epidemiological Transitions and Mortality on the Yakama Indian Reservation, 1888–1964.* East Lansing, Michigan State University Press, 1997.

————. *The Nez Perce.* New York: Chelsea House Publishers, 1992.

Trafzer, Clifford E., ed. *American Indian Identity.* Newcastle, Calif.: Sierra Oaks Publishing Company, 1989.

————, ed. *American Indian Prophets.* Newcastle, Calif.: Sierra Oaks Publishing Company, 1986.

————, ed. *Indians, Superintendents, and Councils: Northwestern Indian Policy, 1850–1855.* Lanham, Md.: University Press of America, 1986.

————, ed. *Looking Glass.* San Diego: San Diego State University Press, Publications in American Indian Studies, 1991.

————, ed. *Northwestern Tribes in Exile.* Sacramento, Calif.: Sierra Oaks Publishing Company, 1987.

Uncommon Controversy. A Report Prepared for the American Friends Service Committee. Seattle: University of Washington Press, 1970.

Vizenor, Gerald. *Manifest Manners: Post Indian Warriors of Survivance.* Hanover, Conn.: Wesleyan University Press, 1994.

Walker, Deward E. *Conflict and Schism in Nez Perce Acculturation: A Study of Religion and Politics.* Pullman: Washington State University Press, 1985.

Wendt, Bruce. "A History of the Warm Springs Reservation." Master's thesis, Washington State University, 1982.

Williams, Chuck. *Bridge of the Gods, Mountains of Fire*. Hood River, Ore.: Elephant Mountain Arts, n.d.

Yakama Agency Records, National Archives, Pacific Northwest Region. Seattle, Washington, Record Group 75.

Articles and Chapters

Aoki, Haru. "Nez Perce and Northern Sahaptin; A Binary Comparison." *International Journal of American Linguistics* 28, no. 3 (1962): 97, 172–82.

———. "Nez Perce and Proto-Sahaptian Kinship Terms." *International Journal of American Linguistics* 32 (1966): 357–68.

Boas, Franz, ed. "Folk Tales of Salishan and Sahaptin Tribes." Collected by James A. Teit, Marian K. Gould, Livington Ferrard, and Herbert J. Spinden. *Memoirs of the American Folklore Society*. Lancaster, Pa.: American Folklore Society, 1917.

Brown, Alanna K. "Looking Through the Glass Darkly: The Editorialized Mourning Dove," in Arnold Krupat ed., *New Voices in Native American Literary Criticism*. Washington, D.C. Smithsonian Institution Press, 1993.

———. "The Bridge of the Gods in Fact and Fancy." *Oregon Historical Quarterly* 53 (1952): 29–38.

Clark, Ella. "George Gibbs' Account of Indian Mythology in Oregon and Washington Territories." *Oregon Historical Quarterly* 56 (1955–1956): 293–325; 57 (1955–1956): 125–67.

———."The Mythology of the Indians in the Pacific Northwest." *Oregon Historical Quarterly* 54 (1953): 163–89.

Ferrand, Llivington. "Sahaptin Tales." *Memoirs of the American Folklore Society* (1917): 35–79.

Gibbs, George. "Tribes of Western Washington and Northwestern Oregon Published with Extensive Vocabularies." In *Tribes of the Extreme Northwest Contributions to North American Ethnology, for United States Geographical and Geological Survey of the Rocky Mountain Region*, edited by W.H. Dall, 163–361. Washington, D.C.: Government Printing Offices, 1877.

Gunther, Erma. "An Analysis of the First Salmon Ceremony." *American Anthropologist* 28 (1926): 605–17.

———. "Historic Perspective in Indian Languages of Oregon and Washington." *Pacific Northwest Quarterly* 28 (1937): 55–74.

———. "Northwest Sahaptin Texts, I." *University of Washington Publications in Anthropology* 2 (1929): 175–244.

———. "Northwest Sahaptin Texts, I." *Columbia University Contributions to Anthropology*, No. 19. New York: Columbia University Press, 1934.

———. "Northwest Sahaptin Texts, II." *Columbia University Contributions to Anthropology*, No. 19. New York: Columbia University Press, 1937.

———. "Sahaptin Kinship Terms." *American Anthropologist* 34 (1932): 688–93.

Jacobs, Melville. "A Sketch of Northern Sahaptin Grammar." *University of Washington Publications in Anthropology* 4 (1991): 815–92.

Joseph, Young Chief. "An Indian's View of Indian Affairs." *North American Review* 128 (1879): 412–33.

Ray, Verne. "Tribal Distribution in Eastern Oregon and Adjacent Regions." *American Anthropologist* 40 (1938): 384–415.

———. "The Blue Jay Character in the Plateau Spirit Dance." *American Anthropologist* 39 (1937): 593–601.

———. "Native Villages and Groupings of the Columbia Basin." *Pacific Northwest Quarterly* 27 (1936): 99–152.

Ray, Vern et al. "Tribal Distribution in Eastern Oregon and Adjacent Regions." *American Anthropologist* 40 (1938): 384–415.

Red Hawk, Richard. "Neither Saint Nor Savage." *True West* 35 (1988): 30–39.

Spinden, Herbert J. "Myths of the Nez Perce Indians" *Journal of American Folklore* 21 (1908): 13–23.

Strong, W. D., and W. E. Schenk. "Petroglyphs Near the Dalles of the Columbia River." *American Anthropologist* 25 (1925): 76–90.

Teit, James A. "Salishan Tribes of the Western Plateau." *Bureau of American Ethnology* 145 (1927–28): 23–396.

———. "The Salish Tribes of the Western Plateaus." *Bureau of American Ethnology*, 45th Annual Report (1930): 23–396.

Trafzer, Clifford E., and Margery Ann Beach. "Smohalla, The Washani, and Religion as a Factor in Northwestern History." *American Indian Quarterly* 9 (1985): 309–24.

Trafzer, Clifford E. "Chief Kamiakin: Bearer of Two Crosses." *The Big Smoke: Journal of the Pend Oreille Historical Society* (1985): 3–12.

Trafzer, Clifford E., and Richard D. Scheuerman. "The First People of the Palouse Country." *Bunchgrass Historian* 8 (1980): 3–18.

Trafzer, Clifford E. "Grandmother, Grandfather, and the First History of the Americas." In *New Voices in Native American Literary Criticism*, Edited by Arnold Krupat, 474–87. Washington, D. C.: Smithsonian Institution Press, 1993.

———. "'This land is your land and you are being robbed of it': Dispossession of Palouse Indian Land, 1860–1880." *Idaho Yesterdays* 29 (1987): 2–12.

Wells, Merle W. "The Nez Perces and Their War." *Pacific Northwest Quarterly* 55 (1965): 35–37.

Trafzer, Clifford E., and Richard D. Scheuerman, ed. A Palouse Indian Speaks: Mary Jim Remembers." *Bunchgrass Historian* 8 (1980): 20–23.

Trafzer, Clifford E. "The Palouse in Eekish Pah." *American Indian Quarterly* 9 (1985): 169–82.

Trafzer, Clifford E. "Washington's Native American Communities" In *Peoples of Washington: Perspectives on Cultural Diversity*, edited by Sidney White and S. E. Solberg. Pullman: Washington State University Press, 1989.

DATE DUE
